# Top Stories in Funeral Service

## FuneralVision.com Looks Back at 2024

**By Thomas. A. Parmalee**

**Founder of FuneralVision.com**

# Introduction

According to the U.S. Bureau of Labor Statistics, about 25% of businesses fail in the first year – and within five years, almost *half* of businesses fail.

But here I am running FuneralVision.com for a second year and traffic to the site continues to increase and it's earning a profit.

I think part of the reason that's the case is that I started the site not to earn money, but rather to continue doing what I love: write about funeral service.

I enjoy being able to write about whoever and whatever I want, which is not always the case when you are working for a firm that has a larger staff to support.

Oftentimes, when it comes to running a publication, the stories that get priority come from the people with money to spend, which means a lot of stories go untold.

I've never liked that – and some of the stories I've enjoyed telling the most the past year have come from people who I know are very unlikely to advertise on FuneralVision.com or throw any business my way. But these stories and the people behind them can be downright fascinating – and by telling them, I get the chance to share valuable lessons with funeral directors or to present solutions to business problems that they may not have known about.

It's also given me the chance to meet some smart individuals, and that is payment in itself. I have no doubt that some of these movers and shakers will make incredible successes of themselves, and I often get to glean their insights in the incubator stage when they are fresh.

Seriously, when you are a committed business journalist, which is what I consider myself, you get a university-level education for free.

This past year, FuneralVision.com also held its first on-site event in conjunction with a partner, and it went so well that I have already booked our next event. It's something I think I'll continue to do as networking in person and helping people forge powerful business connections is a core principle of what the portal is all about.

If you are a fan, partner or collaborator of FuneralVision.com, I can't thank you enough for allowing me to make my dream of turning it into a force to benefit the profession a reality.

And if you've only just stumbled across this book because you're interested in funeral service, I hope you enjoy the stories in this compilation and that you'll regularly visit the site to get insights on honoring the dead and comforting the living.

# Thought Leaders Share Lessons from 2023, Look Forward to the Future

*By Thomas A. Parmalee*

With 2024 in full swing, it's time for funeral professionals to take a look back at the year that just ended – and to envision what lies ahead.

The path you plot forward will be critical to whether you succeed … or fail.

To put 2023 in perspective as you aim to capitalize on opportunities, serve more families and be more relevant in your community, FuneralVision.com reached out to three thought leaders: John Heald, general manager of the funeral home channel at Legacy.com; Alan Creedy, a business consultant who is the co-host of the popular podcast "Two Guys and a Question"; and Michael Anderson, president of @need Marketing.

**What do you think is the most surprising thing or event we witnessed in funeral service in 2023 – and it could be good or bad!**

**Heald**: It's likely at the top of everyone's list but the acquisition of Batesville must be in the Top 3. I thought back to when Aurora was acquired by private equity and then a few years later was successfully sold to Matthews. The Batesville deal is interesting on a few levels but primarily another private equity company wanted to get into the funeral space as they see opportunities and upside on the manufacturing side. It will be interesting to watch the reinvestment dollars that go toward Batesville and what they see and do in this space overall. Is it technology, is it market share grab, more acquisitions? Likely, all the above, but I think it is good. The other big events would be the continued acquisitions of larger funeral businesses and which consolidator got the deal.

**Creedy**: Queen Elizabeth's funeral and *Southern Calls'* article on the Uvalde shooting.

**Anderson:** From a marketing perspective, Google's Local Search Ads (aka "Google Screened") finally launched into the funeral profession. We had been keeping an eye on it for quite some time, hoping that it might solve some of the challenges the funeral profession has faced with traditional pay-per-click. Without a solid strategy to account for these challenges, funeral homes running pay-per-click risked paying for clicks that were not actual leads, such as someone looking for a specific obituary, or paying for calls that weren't actually leads, such as someone calling to find out if it's too late to send flowers for a service.

The introduction of Local Search Ads allows Google to monetize the Google Business platform by charging for leads – not just clicks or calls. Google has elevated the prominence of Local Search Ads and pushed traditional PPC further down the page. My team and I have always said you shouldn't just have to pay for clicks or calls that you can't qualify — and while the jury is still out on funeral service, Local Search Ads seems to be quite effective.

Here's the risk: While this is great for Google and great for local businesses that want to pay for leads, all local companies could be forced to pay-to-play, thus driving up costs and boosting Google's revenue.

**What happened in funeral service (or something that affects the profession) in 2023 that you think is the most *overlooked* occurrence – something that people may have heard about but haven't thought about enough?**

**Heald**: I would answer the question this way. It's not about "what happened," it's more about what is continuing to happen with respect to companies going direct to consumer that has an impact on funeral providers. Whether it be direct cremation providers, casket and urn companies, or funeral concierge offerings, they all affect those who operate in this space. Take Titan Casket for example. It is largely a direct-to-consumer company, but it also supplies funeral homes with specialty caskets. The company seems to be gathering momentum, and while the impact to an individual funeral home will be very low, meaning maybe they get one family per year to buy a casket, across the country this number continues to grow.

**Anderson**: Those who were watching consumer trends closely in 2023 may have noticed a significant shift in behavior that will have a significant impact on the profession as a whole, which is that families began choosing funeral service providers that aligned with their values and expectations of quality service and care rather than choosing those that most closely aligned with their demographics. Historically and across the nation, funeral service has been a segregated business as people often chose the provider who they identified with. This could be a geographical preference; this could be from a religious perspective – Catholic funeral homes, Jewish funeral homes, etc. Race and ethnicity also played a part — Caucasian funeral homes, Black or African American funeral homes, etc. In the past year, we have seen (and helped) funeral homes reach a more diverse audience than ever before. This is important and reflects the shifting demographics in the U.S.

**What are three things that every funeral home owner or senior executive should do to start off this year?**

**Heald**: I recommend three things.

1. **Do a website audit** and ask your web provider three questions: 1) Where do I rank in search organically as well as for keywords? If the results aren't strong, consider making a change 2) Take a look at your market from a competitor call volume perspective. Get an up-to-date report that shows call volume for 2023 and moving forward, so you can know what is happening. I know where you can get said report. 3) Ask for a detailed report of e-commerce transactions and breakdowns. If what you see is not favorable, consider a change.
2. **Set a growth goal**. Whether it be at-need volume or preneed contract growth, having something to measure against is so important. Then, what are the mechanisms in place to help you attain those goals?

3. **Get help**. Your business is likely successful because of your reputation in the community, your service, your staff and your facilities. Notice I didn't mention price but resting on these laurels allows for an unexpected competitor to surface. So, expand upon what you've done in the past, try new partnerships with companies you can hold accountable and that will help your business accomplish your outlined goals.

**Creedy**: I recommend asking three questions:

1. What challenges are we most concerned about?
2. What can we do to mitigate or prepare for those challenges?
3. Who's going to do it?

**Anderson:** Really, I have one solid suggestion that is multifaceted, and that is to have a simplified marketing plan to grow and sustain your business. Within that, there are several aspects, which are:

- Have clear business objectives for the year (ideally margins, revenue, or market share for existing businesses; call volumes for new businesses).
- Design strategies that ladder up to those objectives.
- Invest in tactics that ladder up to the strategy and objectives and either stop investing in tactics that align and are hard to abandon (ex. the annual church calendars that don't seem to be generating a return, but abrupt discontinuation could negatively impact relationships).

I put all my eggs in this basket for several reasons. When you consider some of the biggest challenges facing the profession, such as declining average funeral service value and the increasing cost of doing business, it becomes clear that we can't just sit back and assume that families will continue using funeral homes the way they always have. Funeral service providers are now in the position of needing to *convince* families to spend their hard-earned dollars on ceremony, and for that to happen there needs to be a plan in place.

I also look at the important trends going on:

- The cremation rate was estimated to reach 60.5% in the U.S. and by 2035, there are estimates that the cremation rate will reach 80%.
- The rising influence of the "Religious Nones," or those who don't affiliate with a particular religion.
    - This cohort will continue to increase significantly over the coming years.
- The rise of gray divorce.
- 60% of people no longer live in their hometown.
- 30 million people will move in the next 12 months.
    - Of the 30 million that move, 3 million are 65 years of age or older.

**What is the number one thing that you see funeral home owners and senior managers continue to do wrong, and how can they fix it in the year ahead?**

**Heald:** They overwork, underpay and don't invest in employee growth. Too often, they have a mindset of "this is what I had to do." This is hard because most of the owners today grew up either in the funeral home or around it, and it's all they know. The work ethic these days is simply different, and I am not saying that in a bad way, because I come from the camp of the previous generations. However, limited inventory in terms of help means the inability to be a little bit more flexible could have a detrimental effect on your firm.

**Creedy:** Funeral service is in dire need of reinvention. As a result, licensees and owners will need to learn different skillsets. In the late nineteenth century, they had to learn embalming and abandon coffin-making. In the late twentieth century, they had to learn about the internet and reduce the focus on merchandise. Today, it is about managing the feelings of customers and guests. This requires a change in focus from how you do things to how you treat people. We need a shift from merchandising skills to social skills. In particular, we need to master curiosity as we employ appreciative inquiry to help families explore options they haven't considered.

**Anderson:** It's not my place to tell funeral home owners and senior managers what they are doing wrong, but rather help them understand opportunities for growth.

From a marketing perspective, I think we've learned that 1) digital marketing continues to grow and 2) it's important to understand how to leverage the many different options that are available, so funeral homes don't overinvest in one channel (i.e. social media) while underinvesting in another channel (i.e. pay-per-click or search engine optimization).

This also comes down to having realistic expectations of each channel. For example:

- At-need families with no affiliation or brand loyalty to a funeral home are not searching social media for a funeral home when they have an at-need situation on their hands – they are going to Google.
- Preneed families are open to social media, but you need to be clear about strategy, expectations and budget management.

Note: This doesn't mean these channels aren't useful, you just need to know how to leverage them, so you don't waste money.

**How do you think funeral homes have navigated the pull-forward effect of COVID-19, and what do you think the future will bring in terms of the death rate?**

**Heald:** I think most funeral homes didn't understand the pull-forward effect of the COVID-19 pandemic in the death rate until it happened. That's not good or bad, just reality. It's the readjustment back to the death rates pre-COVID that is the challenging part. This is the same for suppliers, as we all saw inflated numbers, but the reality is you must go back to the year(s) pre-pandemic and realize we may see a flat death rate or perhaps a slow increase.

**Creedy**: Candidly, without proper planning or perspective. "We take it as it comes" is the prevailing attitude.

**Anderson:** The funeral profession handled the pull-forward effect of COVID-19 really well in my opinion. There were some pretty heroic stories from funeral homes like Ballard-Durand Funeral & Cremation Services in New York to O'Connor Mortuary in Orange County.

According to the Pew Research Center, there are 71.6 million baby boomers living in the United States between the ages of 60-78, so it is expected that the death rate is going to continue to increase for years to come.

**We continue to hear about a variety of different options as far as means of disposition, including natural organic reduction (or human composting) and alkaline hydrolysis. Any thoughts on these options?**

**Heald:** I don't think it's necessarily a newer or unheard-of option but more the continued interest and growth in these alternative disposition methods. It's been interesting to see the growth in businesses like Better Place Forests, which allow cremated remains to be buried or scattered around a memorial tree in a forest. It is 100% consumer driven and focused. Green burials, alkaline hydrolysis and the like will continue to grow, but I don't think in any large-scale way – but enough to support businesses that offer these services.

**Creedy**: Funeral homes in Canada are offering their facilities for assisted suicides. Consequently, nothing can surprise me anymore.

**Anderson:** A lesson I learned in business school is that consumers like options. Whether it's burial, fire or water cremation, alkaline hydrolysis, green burial or natural composting, consumers will value having options available to them.

Of course, there are hurdles for each:

- Regulatory hurdles will slow adoption across the country until these forms of disposition are mainstream.
- The value proposition will need to be clearly understood by consumers. For example, just because you offer alkaline hydrolysis doesn't mean your community will understand it. So, messaging and marketing is important.
- There are also logistical hurdles, such as the proximity to the nearest green cemetery option.

**What book would you recommend that funeral professionals read as soon as possible and why?**

**Heald:** "Turn the Ship Around" by L. David Marquet, which is "A True Story of Turning Followers into Leaders." The title and subject alone are compelling enough to want to read. I'd bet there are some followers in your business that will make great leaders, they just need a leader to help show and teach them.

**Creedy**: "The Art of Gathering" by Priya Parker.

**One sentence summary:** Human gathering, for whatever reason, should always have a purpose; we gather because we need each other.

**One surprising fact:** A venue comes with scripts. When you choose a venue (a church, chapel or funeral home) for logistical reasons, you are letting logistics override purpose when, in fact, the venue should be working for the purpose.

**One important quotation:** *"When we don't examine the deeper assumptions behind <u>why</u> we gather we end up skipping too quickly to replicating old, staid formats."*

**Anderson:** This is an oldy but a goody — "Break Through Marketing Plans" by Tim Calkins. Essentially, it was written to simplify the marketing planning process, which is important for funeral service, so owners and staff can focus on serving families. It's easy to read and provides a good framework, but here is the idea in a nutshell:

1. Develop 1-2 business objectives for the year (margin, revenue and/or market share target).
2. Identify the strategies to deliver those objectives.
3. Invest in specific tactics that will drive the strategies and the objectives.

Once established, funeral homes can implement their strategy, monitor their budget and track results to find out what works and what needs to change over time.

**One key takeaway:** Our role as funeral directors has undergone radical change for the fifth time in our 175-year history. We are no longer facilitators and undertakers following society's expectations. We are hosts and collaborators facilitating an outcome. Each outcome is inextricably tied to purpose and purpose is tied to our immediate family and friends. As hosts, we have implicit authority in this event –and when we abdicate that authority (as we almost always do) – we create confusion and anxiety. Every time people gather, they are brought into the opportunity to help one another, to do what they couldn't do or think up or heal alone. It is in gathering that we meet those who could help us.

**What website, resource, app or other tool would you suggest funeral professionals look into as soon as possible, and why?**

**Heald:** I recommend subscribing to ALL things funeral service. All websites that provide news and updates on our profession. Sites like FuneralVision.com, Funeral Business Daily, Connecting Directors, Undertaking the Podcast, A Brush with Death Podcast and A Grave Affair to name a few. Also, the standard trade publications like The Director, American Funeral Director, Funeral Business Solutions and the Funeral Home and Cemetery News (formerly the YB News). I love reading newsletters from Johnson Consulting Group, The Foresight Companies, Ring Ring Marketing, Selected Independent Funeral Homes and more. All these sources, both traditional and digital media keep you informed on what is happening in our space.

From a consumer side, I just set up a Google news feed with keywords important to me and then get results delivered when a search comes up.

**Anderson**: Of course, artificial intelligence, or AI, is and will continue to change the world every day. @need has been using AI directly (i.e. content creation) and indirectly (i.e. pay-per-click) for some time now, and it has enhanced quality and effectiveness in multiple areas.

If you haven't already, start using the AI platforms like ChatGPT simply to gain experience and comfort using AI. To illustrate my point, I asked ChatGPT to write an answer to the question, "Why should funeral directors use ChatGPT?" and the response is below. Note that it took me less than five seconds to type in the question and less to get that result from ChapGPT. Impressive. Efficient.

"Funeral directors can benefit from incorporating ChatGPT into their services for several reasons:

1. **Efficient Customer Support:** ChatGPT can be employed to enhance customer support services. Automated chatbots powered by ChatGPT can handle routine inquiries, providing timely and efficient responses to common questions about funeral services, pricing, and arrangements.
2. **24/7 Availability:** Unlike human staff, ChatGPT can operate around the clock. This ensures that families inquiring about funeral services or seeking information can receive prompt assistance even outside regular business hours.
3. **Preplanning Assistance:** ChatGPT can assist individuals in the preplanning of funeral arrangements. It can provide information about available options, answer questions related to preneed services and guide users through the planning process.
4. **Educational Resources:** Funeral directors can use ChatGPT to provide educational resources to clients. This includes information about different funeral traditions, religious practices and the various services offered by the funeral home.
5. **Cost Estimations:** ChatGPT can help users get preliminary cost estimations for different funeral services. This transparency can be valuable for families in making informed decisions about their budget and preferences.
6. **Streamlined Appointment Scheduling:** ChatGPT can facilitate the scheduling of appointments with funeral directors. It can gather necessary information, check availability and assist clients in setting up meetings or consultations.
7. **Language Accessibility:** ChatGPT's language capabilities make it a valuable tool for communicating with individuals who speak different languages. This can enhance inclusivity and ensure that a diverse range of clients feels comfortable engaging with the funeral home.
8. **Privacy and Sensitivity:** Automated systems like ChatGPT can handle inquiries with a level of privacy and sensitivity. Users may feel more comfortable asking sensitive questions or seeking information about bereavement support through a digital interface.
9. **Resource for Grief Support:** Funeral directors can utilize ChatGPT to provide basic information and resources related to grief support. While it doesn't replace professional counseling, it can offer initial guidance and direct individuals to appropriate resources.

10. **Adaptability:** ChatGPT's adaptability allows funeral directors to customize responses based on their specific services and policies. This ensures that the information provided aligns with the funeral home's approach and offerings.

By integrating ChatGPT into their services, funeral directors can enhance customer engagement, improve efficiency, and provide valuable support to individuals during the challenging and emotional process of funeral planning. It complements the human touch of the funeral director, offering a technology-driven avenue for information and assistance."

Voila!

**What trends are you seeing in the mergers and acquisitions space, and what do you think we'll see in this area for both funeral homes and suppliers to the industry in the year ahead? Will there be more or less consolidation, etc.?**

**Heald:** Continued acquisitions on the funeral home side but perhaps at slightly less valuations due to interest rates and acquirers being very selective in the types of businesses they want to bring into their portfolio. Same for the supplier's side. While there aren't as many opportunities for suppliers in terms of the number of businesses available, if there is a software solution or product from a consumer side that makes sense, those are up for acquisition consideration as well.

John Heald

**Creedy**: The increase in interest rates has had a delayed impact. I expect that some of the smaller consolidators could be forced to merge with other, better capitalized entities. Unless you are a premium opportunity, multiples have gone down but only slightly. During 2023, the actual raw number of acquisitions seemed to decline slightly but seems to be picking up.

**Anderson**: The death-care profession continues to be relatively stable industry. With 71.6 million aging baby boomers now into their 60s and 70s, demand for death care will continue to increase. As such, we should expect continued M&A activity with funeral homes and suppliers.

Additionally, companies continue to improve operational efficiencies and the benefits of scale. However, increasing interest rates can really slow this down through the increasing cost of capital. We can expect that financing acquisitions through debt will be more challenging and business valuations will decrease, causing some owners to hold onto their businesses longer.

**What recommendations do you have for funeral homes to attract and retain high-quality staff, and what staffing suggestions would you offer to keep funeral home operations efficient?**

**Heald:** This is a hard one but seems simple. I often see well run funeral homes and try to identify some of the factors that make them successful, and it always comes back to employees. Most successful ones have employees that have been their 10+ years and much longer. Without even asking how or why, I can assume a few things. The work environment and culture are a positive one, staff are well compensated, not overworked, and there are solid and fair schedules and support systems in place. The funeral home reinvests in employee development for future personal and professional growth.

**Creedy:** The staffing shortage is, in part, a consequence of an outmoded business model. Funeral homes are attempting to staff their firms as if all their business was burial. The increase in cremation with its (largely) lower service profile should have increased per unit productivity, and it hasn't. The situation is exacerbated by the insistence of many licensees to do non-licensee work on top of their own. A similar shortage occurred in the nursing profession. At that time, that shortage was largely resolved with the advent of nurse assistants and LPNs. Funeral service laws need revisiting and updating to encourage a similar model.

Alan Creedy

**Anderson**: It's no secret that staffing has been the No. 1 challenge facing funeral homes for quite a few years. My team and I are blessed to work with many of the leading funeral homes across the country, and we've learned that the best do the following:

- Invest time, energy, and money in building a company culture which creates a place where people *want* to work.
    - This improves retention as people don't want to leave.

- - This makes staffing easier as the word gets out – people hear about it or see it and want to become a part of it.
  - Never stop building the recruiting pipeline — always be on the lookout for great talent.
  - Maintain a strong relationship with mortuary schools to identify the best of the best coming out of school and get their attention early.
  - Keep in close contact with funeral directors from competing firms that have a good reputation in the community. You can often identify those individuals by combing your competitors' Google reviews as funeral directors are often mentioned in the reviews.
  - Leverage platforms such as LinkedIn throughout the year to advertise that you are always looking for talented people to join your organization.
  - Make it easy for candidates to apply by having an application on your website.

**What would you like to see the national death-care associations do that they currently are not doing, or what need do you see that they are not meeting or need to do better?**

**Heald**: This is a challenging one. As suppliers, we spend a lot of time and money supporting several different organizations, annual meetings and more, which has served many companies so well. However, the landscape continues to change. Consolidation will continue to happen on the funeral home side and supplier side, and I often wonder if it will or should happen on the association side? There's a dream among suppliers of holding a weeklong trade show where *everyone* can participate. Like the Consumer Technology Association event in Las Vegas every year, this would be similar. It may be unrealistic perhaps given current structures, but given the amount of money spent by each supplier with diminishing or unmeasurable returns, it causes you to think about what to do, where to invest, how can we do it differently and how or will this part of our business change as much as funeral service continues to?

**Creedy:** Unfortunately, the politics of these organizations impede their ability to do much that would be effective.

**Anderson**: Maybe it is the space where I operate, but a question that I often hear from funeral home owners is the following: *"How are you going to help me grow and sustain my business?"* That's a question I must answer from the perspective of a marketing agency, and state and national associations are being asked the same question. If a company or organization can't effectively answer that question, especially with the younger generation of owners, it's tough sleddin' ahead.

I think it is important for any business or association to revisit their value proposition to understand if the value they are delivering today still resonates with their customers as it once did years ago. For example, is the value that my dad received from a national organization when he was in the business still relevant to my brother who now runs the business? The business today is very different: the consumer is changing, competition is increasing, margins are lower, cremation is rising, staffing is more challenging, etc.

The Texas Funeral Directors Association is a very forward-thinking group as Jason Harrell, Starlyn Aurit, and Harvey Hilderbran have been addressing this opportunity with the goal of increasing member engagement and participation throughout the state of Texas. Many other associations could look to them for inspiration.

This is also a question that I hear from other suppliers at conventions. Conventions used to be a place where suppliers could expect to see many of their existing customers while engaging with prospects, but convention attendance has been declining while costs to attend and/or sponsor continue to increase. Thus, the value of convention support will continue to be called into question.

Michael Anderson

**What other thoughts do you have to share for funeral homes to position themselves for success in the year ahead?**

**Heald**: Stay focused. Run your business like you're a startup and everyone is coming for you. If you're a funeral home, families first! For me at Legacy, it has and always will be funeral homes first!

**Creedy**: Learn the skill of appreciative inquiry, be bolder and more assertive in arrangements, learn to delegate.

**Anderson:** From a marketing perspective, I would say this: embrace change. Online marketing continues to change, whether it is a new offering from Google such as Local Service Ads, a new channel such as over-the-top advertising, a new social platform that captures the target audience, or a new technology such as AI. In all things, exercise discipline and have a plan for the future — but don't be afraid to pivot when things change.

# Tom Johnson, Founder of Prime Succession And Johnson Consulting Group, Dies at Age 73

*By Thomas A. Parmalee*

Thomas H. Johnson, the founder of Prime Succession and Johnson Consulting Group, died Dec. 21, 2023. He was 73 years old.

After beginning his career in banking and then serving in several key positions with Batesville Casket Company, Johnson became president and CEO of Pierce Brothers Mortuaries & Cemeteries in Los Angeles, according to his biography on the Johnson Consulting Group website.

There, he grew the company from 17 locations to a total of 64 funeral homes and 14 cemeteries, making it, at the time, the largest regional independent funeral and cemetery operation in the United States. When Pierce was sold to Service Corporation International, he left the company and founded Prime Succession, which grew from no operations to 146 funeral homes and 17 cemetery locations in only three years, becoming the largest national independent operation in the country.

After Prime Succession, he started Johnson Consulting Group, which has become one of the premier consulting companies in the death-care profession, focusing on mergers and acquisitions, business valuations and appraisals, accounting services, management services and training and business financing.

One of his greatest legacies will be his formation of the long running Memorial Classic Golf tournament hosted annually to honor and remember his friends in funeral service. The tournament provides scholarships in conjunction with the Funeral Service Foundation and the ICCFA Educational Foundation.

Kim Price, a regional vice president at National Guardian Life Insurance Co., has been the coordinator of the Memorial Golf Classic for many years. She first met Johnson via a phone interview for an executive assistant position at Prime Succession.

"Even over the phone, I could sense his dynamic and magnetic personality," she said. "I remember sitting in his mother's kitchen with him using an old-fashioned typewriter to get things started. As the first employee of Prime, I got to watch firsthand as he built the company. He led with certainty, kindness, incredible vision and a big heart. I don't think I have ever known a more charismatic leader."

The two remained friends even after Price left Prime Succession, and she continued coordinating the golf tournament that has been a staple of the profession for so many years.

"There were several trials and triumphs along the way, but each year we were proud to make it better than the last," Price said. "Tom was passionate about honoring his friends and colleagues that had contributed so much to this profession."

Johnson's focus on friendship and maintaining professional relationships will sustain the Memorial Golf Classic for many years to come, Price said. "As he takes the top rank on that leader board in my mind, he would want us to remember that we should pull together as a team to continue that fine tradition and create opportunities for those to come in the future," she said.

Marilyn Jones Gould, a founder of MKJ Marketing and a consultant to Tribute Technology, knew Johnson as a great co-worker at Batesville, a first-class client and a trusted friend. "But my favorite working relationship memory was when we served together as trustees for the Funeral Service Foundation," she said. "Everyone knows of his business success, but his true genius as a builder of organizations is what he accomplished in his years on the board."

She explained that while all board members contributed time and money, it was Johnson who two decades ago used his business acumen to establish systems that still contribute to the foundation's success today. "He took the faltering FSF Golf Outing held annually right before the National Funeral Directors Association convention, and the first year brought record registrations and contributions," she said. "He didn't stop there. His own company's event became another way of generating record contributions for FSF. He was known for creating revenue streams that never dried up. In his life, he issued a challenge to all of us in the industry to use our talents to establish ventures that keep running and benefit the industry even after our death."

Glenn H. Gould III, a founder of MKJ Marketing and a consultant to Tribute Technology said Johnson's incredible vision and charismatic personality stick out to him the most. "In a private conversation decades ago, he foretold that the majority of funeral businesses in the country would change ownership at least twice, which has proven prophetic," he said. "Second, Tom's charismatic personality enabled him to create strong bonds with people important to him. It allowed him to build businesses he ran for others, as well as the businesses he founded."

He concluded, "When you consider the most significant individuals in the twentieth century to the funeral industry, there's Robert Waltrip, Dan Hillenbrand, Wilbert Haas and Tom Johnson."

John Heald, general manager of the funeral home channel at Legacy.com, who serves on the board of trustees and is the fund development chair of the Funeral Service Foundation, called Johnson "a true icon in the world of funeral service." He added, "Since starting the Memorial Classic, the Funeral Service Foundation has been awarded $700,000 to support the mission of 'lifting up grieving communities by investing in people and programs that strengthen funeral service.' He has left a significant mark on this profession that lives on through his son, Jake, Johnson Consulting Group and all those across the world of funeral service that he impacted. He will be missed dearly, but his legacy will live on."

Jake Johnson, who took over Johnson Consulting Group as president and CEO from his dad when he retired, said there are many things he's always admired about his father. "He was an image guy, and image brought success for him," he said. "Whether he was having a bad day or not, it would be hard to know if you were talking to him. Dad always brought his leadership image with him when he arrived at work. He was calculating to be sure that image was never put in harm's way."

His father strongly believed that staying positive could strongly influence someone's success, Jake Johnson said. "Dad was very busy during his career, but as his son, I can confidently say that until later in life, he was ready to do things on the weekend and took his children on great trips that I still remember to this day."

He was also always generous with his time and resources, Jake Johnson said. "I've listened to many lately on how Dad touched their life and helped them excel in their career and achieve financial success," Jake Johnson said. "Dad enjoyed doing that for people and always erred on the side of giving rather than taking. He was also a presence in any room, and his presence drew respect without ever asking for it."

Michael DiBease, who retired as senior vice president of strategic markets at Batesville and now operates Michael DiBease Consulting, considers Johnson to be one of his greatest teachers. "Tom was a great mentor — we talked about a lot of things, and we would bat things around," he said. "That is the kind of relationship we had, and it was very special."

Johnson was the one who hired DiBease when he started at Batesville more than 40 years ago, he said. Johnson's father was a bank president, and the family had deep roots in Batesville, according to DiBease.

"By schooling, Tom was a banker more than anything else," DiBease said. "He just knew he had a good opportunity at Batesville Casket Co., as he had been around it all his life in some shape or form."

The most significant mark Johnson left on the profession — other than the number of people he helped — is how generous he was to others, DiBease said.

"He had a personality and character that was bigger than life itself, and he was a born leader," DiBease said. "He was also an extremely competitive man. Whether it was business, sports, golf, cards, fishing or any other aspect of life, he was incredibly competitive."

What will always stand out most to DiBease, however, was Johnson's sense of fairness and generosity, he said.

"He would take time to answer any question or to give advice," DiBease said.

For 47 years, Johnson was one of DiBease's best friends. "We had so many adventures together," he said. "Both in business and personally. We traveled together, golfed together, hunted together and fished together. He will be sadly missed by so many. I was blessed and am grateful that he was a part of my life."

Steve Shaffer, president, CEO and board chair of Homesteaders Life Company, said, "One of the most challenging parts about being part of a profession for so many years is losing those partners, friends and mentors who have helped you along the way. When I heard Tom Johnson had passed, I was both shocked and saddened. Tom has been such a huge figure in the profession for so many years it is hard to conceive of him passing."

He continued, "Tom gave me my first job in the funeral profession at Prime Succession in 1994 as a 'wet-behind-the ears' accountant. He introduced me to so many people since his team was so well rounded and experienced in the profession — they taught me everything I needed to know about the important work that is done in funeral service, and most importantly, how important the people are who do this work. Tom always treated people with respect though he expected a lot out of his team. He was a force that attracted talent, drove a vision and achieved immeasurable success by doing right by the profession and the people he worked with. He was a strong advocate for the funeral profession, and because he did things right, he made lifelong friends along the way. Tom will be truly missed, and I will always be thankful for all that he did for me personally, professionally and for funeral service!"

Jim Price, who has also blazed a trail in funeral service and knew Johnson for decades, called him "a huge giant in our profession." He said, "My first contact with Tom was in the late 1970s. I was on a Batesville plant tour when I was a location manager for International Funeral Services. Shortly thereafter, he joined us at IFS and continued to be a mentor for me. He went on to be the president and CEO for Pierce Brothers Mortuary & Cemeteries. There are hundreds and hundreds of individuals in our profession that Tom made a significantly positive impact on, both personally and professionally. I've been truly blessed to have had him as my friend and my mentor."

Jay Waring, president of Service Corporation International, said, "Tom truly loved our profession and everyone associated with it. As the old saying goes, 'Everything in life is relationships.' Tom certainly over-indexed in this area."

He added, "He was a bottomless well of optimism and had the charisma, collegiality, deep loyalty and swagger to go along with it."

You're only a leader if someone wants to follow you, and Johnson certainly had a huge following, Waring said. "A natural leader, he was always there to listen and offer advice and support," he said. "He succeeded in every key and pivotal leadership role that he ever had – whether running Greenwood in San Diego, Pierce Brothers, Prime Succession or Johnson Consulting. Along the way he helped thousands, always gave back to our profession, and we will miss him immensely."

Anthony Kaniuk, director of industry relations at the National Funeral Directors Association, said, "Tom was a business guy; he was the one who told people to work *on* their business versus *in* their business. He passed that down to Jake. What a sad day for funeral service."

When Kaniuk first began working in funeral service decades ago under Adrian Boylston, the late former publisher of Kates-Boylston Publications, he was told that whenever he had a question about funeral service, to reach out to Johnson. "He was the one who would know what is going on with anything related to the business side of funeral service," he said.

Doug Gober, a partner at The Foresight Companies, said that while some considered Tom Johnson his competitor, he never did.

"I have known him for more than 30 years going all the way back to the Prime Succession days," Gober said. "My fondest memories of Tom were when he was building something."

It was incredible watching Johnson build and maintain relationships, Gober said. "We certainly had our differences of opinion along the way, but he and I always got along quite well," he said. "The relationships that he established and continued throughout his entire career is really what this business is all about and what Tom Johnson was all about."

Gober also admires how Johnson was able to successfully transition Johnson Consulting Group to his son, Jake.

"They are different people but the same in many ways," Gober said. "I have known Jake since he was a child, and I have seen him blossom into a very solid professional who also has great relationships and a great relationship with us (at The Foresight Companies). It is a unique thing in business today to have the next generation see this business the same way as the first generation."

Rich Darby, founder and president of Operation Honor Guard, a board member at Greenwood, and the retired chief operating officer of Trigard/Sunset Funeral Homes/and Sunset Memorial Park, said, "Tom was a true icon in our industry. He held so much knowledge by being involved as an owner/operator, consultant, broker, and serving on the board of directors at Batesville. Tom believed in relationships and was always willing to take your call. Tom was a fair man that would always be willing to give you his true opinion. I always appreciated that in him." He added, "His knowledge and legacy will live on, as he has shared it with his son, Jake, and so many at Johnson Consulting."

Burial was in St. Louis Catholic Cemetery in Batesville, Indiana.

# A Trove of Bones Provides A Final Lesson to the Students At PIMS

*By Thomas A. Parmalee*

Michael Burns, the dean of faculty and students at the Pittsburgh Institute of Mortuary Science, knew there were unidentified human bones sitting in storage. He just never realized how many.

When it was discovered that 24 skulls and over 800 bones were sitting in the institution's basement, it became evident that something needed to be done.

"We don't know when the bones started to arrive," he said. "The bones could be from the 1940s, the 1950s or the 1960s. We could have inherited them from somewhere else. We have no record where they came from."

The bones included two full skeletons, with the other bones being an assortment of anything you can think of: smaller bones from the hand – some wired together and some not – tibias, femurs and various other body parts, Burns said. "We are not anthropologists, but they seemed to be mostly adults," he said. "The skulls seemed to be fully developed."

Regardless of where they came from, there they were, in metal boxes, and it only became clear how *many* there were when PIMS recently took an inventory of items.

"Then we thought, 'This is a shame, that they are collecting dust,'" Burns said. "No one had touched them in 10 years. I went to school here 35 years ago, and I did not know they existed."

The bones were not abandoned, however: They were stored in a nice area in clean metal boxes. "These bones provided lessons for students," Burns said.

But the more Burns and other faculty members at PIMS thought about it, the more they had a feeling of unease … it just didn't feel right.

"These are the remains of human beings," Burns said. "Even though we had no idea where they came from, we knew they did not belong in the basement."

Dr. Barry Lease, president and CEO of PIMS, agreed, so he presented the issue to the board and said the institute needed to make it right.

The board gave the staff its blessing to spend the funds necessary to provide the bones with a proper burial, Burns said.

Michael Burns

## A Teaching Moment

PIMS, however, did not simply cremate or bury the bones and call it a day, however. The faculty used it as a teachable moment – one where the remains could provide students with a final lesson.

"We did not want to opt for cremation, because we did not know what religion they were or what they believed in," Burns said, referring to the remains.

Separate committees of students were formed as PIMS gave the bones the sendoff they deserved, and the entire funeral service community rallied around the idea, with Haven Line Casket donating a nice 20-gauge sealer casket.

Henderson Funeral Homes, which is owned by the father of a PIMS student donated several hundred dollars. And Jefferson Memorial, Cemetery, Funeral Home and Crematory really stepped up.

"We went to Jefferson Memorial Park, and they donated a space, including a vault and an opening and closing – it was totally free," Burns said, noting the funeral home also donated the use of its chapel. All told, the donation was worth over $4,000, he said.

Even with everyone rallying around the institute, however, the PIMS board still spent several thousand dollars to make sure the bones got the burial they deserved and that students were given a final lesson in the process, Burns said.

"There was a clergy committee, and a committee for the cemetery," Burns said. "There was a committee for pallbearers and one focusing on veterans organizations."

Students on each committee did a stellar job – for instance, the casket committee engaged in outreach to get the casket donated, and the cemetery committee reached out to the cemetery, Burns said.

The day before the funeral ceremony, which was Nov. 22 (the day before Thanksgiving), PIMS held a visitation at the school, which lasted about four hours, Burns said. "Really the only people who visited were the students, but they signed the register book and took a prayer card. We had flowers there. Students swung by after class it paid their respects."

There were some moments, however, where PIMS was not sure how to proceed.

"We contacted the state of Pennsylvania to ask about the permit, but they said there is no permit to give … and they wrote a letter, which we presented to the cemetery," Burns said.

The bones all fit snugly in a single casket and were buried in a full-size casket in a full-size plot, Burns said. "The bones were put in a body bag and zipped up," he said.

A rabbi, Lutheran minister and Catholic priest each came and said a few words, Burns said. A PIMS student who is Muslim also said a prayer. Since the institute did not know the religion of the various people whose remains were being buried, it wanted to be sure a multitude of faiths were represented, he explained.

"I also said a few words – how these bones provided a final lesson and how we did the right thing," Burns said.

After the service in the chapel, the remains were brought straight to graveside, as the cemetery and funeral home are on the same property. "There, we had a bagpiper pipe us in and pipe us out, and we had a brief graveside prayer," Burns said. "A veterans service organization played taps and folded the flag, which was presented to our president and CEO, Dr. Lease."

Students – about 125 of them – attended and then ate a box lunch. "It was very well attended," Burns said, who noted that PIMS did not seek to get any press to attend the service.

"We thought about press coverage, but that is not what we were after," Burns said. "We could have done that, but we were not looking for fanfare. For us, this was about providing proper dignity to the deceased, and the students felt the same way."

He added, "While this was overdue, now we feel good because they are in the right place – in a casket and buried in a public cemetery. These bones provided a final lesson which is how to properly bury them and make arrangements for a funeral."

Burns expressed his appreciation to everyone who stepped up to help PIMS do the right thing while providing students with a lesson. "Once we explained what we were doing, no one hesitated – everyone jumped right on board as they knew it was the right thing to do," Burns said.

There is still some work to do, however.

"Our next step is to see if we can get a marker," Burns said. "We want to see if we can get a good price. We are not sure what we will write on the marker … maybe we will say 'Known only to God,' but we do not want to get too religious. But we need a phrase to tell what is buried there."

Burns knows the students at PIMS will remember the final lesson the bones taught them for the rest of their lives.

"When something needs to be done, it takes lot of work, a lot of energy, and sometimes lot of time, but if it is the right thing to do, you *have* to do it," Burns insisted. "We could have taken these bones and put them in a biohazard box and forgotten about them, but we did not want to do that. We could have mass cremated them and thrown them in a box somewhere."

In the end, however, the PIMS faculty and the students knew that was not the right thing to do, and Burns is pleased that everyone came together to give the remains the final tribute and burial they deserved.

*Visit https://www.pims.edu to learn more about the Pittsburgh Institute of Mortuary Science.*

# First to Strike: Central Cremation Center Provides Families in Illinois with an Affordable Option

*By Thomas A. Parmalee*

If you want to start a funeral home from scratch, you might want to take a look at the business Jason Murphy has built with his partner.

Murphy, 36, the co-founder and chief operating officer of Central Cremation Center in Forsyth, Illinois, launched the business with Tom Cantwell, who serves as the company's CEO. It opened its doors on Nov. 1, 2021.

In just two years, the firm has already served more than 700 families, and in 2023, it served several dozen families more than the previous year, even with the "pull forward" effect that COVID-19 has had on the death rate.

On average, the firm is serving about 30 to 40 families per month, with its busiest month being December 2022, when it served 62 families, Murphy said.

**Pursuing a Dream**

Murphy and Cantwell only knew each other for five months before deciding they'd go into business together.

To some, that may seem risky – and even Murphy admits it was a bit nuts.

With three boys and a girl at home – all in elementary school – Murphy knew full well he had to keep putting food on the table. But he also felt like it was time to step on the gas and travel out of his comfort zone.

Cantwell was in exactly the same place.

"We are very like-minded individuals," Murphy said. "A lot of people thought we were brothers for the longest time as we are both very driven and competitive. His background is in health care, and he served nursing homes and facilities like that around this area, and he is well-connected there. He got interested in this industry because he lost both of his parents in the last six years. He's in his late 30s and has that marketing sort of brain, so we dubbed him the CEO. I am the COO because I have the industry experience."

Part of the reason the partnership has worked out is that both men found themselves at similar stages of life at the same time – and they both wanted the same things.

"His boy is my youngest son's age, and his daughter is my daughter's age," Murphy said. "We were both honestly tired of the corporate world."

Striking out on their own – neither one of them had ever owned a business – was a risk, but a *calculated* risk, Murphy emphasized.

"We spent a lot of time on it, including late-night phone calls," he said. "We got our ducks in a row before we took off. Also, if you really want to go into business with someone, you want to find out about their personal life a bit – their background, their family, their past career and things like that."

**Lessons from the Gridiron**

Unlike many funeral home owners, Murphy was not born into the profession … he just happened to fall in love with a woman who was.

Like so many other things involving love, the rest, as they say … is history.

The woman in this case is Lindsey Murphy.

Like virtually all boy meets girl stories, the way they met is an interesting story.

"I played football and basketball at Illinois College, and she was part of the volleyball team," he said. "The funny story is that we first met because her high school boyfriend also went to IC, and ironically, he was the one who was in charge of helping recruit/mentor me before my freshman year."

The two met when Jason Murphy visited the college on a recruiting visit, and she happened to be with her boyfriend, who was showing the standout athlete around.

"Now, it took two years after that first meeting for us to start dating, but I knew I liked what I saw from that first interaction back in 2005," he said.

After college, Lindsey Murphy went to work at one of her family's funeral homes in Danville, Illinois. At first, Murphy chose a different direction.

"I graduated in 2009, and the job market was not the best at the time. I tried a couple of other jobs outside the industry, and then a job selling cemetery property earning commission only opened up at their company. So, I hopped on and grew to love it and had a passion for it."

It was a path Murphy never foresaw, as he was dating Lindsey for about six months before she even told him her family owned and operated funeral homes. "I never had any involvement with funeral homes or the death-care industry growing up, so I was clueless," he said. "Honestly, it wasn't a big deal at all in college for us, and we never really talked about it much until we graduated and got involved in the business."

After joining the family business, he worked his way into a sales manager role, hustling for about 12 years. His wife was a member of her family funeral home's marketing staff from 2009 to 2020, rising to the position of director of marketing.

In 2020, the couple left the family business and never looked back.

"It was a situation where the next generation was coming up and some kids were getting involved, my wife being one of them," Murphy said. "There were disputes as to where the company was going to go, and we parted ways."

He ended up working at Graceland-Fairlawn Funeral Home, Cemeteries and Cremation in Decatur, Illinois, which is owned by NorthStar Memorial Group. That is where he and Cantwell met.

"We were both family service advisers, and we developed a connection," he said. "We had years of experience seeing cremation growth, as well as the need and desire of people wanting more affordable options."

The funeral homes Murphy had worked for in the past, he explained, did not have an affordable option and steered clear of using the words "direct cremation."

"That was not even an option," he said. "If the family said, 'direct cremation,' the funeral director would get upset and ask if they wanted a memorial service or something. It was taboo to focus on that."

Murphy and Cantwell, however, envisioned something different that would allow them to focus on both.

"We developed our firm to be a low-cost, affordable option. Yes, we are probably the lowest priced in our area, but we can still provide the services of a full funeral home. The only thing we *can't* do is have a large, public visitation at our facility. But everything else operates like a funeral home."

Central Cremation Center offers families the most affordable prices "by far" in Central Illinois, according to Murphy.

"Our Heroes Package (veterans and first responders) is a cremation price at $795. Our Direct Cremation Package is a cremation price of $995. Our Immediate Burial Package is $1,495 with the casket, vault and cemetery charges not included in the package price. So, those would be added in. Usually, it ends up around $3,500-$4,500." He added, "Other funeral homes have recently tried to mimic our pricing structure and marketing strategies, but typically the general public can see right through that."

Price seekers are never discouraged from opting for a direct cremation or keeping it simple, Murphy said. "But if a family comes in and wants bells and whistles, we can do that, too. We think that makes us unique compared with other, low-end providers in our area who contract out and don't put much money back into the business."

Central Cremation Center prides itself on being "as close to a full traditional funeral home we can be without the price tag," Murphy said. "We have taken market share away from other funeral homes, so we are not popular."

With everything, the firm tries to simplify.

"With bigger firms, the arrangement process can be grueling for families," Murphy said, noting even getting obituary information can be tedious – and for a family, it often results in them feeling pressured to spend and opt for *more*.

"We didn't want to do that," he insisted. "We wanted to be listeners first for these families and let them tell us what they need. We want to meet them where they are. We want a simple structure."

The business has about 30 urns on display along with some keepsakes, and it also provides families with a simple catalog, Murphy said. There are also online catalogs for caskets and vaults, which are not on display, he said. "We have all the options you can think of, but we tried to make it simple for people, so they are not stressing over these decisions," he said.

That idea of making everything easy has been key to the firm's success, Murphy believes.

"Families can come in and be out the doors in 30 minutes to an hour and not feel as though they have been shorted anything," Murphy said. "We give them 100% of our attention and all their options and let them guide us through the process."

He added, "With funeral service, you hear a lot about 'directing' families – you 'direct' them to the casket, to the vault and to the service they need. Well, *we don't believe in that*. We believe that we listen first, every family is different, and we meet them where they are at."

*Central Cremation Center.*

**Overcoming Challenges**

Neither Cantwell nor Murphy is a licensed funeral director. Starting a funeral home from scratch was a huge leap of faith for both men, Murphy said.

"The risk and stress and uncertainty were enough to take you under," he confided.

Cantwell knew of a building near his home that he felt would be perfect for a funeral home, and the duo started there.

"We were able to get it at an affordable price," Murphy said. "We created an LLC, and my wife helped create the logo. We wanted the name to be simple."

The partners took a big hit from their savings and invested a lump sum of cash. They also took a loan from a bank.

"I went to college with the marketing manager, Jon Valuck, of Prairie State Bank in Springfield, Illinois, and we got a tremendous deal," Murphy said. "We were approved really quick. They are amazing to work with!"

As for the building they bought, it used to be a large warehouse, and it's broken into three sections, with the first part being an office area that includes a large conference room, bathrooms and a small arrangement lounge.

There is also a section they use for storage, and a third section where they house their retort and cooler.

"We do everything under one roof," Murphy said. "We don't contract out, and that was our goal from the start. We want families to have peace of mind. Once they are in our care, they don't leave our care. We make all our own removals unless there are unavoidable circumstances, in which case we use a trade service, but we always maintain communication with the family, and those contracted removals are few and far between."

The building, which used to be home to a billboard company that relocated, is about three blocks from where Cantwell lives. Murphy commutes from about 45 minutes away.

"The facility had to be a certain distance away from where my former employer had locations, and it worked out perfectly," Murphy said. "It satisfied my requirement. There are already quite a few funeral homes in the area, but at the time we launched the firm, there were no affordable cremation options." He added, "We wanted to be the first to strike, because this is the way the industry is going."

Since neither Cantwell nor Murphy is a licensed funeral director, they teamed up with a trade service to serve their first dozen or so families while keeping their heads down and searching for the right people to hire, Murphy said.

"Within two or three weeks, we had a couple interviews lined up," Murphy said. One person joined the firm and stayed on for only a short time, although they knew she planned to move when they hired her.

"But then two great ones fell into our lap – one was referred to us and the other found us online."

Keith Epperson has been with Central Cremation Center almost two years, and Ali Davidson has been with the company seven months. Both are licensed funeral directors/embalmers and licensed crematory operators in Illinois.

**Competing to Win**

As the two have grown the business, Murphy has leaned on the lessons he learned as a standout football player.

"I was a middle child and grew up in a competitive and athletic sports family," he said. "Football was my top sport through high school and into college. I played four years at as smaller school, Illinois College in Jacksonville."

In high school, Murphy played wide receiver and cornerback on defense. In college, he played three years at cornerback and during his senior year, he moved to free safety. He made the All-Midwest Conference all four years while at Illinois College.

If football is not the most physically draining and emotionally demanding sport, it's right up there, Murphy said.

"Like funeral service, it's a grind," he said. "All the hours of evening and early morning work. You have to get up and do it every day."

But the way a football team is organized sheds some lessons on how to run a good funeral home, Murphy believes.

"On the football field, you have very skilled positions – not every guy can do everything. It's not like basketball, where everyone needs to be able to dribble and shoot. In football, you are not going to ask a lineman to play quarterback. Everyone has a special role, and when they do that well, the team is successful."

It's similar in funeral service, Murphy said.

"Even if you are a licensed funeral director and paid the same salary and have the same title as someone else, you don't have to do the same things to help your company," he explained.

For instance, one of Central Cremation Center's funeral directors meets with more families. That funeral director is better at developing relationships and has higher average contracts, but the other one is great "in the back," embalming, doing paperwork and such. Both can do what the other does *if needed* … but they prefer specializing in a certain area, just like specialists on a football field.

"The way we have structured our company is we cater to their individual skillsets," Murphy said. "While they are both great embalmers, one is better than the other – and one *likes* to do it. The other not so much. Whatever one may lack, the other excels in. We don't want to force either of them into situations they are not comfortable with."

**Delivering Services and Value**

Given the name – Central Cremation Center – it should come as no surprise that 85% of the families the business serves opt for cremation.

"We've had about 50 burials in the last couple of years, and of those, about 75% have been embalmed and the others have been direct burials," Murphy said.

Catering to families that may not have the highest income and who want an affordable option was quite intentional, Murphy said.

"Out of the gates, that was our focus," he said. "We want to cater to lower-income people who do not want full-fledged funerals."

With that said, Murphy has been somewhat surprised that the firm is doing business with a number of families in a higher income tax bracket. "They just don't see a ton of value in having a viewing or burial," he said. "So, we've been able to appeal to a large amount of the population and wide demographics."

Even though the firm focuses on simple, it still has a "good amount" of people who have a memorial service after the cremation. "We have an area at the facility where a family can have a private viewing, although it really can only accommodate 20 to 30 people," he said.

If a family wants a few hours to say goodbye before the cremation, Murphy and his team allow that as well.

There are also a few churches in the area that have opened their doors, so the cremation center can offer families a chapel. "And there is an event center in town about 15 minutes away, and we have used that as well" he said. "Families understand that – our building is not a chapel and is not a traditional funeral home so to speak, so they don't expect to have a full visitation at our place. We communicate that to them: We don't accommodate that, but we can help you find a location."

About 25% of the families the firm serves opt for some sort of service or viewing, Murphy said. It charges $200 for a private viewing, or it can help facilitate a memorial service for $450. The churches it has worked with as well as the event center have provided their venues free of charge, but if that ever changes, the firm will simply pass on the charge to families, he said.

So far, the business has served a larger geographic area than Murphy anticipated.

"As of now, we've served 41 counties in central or southern Illinois," he said. "Our reach has been outstanding."

The firm has done numerous commercials, particularly with a local station, WAND, out of Decatur, which reaches a wide swath of the state.

"Our bread and butter has always been our TV commercials," Murphy said. "We rotate out messages. Our first message focused on price, and how we wanted to be transparent and offer a low cost. A couple months later, we put out a commercial on preplanning. Then we touched on preneed transfers. A lot of people may have planned years ago with XYZ, but you can get the same service with us for a lower price, so come to us, and we can help you with your preneed transfer process. I am very well versed in that and know how to get it done. A large portion of our preneed program has been preneed transfers."

The company has also experimented with billboard advertising, but it seemed expensive, and so it has backed off that. "We've also done a little radio – not a ton," Murphy said. "We also do community seminars at our location, or we find a restaurant where we can do a lunch and learn."

The COVID-19 pandemic may have paved the way for the firm to serve a larger area, since more people are now comfortable making virtual arrangements or seeking information online.

"People started using things like DocuSign, since they are COVID conscious and do not want the interaction," he said. "They are still using those tools, especially if their family member was two or three hours away. They do not want to come back and make arrangements in person, and sometimes they do not want a service."

He added, "We can ship cremated remains to the family. We can do everything through email, DocuSign and a phone call. We don't actually have to meet in person to make arrangements."

**Staying Involved**

On top of providing an essential service to the community at an affordable price, Central Cremation Center made getting involved in the community a priority from day one, Murphy said.

"We introduced our Central Cremation Give Back Program," which entails giving a small percentage of the company's profits to a community organization each month. "We donated to the Salvation Army one month. Another month, it was the American Legion hall. We are very involved, and anytime there is a community event that we are allowed to be at and makes sense for us, we are going to be there."

Monthly donations through the Give Back Program have been in the $500 to $2,000 range, he said. "They are always appreciated," he said.

"We've done better than we thought we would do out of the gate," Murphy said. "But we always knew – especially in this area – that there was a need for something like this. But we did not anticipate the amount of growth or the massive area and territory that we'd be able to serve. That has created logistical challenges, but with the use of technology and fancy scheduling, we've been able to please the families we serve."

Drawing on his expertise as a preneed salesperson, Murph, who was previously a preneed and cemetery sales manager, has also made sure the firm focuses on helping families preplan. "I have always known preneed is important," he said.

In short order, Central Cremation Center has almost achieved a one-to-one preneed to at-need ratio of families served, Murphy said.

"This is in large part due to the efforts of our director of public relations, Brett Zerfowski," Murphy said. "He's very well known in our area. Whether it's from his days working as a postman, or his time as a PA announcer for Macon Speedway, Millikin University games or radio advertising, people love the guy. He's a very genuine person, and out of all my years working with preplanning advisers, he's at the top of the list! He truly cares about what's best for the families he meets with — and that goes a very long way!"

In only two years, the company already has 600 preneed contracts on the books, he said.

Looking ahead, Murphy sees the greatest challenge as growing but at a responsible pace.

"We are kicking around what is our next step," he said. "Our model has proved successful, and we are serving a large area. We know if we can get the right resources in place, we can grow this. But whether that means opening another center somewhere else or franchising this, we are not sure. If we were to do that, we'd need the capital and staff … and possibly investors."

All Murphy knows is he needs to figure it out – and quickly.

"We want to grow this for the future," he said. "We know that if we don't, someone else will do it – and we don't want to be late to the party."

*Visit www.CentralCremationCenter.com to learn more about Central Cremation Center of Illinois.*

# Full Circle Aftercare Provides A Safety Net For Families and Funeral Homes

*By Thomas A. Parmalee*

Matthew Van Drimmelen was a civil engineer working in the government sector. It was the type of stable job most people spend years trying to get – and when they get it, they hunker down and stay put.

But he realized pretty quickly that he was not going to last.

"I was getting reprimanded for doing a good job and creating high expectations for others," he said.

For someone who was striving for excellence, it was frustrating. "I decided I wanted to shift, and I had a friend who owned a preneed general agency," he said.

And so began his journey into the world of death care.

"My friend was lamenting how none of the families wanted to talk about buying preneed … there was simply too much else going on," he said.

There were also challenges on the sales side of the business, as many funeral directors were reluctant to push too hard on preneed, Van Drimmelen learned.

His engineering mind was intrigued, and he started asking questions, such as whether or not these challenges were contained to only certain types of firms or certain types of people. And the answer he heard was no – it was across the board.

So, he joined his friend at a company called Final Assistance, which eventually became Full Circle Aftercare, with Van Drimmelen taking over as the sole owner in 2016.

"His desire was to create something very automated and technology-based, and I wanted to create something that would have that human connection," Van Drimmelen explained, when asked about the pivot. "So, I bought him out and kind of revamped the company."

He grew the business, aiming to make everything as affordable as possible, focusing on two channels: Funeral homes and hospice care organizations. The company has only recently expanded into a third channel – law firms.

"The main thing that is happening there is they are using our services for probate cases," he said. "We do things the attorneys don't do that families want done. *I don't want to call Verizon Wireless – can you do that for me?* They add our services to help families during the probate process."

Sometimes, Full Circle Aftercare finds itself in the position where it may need to recommend legal services, although it generally does not collect referral fees, he said.

Today, Full Circle Aftercare serves clients in 38 states as well as two provinces in Canada. All told, it helps about 1,700 families per month.

It started working in Canada last year, which Van Drimmelen is excited about.

"We will serve every province except Quebec," he said, noting its laws vary from the rest of the country. "We came into Canada because we had a firm in the United States that also owned several Canada locations, and they wanted us to serve all of them."

He added, "We started in the West, so we have grown most in the West," Van Drimmelen said. "We could definitely grow more in the Northeast and the South."

Asked about what "aftercare" really means, Van Drimmelen observed that if you ask 100 different funeral home owners this question, you'd probably hear 100 different answers.

"It is this nebulous thing that they are told they need to do, and yet it has not been defined," he said.

Often, when Van Drimmelen asks a funeral home owner what they do in regard to aftercare, their response will be "not enough." It is generally an afterthought, he said.

Many funeral home owners seem content with having some type of follow up, which has led to text messaging and the mass mailing or emailing of cards, Van Drimmelen said.

"I'm not saying that's not nice … but it's just kind of fluff," he said. "It is not actually serving families. For funeral homes that are looking to provide actual services to families, that's going to be estate closing services or grief services like ours."

Funeral homes have to be careful not to lump in aftercare with preneed, he said.

"It needs to be its own thing in my opinion," he said. "If someone calls you to help you, but really they are just trying to sell you something, families can feel that, and it feels disingenuous. When you are able to jump in with no ulterior motive, that is where the magic is. That is where you create delighted customers who are loyal to your brand … and that sells more preneed. You can't go directly at it."

Aftercare typically ends up being more of a strategy than part of operations, Van Drimmelen said. "You need to take a step back and think how you grow your business over the long term – and aftercare needs to be a piece of that."

**The Big Pivot**

Full Circle Aftercare didn't really hit its stride until it moved from a direct-to-consumer model to a business-to-business model, Van Drimmelen said.

The ah-ha moment came after the company helped a family member with ownership in a hospice company who mentioned he'd love to leverage the solution as a business owner.

Today, hospice care organizations account for about 35% of Full Circle Aftercare's business.

"They are great clients," Van Drimmelen said of hospice care organizations. "One thing we are really working on is how to get families from hospice back to the funeral home." He added, "One of our goals is to educate hospices on the value of funeral services and how it helps families."

The majority of its clients – 60% — are funeral homes. The remaining 5% consist of law firms, Van Drimmelen said.

Going B2B instead of direct to consumer has proved to be a winning formula, largely because of what Van Drimmelen calls "The Home Depot effect.'"

He explained, "When you are at Home Depot and looking at something and seem kind of confused, an employee usually comes up to you and asks, 'Can I help you?'"

And the typical response is for an individual to *refuse* the help, and later, they often second guess themselves, wondering why they didn't take the employee up on their offer.

Van Drimmelen and his team noticed the same thing happening with the families it served: They thought they were OK, but they really were not engaging in a conversation.

"But when we started going B2B and white labeling our service under the hospice or funeral home, families started engaging more," he said.

Since families already had established relationships with hospices and funeral homes, they ended up seeking and receiving more help from Full Circle Aftercare, which was important to Van Drimmelen.

"My goal is to help a family as completely as possible," he said. "We can accomplish that better as B2B compared with direct to consumer."

The move paved the way to embark on a whole new mission: to help funeral homes provide more services to families while boosting the value of their own businesses.

"I realized funeral homes are looking to differentiate and add value to families," he said, noting that firms that work with Full Circle Aftercare end up selling more preneed services and collecting more positive Google reviews.

**Overcoming Challenges**

As an engineer, Van Drimmelen is inclined to want to "optimize things," which was the biggest challenge to overcome as he sought to grow the Full Circle Aftercare business, he said.

"What do you get when you optimize?" he asked. "You go from orange juice to Tampico, and pretty soon, there are no oranges in the juice – just sugar, orange coloring and orange flavoring.

Everyone would rather drink fresh OJ. So, the big challenge for us is we wanted to keep things authentic for families."

The goal for the business has always been to provide "a real service and not something made out of fluff," he said. "Keeping things simple is really hard, it takes a lot of effort, but it is such a better experience for everyone involved," he said.

The "simple" in this case is doing the hard work after a loved one dies to keep everything simple for families, Van Drimmelen said.

"Making that decision over and over is hard. It hurts the bottom line – it is hard to scale and to keep your quality control up," he said.

Another big challenge has been to avoid taking on debt or investors, which Van Drimmelen admitted has been tempting.

"It has been hard seeing other companies come in with a bunch of investors and they grow very quickly," he said. "Most of our growth comes through word-of-mouth referrals. We don't have a big marketing budget. But our growth has been slow and powerful. We lose almost no clients." He added, "It's great being able to own and control the process, but it's difficult growing slowly and living on that shoestring budget."

**How the Service Works**

Full Circle Aftercare offers white labeled services that are sold by the funeral home or hospice care organization, Van Drimmelen said.

"When families are sitting across from a funeral director, the funeral director usually asks, 'How many death certificates do you want?' And the family usually says, 'I don't know, what do I need them for?'"

And then, the funeral director will typically pull out a list of everything the family needs a death certificate for, he said.

"Families start looking at that list, and it's like someone put two big sandbags on their shoulders," he said.

When a funeral home owner works with Full Circle Aftercare, however, they can then tell the family they have a team that will help them with all that they have to do – and that it's included with the funeral service at no charge.

"Most funeral homes include our service in the cost of the funeral," Van Drimmelen explained. "Few sell it."

After that interaction, someone from the Full Circle Aftercare team will call the family on behalf of the funeral home to help them close out the affairs of their loved one. They set up an appointment and go through important items, such as the credit report of the deceased, any insurance they had, what money is coming in and going out and what subscriptions might need attention.

"We come up with a plan of what needs to be done, and some things we can do for them," Van Drimmelen said.

One of the primary ways Full Circle Aftercare can serve families is by assisting in transferring Social Security benefits to the surviving spouse, Van Drimmelen said. "We get on the phone and do that dialing," he said, noting that families can often spend several hours on the phone at a difficult time, adding to their stress, when his team can typically get everything done in two hours.

"We know what to say, what to do and how the process works," he said. "We can do it in a more efficient manner and protect the person from being on hold saying their wife just died." He added, "That is a raw emotional state for a family member to be in, and the person on the other end of the phone is ready to have a business conversation. We act as an intermediary, where we can have that business conversation while protecting the emotions of the family."

The whole process of transferring Social Security benefits is a bigger chore than most funeral professionals realize, Van Drimmelen said.

"What does every funeral home owner say to the family? 'Don't worry about Social Security, I will take care of it,'" he said. "And what they really mean is don't worry about notifying them of the death. But you need to go in person to claim your lost payment and deal with survivor benefits. Most families walk away thinking they don't have to worry about Social Security, but that's simply not true."

Many times, in fact, the surviving spouse is missing out on their full survivor benefits, sometimes as a result of miscommunication with the funeral home.

"Funeral homes are not doing this to be malicious," he said, noting that they are sometimes just not familiar enough with all the moving parts.

"They do not understand that what they do does not help them get benefits … and we explain to them that they do the first part but not the second part."

Often, that is the biggest struggle in Full Circle Aftercare winning new clients – explaining to funeral homes what it can do for families, and why the service is so valuable.

Typically, a family may take 14 to 18 months before taking care of all the affairs of a recently deceased loved one. With the help of Full Circle Aftercare, however, it's usually all taken care of within a week, he said.

Moreover, there is no limit to the service Full Circle Aftercare provides, according to Van Drimmelen.

"There are some things we must assign a family to do, and we provide clear instructions," he said. "For instance, we cannot close a bank account, but we *can* provide them with paperwork and coach them through the process. They might need an outside service, like a law firm or tax adviser. We don't pay for those, but we won't charge the family anything through the process. And we don't upsell them. Our job is to represent the funeral home."

Along the way, it provides the funeral home with some valuable deliverables Van Drimmelen said. The first is that families are often overjoyed and "blown away" that the funeral home has gone the extra mile to help them. "They do not expect that the funeral home will be there to help them after the service is over," he said. "This creates goodwill, loyalty and word-of-mouth referrals."

By interacting with the family, the Full Circle Aftercare team also gets to know the family fairly well, and they get to ask what the funeral home did well or what it could have done better.

"I call what we provide a safety net," Van Drimmelen said. "We get so much feedback that they would never write in a survey or a review, and we send all that feedback to the funeral home."

When there is a problem, the funeral home learns about it right away, and if Full Circle Aftercare hears a particularly good *compliment*, it asks the family if the funeral home could use the testimonial in their marketing. "We get verbal confirmation, and we'll send that back to the funeral home," Van Drimmelen said. The funeral home, in turn, may make a social media post out of the comment or use it in some other way.

And obviously, if the Full Circle Aftercare team likes what it hears from the family, it will send them a link, so they can write a review of the funeral home on Google. "We have a very high success rate with Google reviews," he said. "In November alone, we were able to generate 300 Google reviews for our clients, which was awesome."

But perhaps the most critical deliverable that Full Circle Aftercare provides to funeral home clients is it helps bridge the gap between the at-need services a funeral home provides and its desire to help more families prearrange. As a result, a number of preneed marketing companies and preneed insurance providers encourage funeral homes to include the Full Circle Aftercare solution with every funeral service, Van Drimmelen said.

"What usually ends up happening is a family comes to a funeral home, has a service, and then the service ends – and then a month later, they get this call from a preneed salesperson asking if they want to buy something else," Van Drimmelen said.

Some families end up feeling as though that experience cheapens what they just went through with the funeral home, he said, as they – right or wrong – think the funeral home only wants to make more money.

"We try to bridge that gap," he said. "Eventually, we wrap up the deceased's estate … we update beneficiaries, and we educate them about wills and trusts. We are not selling – just educating."

Full Circle Aftercare gently informs the family that its team can assist family members in getting funeral arrangements in place. "We get an average of 40% to 70% of families, depending on demographics and the area, request a preneed agent reach out to them," he said.

Such a turn of events changes the entire dynamic with the family, because now when the funeral home reaches out, it's not a sales pitch – their preneed sales agent is calling to answer questions, Van Drimmelen said.

**Pricing and More Details**

Full Circle Aftercare charges funeral homes $159 per family to provide its service along with a funeral – and $200 to the funeral home if it is offering it as an add-on option to the family.

Law firms sell the solution as part of the estate planning services they provide, he said.

A small number of funeral homes offer it to families as an add-on option, typically charging $200 to $400, Van Drimmelen said.

While the firm does not actively try selling its services directly to consumers, it states on its website that it is available for $499, which is higher than any funeral home offers it for, so funeral homes can correctly say they are offering it at a discount.

Funeral homes that include Full Circle Aftercare with every service (about 85% of funeral home clients approach it this way) don't always pay $159 per family, Van Drimmelen said.

"So, if a funeral home sends us a family who ends up not needing our service –maybe there is not much to do – we just charge a $14 consultation fee," he said. "I don't want a funeral home to pay us for services that we don't complete. So, for a funeral home that uses us, it usually ends up being about $100 per family if you average out our consultations with our full service."

If a firm is creative, it can find a way to do business with Full Circle Aftercare and provide a higher tier of service to families – even if it's serving families that typically opt for less service, Van Drimmelen said.

"We had an online direct cremation company, and they were doing direct cremations for $699 and told us that there was no way they could include our service," he said.

So, what Van Drimmelen proposed was this: Give customers two options — $699 for a direct cremation or $899 for "direct cremation plus," which would include Full Circle Aftercare's services.

The first month the firm gave families the option, 55% of them opted for the higher-priced package, he said.

He added that when a selection of funeral homes polled their customers about how much the Full Circle Aftercare service should cost, the average was $750, so firms are very happy to pay $159 per family as they know they are getting a considerable value at a fair price for families.

Visit *https://www.full-circlecare.com* to learn more about Full Circle Aftercare.

# Everly Seeks to Transform Grief Care

*By Thomas A. Parmalee*

How does someone go from being a chef and owning a stake in a restaurant to launching a platform that seeks to transform the grief care landscape?

In Gabriel Rao's case, it's a heartbreaking story – but one that he hopes will help others cope with loss.

"My brother was killed in Afghanistan, Dec. 5, 2009, and my wife's late husband, Sgt. Jack Martin II, was killed in the Philippines on Sept. 29 of that same year," he said. Both were killed by an improvised explosive device.

The death of his brother has brought him to places he never imagined he would go.

"We spend so much of life keeping thoughts of death at bay," he said. "Really meeting it head on and being present to it has made my life unrecognizable," he said.

In a recent post on LinkedIn, Rao paid tribute to his late brother, Sgt. Elijah John-Miles Rao, on the anniversary of his death, stating, "His sacrifice has been a guiding light in my life, leading me to places I never imagined. In large part to his service and sacrifice, I co-founded Everly."

The company's co-founder and chief operating officer, Ben Harris, has also been hit hard by loss: His brother, Lance Corporal Michael W. Harris, who served in the U.S. Marines, died by suicide Feb. 6, 2012.

Everly, which Rao heads as CEO, offers a platform that supports individuals who preplan and their families, helping them navigate challenging moments and providing resources that they can use to pass on a legacy and help loved ones navigate grief.

With an empathetic and innovative approach, Rao is seeking to make a tangible difference in people's lives.

*Sgt. Elijah John-Miles Rao*

**Coping with Loss**

Rao had what he calls "a relatively healthy" grief experience when his grandfather died a couple years before his brother. "I was there when he took his last breaths, and it was something I could understand," he said. "But with Elijah, it was really different. It struck me to my core."

It also made him question what he wanted out of life and who he was, he said.

"I ended up going to a national seminar (held by Tragedy Assistance Program for Survivors, also called TAPS), and I sat across from another sibling sharing his story, and it was the first time I felt seen and heard during my grief experience – and validated as well," he said.

It was a "transformational experience" – one that compelled Rao to explore how he could give back to others coping with loss.

Even though he was a chef at the Four Seasons in Hawaii, when he had an opportunity to join TAPS full time, which is a national nonprofit that provides ongoing emotional help, hope and healing to all who are grieving the death of a loved one in military service to America, he jumped at the chance.

"I wanted to understand how to have an impact using a retreat-based model, how to engage in activities that foster community and connection," he said. "And also, what subclinical grief support could look like in a grief support setting."

While an expert through loss, Rao found his training as a chef also helped him support others in a grief setting.

Being a chef, he noted, involves having an ability to create environments where people feel comfortable. "I look at the sacred act of breaking bread as an opportunity to share yourself," he said. "It is surprising how translatable a lot of those experiences were."

Leaving that world was not as big a leap as you may suspect, since in his teens, he was torn between pursuing social work or becoming a chef, he said.

"I had success and became part owner of a restaurant in Portland," he said. Later, he moved to Hawaii where he had the opportunity to join the Four Seasons.

"I was sitting there looking at a pod of humpback whales thinking, 'Where is the dotted line?'" he said, explaining what it was like when he received the offer to become a chef at the hotel.

While he treasures his time at the Four Seasons, he said he knew there would be a moment when he'd be ready to step outside the kitchen and step forward – and it arrived when he had the chance to join TAPS.

**Embarking on a Mission to Support Others**

Rao led a men's support group at the nonprofit and played a key role in building out and marketing various initiatives. He also helped launch an expedition program that focused on helping people who had suffered a loss two or more years ago.

He enjoyed helping people transition to a new life after loss – one where they realized that their existence was not defined by the death of their loved but how they incorporated that loss into their own story.

Along the way, he climbed Mount Kilimanjaro, got drenched while white water rafting and made some incredible friends. (The picture at the top of this article shows Rao giving a "gender reveal" of one of the two daughters he and his wife adore.)

*Rao on an expedition to the Grand Canyon area.*

"I used to do this retreat every year in Montana," he said. "I would take 40 or 45 men there, and we would fly fish and go to Yellowstone. It was an opportunity for men to do an activity next to each other, and our most powerful words were shared in passing."

It was a powerful experience for Rao, as when he and his brother were kids, they would fish and chat about what they'd like to do one day – and his brother mentioned going to Yellowstone. "And every year I was in Montana, I let the men know that this was something I was going to do with my brother … and although I never had the opportunity to do it in life, death ultimately brought me here … and how powerful that was."

Rao spent more than seven years at TAPS, and he feels blessed for having had the opportunity to serve the nonprofit, even though it was the result of tragedy. "I fit a unique profile," he said. "I had lost my brother in military service and was considered an expert by experience. I received specialized training in supporting the bereaved."

Eventually, however, Rao felt compelled to try something new.

"TAPS was a wonderful chapter of my life," he said. "It was incredible walking alongside thousands of fellow Gold Star family members. But I was ready to embark on building a scalable, market-based solution to have an even greater impact on how individuals and families prepare for the inevitability of death and how grief is experienced afterward."

**Launching Everly**

Rao's urge to build something led to the formation of Everly, which serves everyone – not just men.

With that said, Rao observed that it's particularly common for men to struggle with grief, as they are not as quick to reach out to others for support than women.

"It's not that men do not want or need help – they do," Rao said. "I say marketing has never really been directed at men to reach them where they are." He added, "One of the things we see as a unique opportunity is to be inclusive, encouraging and supportive and to honor the fact that there is room for more messages, more tones and more personalization — and technology allows us to do that."

As to what makes the Everly platform different, Rao said the key word is *experiential*.

For instance, someone can find grief support videos from experts, activities that involve journaling or photography along with messages from a loved one who has prearranged – or a medium with which to share such messages.

Rao had facilitated numerous workshops and regional and national seminars to help people navigate grief at TAPS, but what he saw missing was a scalable solution to have maximum impact.

"The reason Everly is a company and not a nonprofit is that nonprofits are never meant to scale – they are always having to bring money in and never get large enough to meet the need," he said.

He has only great things to say about his co-founder, Harris.

"He was a participant in a couple of events I led, and I knew about his entrepreneurial spirit," Rao said, noting that they decided to team up together to do something to help those in grief. "Originally, we were looking at sibling grief as a stepping stone, as there is more complexity – they are often called the forgotten griever."

Over time, they fine-tuned their concept and began to look at funeral homes as a singular touchpoint where they could have a huge impact. "We really wanted to understand that environment as everyone has to navigate that experience," he said.

Everly was incorporated in September 2021, and Rao and his team conducted market research, learning more about preneed. "Pre-care and preneed was a very interesting space that we wanted to dive into and understand," he said. "We saw an opportunity to positively impact the grief experience for family members and to further deepen the relationship around a preneed purchase."

The Everly team also looked at how it could help prevent suicides "as statistically speaking, you are at increased risk of suicide if your loved one died by suicide," Rao said. "If you look at grief, it is reactionary … we are looking further upstream."

Since introducing the platform, it has been offered to families through independent sales partners, including preneed sales agents and funeral directors.

Some partners – almost 7,000 of them, according to Rao – offer Everly as a core element of the service they provide while others offer it as an "add on," he said.

The company employs seven full-time team members, dozens of contractors and a variety of partners, Rao said.

"We can work across various segments in the industry," Rao said "Coast to coast, we are seeing a variety of partners, from the funeral director to preneed marketing companies to the insurance companies themselves reaching out. We have immense interest from international partners as well."

Rao and his team enter the space with an acute awareness that grief is universal. "The way that cultures and various groups approach grief is inherently unique," he said, adding, "There are enough complexities to allow us to dive in, develop our core understanding and better our service and product before we look at international expansion."

The backbone of the platform is that it's a community for grievers *by* grievers, which Rao said would have been so helpful to him and others who've lost loved ones.

For those who opt in to the Everly platform, the team looks at their individual grief profile. "You can look at it like a Netflix carousel – no two experiences are the same," he said. "The content that will come onto their feed will be unique and different to help them go through the grief process."

When it's included in a preneed contract, anyone in the purchaser's network gets a year's worth of grief support. "That way, they are able to provide support for their families and communities – we help an individual to share their values and life experiences with those they love."

Rao explained more about how the platform works.

"We offer a one-time pay for $500, or you can pay over time for $600. We try to make our services approachable for consumers and strive to not be a part of the subscription-based economy. We want our customers to have the peace of mind that once they've paid for Everly, they are guaranteed the services we provide."

After purchasing Everly, the customer gets lifetime access to its digital time capsule service, he said. "What that customer dies, everyone they love — family, friends, neighbors, co-workers, etc. — gets one year of access to Everly's grief care resources." He added, "Everyone they love, however, gets LIFETIME access to the digital time capsule contents left behind by our customer, to the extent that the contents were shared (/tagged) to that individual or made public."

The goal is to help people experience a healthy death and for their loved ones to have a healthy grief experience, Rao said.

Grief content is regionally specific, so that those on the platform hear from someone that sounds like them in environments they know. "We feature individuals walking various journeys that are relatable," Rao said. "We help strengthen relationships between a preneed purchaser and those they love ahead of their passing … once you are a griever, you are part of a larger community."

The platform allows people to have their loved one's grief and words in the same space, Rao said.

For instance, a preneed purchaser who does not know whether they will live long enough to walk their daughter down the aisle on her wedding day may record a message for what they'd say on that day – or someone might leave a message for their unborn grandchildren or share some words about their family history.

Or, the platform can give a son the opportunity to ask his father what their greatest memory is as a parent. Likewise, a son or daughter can ask their mom to tell them more about the day they were born.

"The platform creates opportunities for connection and engagement," Rao said. "It provides an environment for a family to navigate the end."

Everly views itself as being stewards of last words.

"If John says this is Jane's video, we will deliver that and make sure that piece is there … we deliver those pieces as requested," Rao said.

In a way, the platform is leveraging technology to bring back something that we used to have that has largely been lost.

"We used to have a will and testament … that was the norm," Rao said. "But then we lost the testament. It could be that this is a modern take to share those words."

While Everly currently focuses on offering pre-care (for those who preplan and their loved ones), it is working on introducing an aftercare solution to the market as well, Rao said.

"Aftercare will be coming in mid-2024," Rao said. "Our primary focus right now is on the proactive nature of pre-care and how beneficial it can be to families. But we do want to make an impact on the at-need equation as well."

*Visit www.everly.care/partner to learn more about Everly.*

# Will Andrews Talks About A Robust Pipeline and the Future of Anthem Partners

*By Thomas A. Parmalee*

When Will Andrews left his job at Batesville, most people were surprised.

That he was leaving *not* to join another supplier but to serve as president of a new privately owned consolidator of funeral homes and cemeteries only turned the surprise into – for some – a level of shock.

But Andrews, who left Batesville after more than 20 years, says the opportunity to join Anthem Partners was too good to pass up. It was also a natural move that allowed him to leverage his considerable talents.

"Most of my work with Batesville was around supporting funeral homes through consulting and not actually selling products," he explained. "Thus, I was well versed in HR, legal, finance, community outreach and marketing of funeral homes."

In short, he paid no mind to the naysayers who raised their eyebrows when he announced his move.

"There are many executives within our industry without a funeral background who are very successful due to their business sense," he said. "I really felt like I could bring the knowledge gained at working for a major corporation, plus the learning of the good and bad transitions of some of the consolidators within the space, and merge that with my leadership capabilities."

So far, what some may have perceived as a gamble, has paid off: Three years after opening for business, Anthem Partners has more than 70 locations in five states and three Canadian provinces and is on a trajectory to enjoy steady growth.

The company began when it acquired its first seven locations in Central California before making large acquisitions in Canada, Tennessee, California, Arkansas, New Mexico and Nevada. "After the first 12 months, we were at around 50 locations and acquired the rest in year two," Andrews said. "Year three has been about effectively integrating our operations and working on being a world-class operation company."

We recently caught up with Andrews to learn how he made the transition from being a Batesville legend to becoming the president of Anthem, along with his goals for the future.

**Tell us a little bit about yourself.**

I am married to my college sweetheart, Courtney, and we have three wonderful daughters, Ellie, Sydney and Mallory. We live in Frisco, Texas, and I suffer through being a diehard fan of Auburn University, the Dallas Cowboys and FC Barcelona. I love to travel, whether to Europe or Disney with my girls. I also love exploring the world of wine, while also watching a lot of sports.

**Many people were very surprised when you left Batesville. What led you to leave?**

I had always wanted the opportunity to sit on the other side of the desk. I had worked so closely with many of the top operators in funeral service and wanted to try my hand at it. It was very difficult to leave my Batesville family, but the timing was perfect for accepting this opportunity.

**When you got out of college and began looking for a job, did you actively seek out a job in death care?**

I actually just answered an advertisement in a local paper back home in Alabama for "vault sales" with Vantage Vault. I got a sales territory covering Alabama and Mississippi for them. It was the perfect job right out of college, staying in hotels and traveling the South was a lot of fun. After a year with Vantage, I got the opportunity to work for Batesville and after attending some conventions, I knew they were the company to work for within the industry, at that time.

**You made a big mark in the profession at Batesville, rising to division vice president of sales. What did you like most about that job?**

No doubt it was the customers. Getting to know funeral directors and business owners across North America was fantastic. I never pictured myself ever having much reach outside of the South and traveling to the West Coast, Canada, New York, etc. was so exciting. Understanding their businesses and forging personal relationships that have lasted over the years is something that I cherish very much.

**Who were your biggest mentors at Batesville – what did you learn from them?**

I had many over the years in multiple capacities, but Ray Armstrong and John Schutte would be the two that really stood out. Ray taught me to not back down from my opinions. If I believed something was best for the customer, to stand firm and not just be an order taker. Schutte taught me to be authentic and not lose "who I am" no matter the situation. His passion for the company, employees and customers was greater than anyone I ever worked with during my tenure in the profession. He cared so much and with every decision he made, he would weigh its impact on those around him.

**What is the Anthem-wide cremation rate and how does that compare with the average of the states you are in?**

Anthem's cremation rate varies substantially from locations at over 80% in Canada/California to some in the 40% range in Tennessee. We typically are very consistent with the markets we participate in.

**What does your acquisition pipeline look like – and what do you look for when deciding whether to consider buying a firm?**

Our pipeline is very robust. The challenge coming out of COVID is the valuation process. Balancing the spike from COVID with the tightness of the market is challenging. We like to look for a group of firms within a market. These regional consolidators give us the ability to draw efficiencies within the group.  That, along with our corporate buying power allows us to enhance profitability without making wholesale changes at the local level.  After we establish a presence in the market, we will add "bolt-on" acquisitions within geographies that are already in play.  One of the greatest compliments we receive is when a local funeral home approaches us about buying their firm because of the positive things they have heard from our employees.

**How challenging has it been to operate in a high interest rate and high inflationary environment? What have you had to adjust?**

This has caused us to slow down and effectively integrate the operations at the firms we have acquired.  With the cost of capital being higher, we have used this time to focus on streamlining operations until rates begin to soften.  We have been able to offset inflation substantially due to our buying power and size.  We grew at the right time to begin to negotiate better terms with our vendors and partners.  That all being said, we have had to look at passing along some of the rising costs on to the families we serve.

**Is there ever a chance that Anthem would go public?**

There is the possibility of us going public, and we have had a substantial amount of interest in an IPO.  We do prefer seeking investors with longer-term/forever-hold approaches to the businesses they invest in.  We know this is a very personal business and there are many advantages to being private.  In the end, whether we go public or stay private, we want to choose the path that is best for our employees, shareholders and the communities we serve.

**What are some of the most important lessons you have learned over the past few years running Anthem? What did you wish you knew starting out that you know now?**

The most important lesson is to grow deliberately.  Whenever you start an endeavor such as Anthem, you want to grow as quickly as possible.  It is hard to walk away from deals when people want to sell their business to you, but sometimes the best deals are the ones you walk away from.  Growing fast leads to a lot of growing pains.  Building the infrastructure to support that growth is vitally important.  Patience is paramount.  Also, don't feel like you must be the expert.  I am not a licensed funeral director, embalmer or celebrant, and that is OK, as we have great people in all those areas.  Being curious is the key to success and not a sign of weakness.  Not being the expert gives you the ability to support more thoroughly without prejudice.  Lastly, keeping decisions as close to the field as possible is best for everyone.  The more you empower your local people, the better the families you serve are treated.

**What makes the Anthem Partners culture so special?**

Our organization has a bottom-up mentality when it comes to processes, procedures and decisions.  Thus, we try to empower our people to create our operations manual versus us pushing down to them how to handle themselves. Our leadership team is constantly going on "listening tours" where we try to understand the challenges in the field and with our team. We try to constantly listen to those closest to the families we serve.

**What do you see as your biggest challenges at Anthem moving forward – what about the biggest opportunities?**

The biggest challenges going forward are on the financial side. Ensuring we get our valuations correct on acquisitions is tough in a market with as much volatility as the current one. Continuing to right-size our organization to ensure we have the right mix of employees so that we can be agile as the market shifts is also very important. We are also going to be challenged by the same factors as many other businesses across all industries, such as inflation, retaining top talent and the cost of capital.

Our biggest opportunities revolve around our reputation and the fact that we aren't viewed as "corporate" – yet. I know the larger we become, the more that moniker will apply, but many sellers are looking at us as the protector of their legacy. We have bid on many businesses in our first three years and often win the bid with a lower bid than the other consolidators, mainly due to our reputation and our little to no-disruption policy. We also have a lot of opportunities around the changing industry as many great operators are looking to sell but stay on in the business. They are tired of the HR, finance and technological aspects of their business. We can take care of those items while they continue to focus on families within their communities.

*Visit https://anthempartners.com to learn more about Anthem Partners.*

# A Conversation with Joseph Finocchiaro, the CEO and President of Pierce Colleges of Funeral Service

*By Thomas A. Parmalee*

Pierce Colleges of Funeral Service started the year off with a bang, announcing that Joseph Finocchiaro, who serves as president of one of its schools – the Dallas Institute of Funeral Service – would take on the chief executive officer and president roles for the entire organization.

In addition to its school in Dallas, Pierce Colleges of Funeral Service includes two other institutions that are also accredited by the American Board of Funeral Service Education: Gupton-Jones College of Funeral Service and Mid-America College of Funeral Service.

All three schools are single-purpose institutions offering an associate degree in funeral service.

Finocchiaro earned multiple degrees in music performance at the University of South Florida and then an associate degree in funeral service education from St. Petersburg College. Later, he also completed an executive juris doctor in law and technology with an emphasis in cyber-law from Concord Law School.

After completing his funeral education, he continued his work at the E. James Reese Funeral Home & Crematory in Seminole, Florida as an intern before earning his full license. When the firm was acquired by the Anderson-McQueen family of funeral homes, he became the funeral director in charge at its Life Tribute-Gulfport chapel before switching gears, taking his first teaching job at Miami Dade College, where he became coordinator of funeral service education before joining the Dallas Institute of Funeral Service in January 2019.

We recently caught up with Finocchiaro to learn more about his march up the administrative ranks of funeral service education, the challenges he plans to tackle in his new role and his thoughts on mortuary science education.

**You were a funeral director and certified crematory operator at E. James Reese Funeral Home and Crematory in Seminole, Florida, for several years before transitioning to becoming an educator. What prompted the change?**

My constant dream was to be a collegiate professor, and this was apparent to me years before I ever thought about funeral service. When I began thinking what my next big step would be, I began looking at funeral service education as a way to enter the field of academia. It was a hard decision to leave funeral directing as I had very strong community ties in Pinellas County, Florida where I worked, but when faced with your dream job, better compensation and benefits, you take the opportunities you're given.

I moved to Texas when they offered me the presidency of the Dallas Institute, since it was an on-campus, student-facing position. I had to move from St. Petersburg, Florida, to Hollywood, Florida, in order to take my job at Miami-Dade College, as there was no distance education program at that college and, even if there was, full-time faculty have to have an on-campus presence.

**Do you still engage in any active funeral directing? Why or why not?**

The short answer is I do not. As a professor, I felt it was very important to remain strictly neutral when working with funeral homes – both corporate and independent. As such, I did not solicit any trade work or part-time work outside of academia once I entered it. To be clear: I absolutely offered my time and talents to anyone in an emergency who would ask me, especially during the pandemic. I would not solicit opportunities to direct otherwise. Lastly, to do well in funeral service education, especially starting off, is an extreme time commitment. Like any teacher, you work countless hours off the clock that is not accounted for.

**You jumped from being a professor at Miami Date college right to becoming president of funeral service and then to being named CEO of Pierce Mortuary Colleges. What prepared you to make that leap?**

I wasn't just a professor at Miami Dade College, I was the program coordinator of its funeral service program. This prepared me well for the next stage of my career since I had both educational experience and administrative experience. It was because of that administrative role I decided to study law, as I felt that would give me an edge if I went further into administration. When you combine the teaching, administrative, and legal/regulatory experience, in my opinion, you get a strong candidate for someone in charge of stewarding an educational organization.

**You worked for a subsidiary of the prestigious Anderson-McQueen Family of Funeral Homes of St. Petersburg, Florida. How closely did you work with John, Nikki and Bill McQueen and what big lessons did you learn from them?**

Anderson-McQueen acquired Reese Funeral Home right as I was finishing my internship. As a line-level director, I didn't work day to day with John, Nikki, or Bill but rather would see them on a week-by-week basis during leadership meetings. What Bill and John did was invest in my development as a funeral professional. I have long attributed my success since then to that investment they made. I think the biggest lesson I learned is that it is entirely possible to do things in the nontraditional way and succeed at it. Anderson-McQueen always innovated new concepts and merchandise into its business model. The McQueens were highly visible and active in national organizations and encouraged their employees to engage in business networking opportunities. I would like to think I was a good employee to them, and I have the highest respect and admiration for John, Bill, and Nikki.

**Can you share an experience where something at a funeral service did not go as planned or as expected, and what lesson did you learn from the experience?**

It's hard to pick just one story as you can imagine. I was at the funeral of the mother of a very dear friend. At the entombment, the lift battery died just shy of where it needed to be in order to load the casket into the crypt easily. Thankfully, the mausoleum crypt was about chest high, and when I looked at the cemetery worker his eyes were wide because he didn't know what to do.

Before anyone could think about what was happening, I walked up to the side of the casket and stated, "This is where I would like to ask the men of the family to please assist me in laying their mother to rest."

They immediately joined me at the casket, I gave some simple instructions on what we were about to do, and we laid their mother gently to rest. After the services were over, my friend who is a licensed medical doctor stated, "I have been to hundreds of these services over the years. I never could have imagined how important and meaningful a service could be until this moment."

To this day, they do not know the battery failing gave them this incredible and powerful moment. They believed this was planned and an important part of the ceremony.

**Do we have enough young people and older people who may be transitioning to a new career interested in funeral service? What can funeral homes and funeral professionals do at the local level to encourage more members of their community to explore a career in funeral service?**

This is a difficult question – I think we have enough people coming into education to meet the needs, but we're having a hard time closing that loop to getting them licensed.

There are several reasons for this and, to be honest, this question alone could be the topic of an entire interview, but I think a primary consideration is that people are coming for a funeral service education with unrealistic expectations of what we do. I think it's very important that funeral professionals engage with educational institutions that offer shadowing opportunities, not just part-time work. Ride-alongs are common in some fields, and we need to paint a realistic picture of what we do on a daily basis.

Shadowing costs licensed practitioners nothing. As a shadow, they should not be participating in any way – they should simply watch and observe. If a shadow wants to take a more active role, then some type of part-time employment needs to be discussed so that they are covered by the firm's general liability policy like any other employee. I think most funeral professionals will be able to tell quickly during the shadowing opportunity whether or not they may wish to invest in that shadow as a part-time employee.

**Can you tell me a little bit about each school under the Pierce umbrella?**

The Dallas Institute of Funeral Service originally began its history in 1900 as the Barnes School of Embalming and later became the Dallas School of Embalming. It was succeeded by the Dallas Institute of Mortuary Science founded by W.H. Pierce and L.G. Frederick. Current enrollment is about 450 students.

The Gupton-Jones College of Funeral Service was founded in 1920 in Nashville, Tennessee, by L.A. Gupton. By 1969, it had migrated to the Atlanta, Georgia area. It moved into its current home in 1992 in Decatur. Current enrollment is about 425 students.

Mid-America College of Funeral Service is a combination of two schools: The Kentucky School of Mortuary Science and the Indiana College of Mortuary Science. The Kentucky School was founded in 1895. In 1972, the school was acquired by the Pierce Organization. The Indiana College of Mortuary Science was established in 1905 in Indianapolis, Indiana as the Askin

Training School for Embalmers by Clifford Askins. It changed its name in 1924. In 1980, both schools merged, and the Mid-America College of Funeral Services moved to its current location in Jeffersonville, Indiana. Current enrollment is about 320 students.

Since the pandemic, a tremendous shift has occurred in education and distance education far exceeds on-campus enrollment. Many schools had to adapt to that trend, and thankfully, we had put emphasis on our distance education programs prior to pandemic, so we were able to adapt relatively easily because of our foresight.

Each campus has its own rich history and personality. Demographics also differ between the three schools, so each school, necessarily, has its own challenges.

**What excites you most about the students you see at Pierce Mortuary Colleges today?**

Today's students genuinely want to get into funeral service for good reasons: to help people and provide support to others in their time of need. A large number of them come with no prior experience in funeral service and start working at funeral homes during or after their funeral service education. This provides both benefits and challenges, of course. But with the evolution of the death-care industry becoming a service-focused industry rather than a merchandise centered industry, the modern graduate is well prepared for their evolving role as a funeral professional.

**What do today's mortuary college students struggle with the most?**

I would say many students struggle with time management and the discipline necessary to succeed in online learning while also juggling their personal lives and employment. Funeral service distance education isn't diluted just because it's delivered in an electronic format. The second thing is students struggle with the nature of the job. It's hard physically and emotionally, and there's not much that can prepare you for it.

**What do funeral homes need to do to appeal to today's mortuary science graduates, so that the best new graduates come to work at their firm? What do students value that perhaps their older peers did not?**

Modern funeral homes have to accept that the business model that existed in the 1980s and 1990s is evolving, and the modern worker is not going to accept the same conditions that Gen Xers and millennials did. The newer generations put emphasis on work-life balance and their own personal physical and mental health. They have a personal identity that is separate from their work identity, unlike previous generations where their work identity/work ethic is strongly associated with their personal identity.

Would you like to see more states allow for a split licensure, or are you in favor of the idea that all licensed funeral directors should also be licensed embalmers?

I unapologetically have a clear preference that all licensees, dual or single, should have the common experience of a full funeral service education in both the arts and sciences.

I'm actually indifferent to the concept of split licensure and there are some compelling reasons why this model of licensure should be adopted. My concerns lie in the customer experience and increased risk of liability.

Traditionally, a family member could meet with a licensed professional in an arrangement conference and that arranger likely had a "dual license." That client could ask just about any question and receive a response based on experience and personal knowledge because the licensee went through school and had experience on both the arranging and preservation side.

My concern now is that a single-role licensee (arranger) will have to defer questions to a second single-role licensee (embalmer). Worse yet, the arranger may answer the question conveniently with no basis in reality, which then increases the firm's liability as they talk about something they know little, if anything, about. To be clear, of course there will always be situations with an arranger making promises they aren't able to fulfill, as unfortunate as those situations are. A dual licensee is at least *knowledgeable* to some extent in preservation techniques and has proved some level of competency as a requirement of their formal education. That is not the case with a single-purpose licensee. This increases the risk of egregiousness when an unsubstantiated promise is made, which then increases liability.

From my decade of experience with those who "only want to be embalmers," when they arrive at mortuary school, I've noted they're choosing the prep room *to avoid contact with clients*. These licensees now have to be able to communicate effectively with clients and *when* those clients ask questions. This equates to your embalmers being interrupted from their expected duties in order to field questions that the arrangers simply have no knowledge of and then resuming duties after they're done talking. This could lead to costly mistakes in the prep room.

Lastly, courts don't change standards quickly, easily, or affordably. Courts may apply existing dual-licensee standards which may lead to increased litigation costs and appeals.

In summary, I'm not opposed to single licensure. I'm opposed to quick fixes that will cause other problems if the situation is not well thought out or planned for. I have single-licensee graduates of my certificate programs who are excellent arrangers and managers. I am just as proud of them as I am the traditional students.

**What do you see as your biggest challenges as the president of Pierce moving forward? What are some of your major goals?**

I think my biggest challenge as the president of Pierce Mortuary Colleges will be to communicate to the industry, regulators, and general public the necessity of a formalized, quality funeral service education in the development of licensed professionals. A secondary challenge will be to educate those same parties on how pre-licensure education and testing is planned and delivered; especially the role of licensees in such things as exam and curricular development. Neither of these things happen in an echo chamber.

As for my goals, I am hoping to increase our partnerships with institutions of higher learning, so that all Pierce Mortuary College graduates have the benefit of transporting their education into baccalaureate and, in the far future, even graduate degrees.

I'm hoping to increase our efficiency as an institution to meet the modern needs of federal and state regulatory agencies while also exceeding expectations in regard to educational excellence.

Lastly, I'm hoping to establish our schools as the institutions of choice, so that both students and those seeking to become educators think of our schools first as excellent places to go to receive and provide instruction.

**Is there a website you'd recommend your funeral service peers visit?**

Please visit the American Board of Funeral Service Education (www.abfse.org) and the International Conference of Funeral Service Examining Boards (www.theconferenceonline.org). Subscribe to their notifications and newsletters, so that licensees can take part in things like subject matter expert evaluations of curriculum or test issues.

As president of the American Board, I'm always surprised that licensees are not more aware of their role in the development of education and pre-licensure certification. It's a very important role they play.

**Do you have any other thoughts to share or add?**

Stay engaged with your state regulatory agencies and state associations. I think it's very, very important that licensees participate in state and national associations to protect their interests and stay engaged in our ever-evolving industry.

*Visit https://pierce.edu to learn more about Pierce Mortuary Colleges.*

# Loose Ends Aims to Help Grieving Families Finish Projects of Love

*By Thomas A. Parmalee*

If you're a funeral director, you talk to a lot of families and hear a lot of stories … and no doubt, you've heard about some unfinished projects that were being undertaken by the deceased.

It's usually up the survivors to finish them, and in the case of completing that kitchen redo or repainting a room, the process is usually straightforward and not so loaded with emotion.

But some tasks carry with them more meaning.

For instance, what if your loved one was working on a book that had consumed them for months or years before their death … if you're not a writer or an expert in whatever your loved one was writing about, that's a tall order – and you may end up feeling like you've let them down by having it sit unfinished.

Another example that may have even more meaning is an unfinished knitting, crochet, quilting or other fiber arts project.

So many people enjoy doing these crafts, and if your recently deceased spouse or loved one was one of them, you don't want to leave it unfinished. And in fact, having it completed may very well result in being gifted with an item that carries incredible meaning.

The Loose Ends Project, which has volunteer finishers from every state in the United States (plus Puerto Rico and Washington, D.C.), as well as in 64 other countries, has stepped up to fill that need, knowing that survivors who are left behind usually cannot finish these projects on their own.

Knitters and nonprofit entrepreneurs Masey Kaplan of Falmouth, Maine, and Jennifer Simonic of Seattle, Washington launched the organization in September 2022 to complete unfinished projects left behind by crafters who have died or who can no longer do handwork due to compromised health. *(The two women are pictured at the beginning of this chapter in a photo by Winky Lewis, shared with permission. Simonic is on the left and Kaplan is on the right.)*

The free, volunteer-based service gives surviving families and friends an easy way to find knitters, crocheters, quilters, rug hookers, or any other crafters needed to complete a project. Skilled volunteer finishers wrap up the projects and return them to their intended recipients.

"We rely on a network of 22,000 volunteers around the world," Simonic said. "These volunteers use their skills that they have honed over years. Project owners are responsible for paying for any costs that happen (if shipping is needed, if extra materials are needed)."

The two women share a love for fiber arts and have been friends for more than 30 years, Simonic said.

Over the years, they've been asked to finish blankets, sweaters, or other projects left unfinished by deceased loved ones. They would always do so enthusiastically, understanding what it feels like to wear something a loved one has made.

Eventually, they launched their nonprofit to serve others on a larger level. They rely on their network of volunteer finishers to help people who submit projects – they don't try to tackle this themselves, Simonic said.

"But with over 1,500 projects submitted, there are so many that make us tear up," Simonic said. "There are ones from Grandma, who never got to meet great-grandbabies, sweaters from loved ones and some projects started by children who have passed on before their parents."

The toughest challenge has been getting the word out about what Loose Ends offers, Simonic said. So far, the organization has not worked directly with funeral homes – although it would welcome any support from the industry.

"Getting the word out to people who have the projects is the toughest thing," Simonic said. "Our volunteers, who are crafters, know how important it is for these projects to get done because we know we will have projects that may be left undone. Project owners — or finders – don't always know what they have or how to finish it."

Projects are often submitted by people who have heard about the organization at craft stores, yarn stores, quilt shops and online, Simonic said. "Whenever a news story gets out about us, we definitely see an uptick in projects," she said.

The items that are finished have been touched by the crafter who has died, so have incredible meaning for survivors, Simonic observed. "They even contain some DNA that has been left behind," she said. "They were usually started with someone in mind. Finishing these items for grieving gives them a tangible item to remind them of that person."

Kaplan added, "Handmade items are gestures of love. The time, expense, and skill that go into making them are impossible to quantify. When you wear something made especially for you, it feels good — the recipient of a handmade gift is thoughtfully considered with each stitch. When a maker dies mid-project, this tangible, handmade expression of love could get lost, donated, or thrown out. Loose Ends volunteers' goals are to finish these projects as intended and give them back to be used and cherished."

There are benefits for the finishers as well.

"Being a finisher gives people a chance to use a skill that they love to help someone else," Simonic said. "That is a magical experience. With the way the world has been these past few years, people have been looking for ways to reconnect. Loose Ends helps volunteers connect with people in their communities that they may never have met if it weren't for this project to be finished. We are reminding people that they can help others."

Crafters tend to be a "generous lot," Simonic observed. "Loose Ends is simply another place for crafters to demonstrate selfless kindness to a stranger," she said.

The organization will match finishers to projects of any textile handwork craft, including knitting, crochet, rug hooking, embroidery, cross stitch, quilting and more, she said. So far, the organization has facilitated the completion of more than 2,500 handwork projects to date.

There are ways to support the organization if you believe in what it is doing, Simonic said.

"People can help in many ways: Sign up to be a finisher, submit a project and donate," she said. "All of this can be done through our website. The one thing we do not take are craft items or yarn. We do have a list of places throughout the United States (by state) that will take these items."

So far, the organization has enjoyed an impressive level of success, landing media coverage in publications such as the Washington Post and Down East magazine.

It also has an alliance with Joann Stores, which trades on the Nasdaq and provides discounts and in-kind donations to volunteer finishers affiliated with Loose Ends. The chain's locations serve as designated meet-up spots for family members and finishers to connect on projects. It has also assisted in helping the nonprofit by allowing customers to "round up" their purchases at checkout or donate.

The Loose Ends Project website is the best place to go to for information about submitting a project or signing up to be a finisher.

**You can also read news articles on the organization by conducting a Google search for the following headlines:**

- *When illness or death leave craft projects unfinished, these strangers step in to help – NPR*
- *Joann Inc. partners with Loose Ends Project to finish what loved ones started – Bizwomen*
- *Loose Ends Project Volunteers Finish the Work of Deceased Fiber Artists – Down East Magazine*
- *They died leaving labors of love undone. Strangers complete their work. – The Washington Post*

*Visit https://looseends.org to learn more about The Loose Ends Project.*

# For Rolf Gutknecht and the Team at LA ads, Inspiration Starts with Being Curious

*By Thomas A. Parmalee*

Whether it's developing marketing for an event, a yearlong campaign, collateral material, or something else, Rolf Gutknecht finds inspiration everywhere.

The president and CEO of LA ads, a full-service marketing firm that serves the death-care market, Gutknecht (pronounced "Goot-neck," which means "good servant" in German) leads a team that finds ideas in every media and content channel there is – from television to Facebook to TikTok to outdoor bulletins, YouTube shorts and routine chats.

"We've had some wonderful work come out of research conversations we've had with our clients' customers and internal folks," he said. "For me, inspiration all starts with being curious," he said. "When you become intentional about being curious, new sources of inspiration can come pouring in. For example, I'll hear a song and then think, "How could I use the lyrics for current project we're working on or something later?""

Ideas are all around, but there's a big, big difference between taking that inspiration and turning it into an idea that "sings like a songbird versus croaking like a frog," he said.

So, how do funeral home owners, cemeterians and death-care suppliers craft messages that resonate and pave the way to building stronger, more successful brands? Gutknecht (pictured at the beginning of this chapter) recently shared some of his insights with FuneralVision.com.

**You might have the most interesting and original name in all of funeral service. What's the story behind it?**

Well, there is a story that I tell folks that speaks to how my first name has helped me maybe stand out in the world of more common names. The story goes like this: Growing up, I can't tell you how many different versions of my name I heard on the school playground and in the classroom – Rolfe Gootnut, Rolph Goodnick, Ralph Goodneck, Rolfe Gootnech, and there's more where that came from. I'd come home and whine to my mom about how my name was being mispronounced by kids and teachers alike. Now being the German mom she was, she didn't see the problem with my name, but she said something to me that I remember to today: *"It's the one thing about your name that makes you different, that will make you love it."* Of course, I didn't believe her at the time, but after years of therapy (not really), she was right. While it still gets hacked up and mispronounced fairly regularly, I'm ok with it because, well, how many people do you know named Rolf? Few if any, right?

**Recently, you wrote an article highlighting advertisements from the Super Bowl. If you had to pick one advertisement that you saw this year that offers lessons for funeral homes – good or bad – which advertisement would that be and why?**

Good question. There were a number of really good commercials this year that I enjoyed but I'd say the State Farm (Arnold Schwarzenegger– "neighbah") spot was my favorite. State Farm understood that while they have had the same tagline/brand positioning for years, it needs to be continually presented and done so in an interesting way. The ending with Danny DeVito clearly mouthing the line: *"Like a good neighbor State Farm is here"* was funny given how Arnold was "struggling" saying "neighbor" throughout the spot. I also liked it because from a marketer's perspective for a commercial – or any general marketing/ digital/ content/ etc. advertising, for that matter – to be effective, it has to accomplish several critical feats: *It has to be different and attract attention, it has to be clear in its fundamental selling message,* so the audience is not in the least bit confused on what is being advertised, *the message has to be compelling,* so that it influences people to want to get what's being advertised, and *it has to be memorable,* so when you walk away from it, you'll associate some level of positive feelings with the product /brand in the future  Again, this applies to all marketing/advertising efforts in any channel.

**I believe you used to be based in Los Angeles, but now you live in the Dallas-Fort Worth area. How are you enjoying Texas, and how has the shift affected business, if at all?**

Yes, L.A. was home for a lot of years, but we're now in the Dallas Metroplex (as they refer to it). We left for a number of reasons, with one reason being that we needed to refresh who we were, and the move has been very positive – both personally and professionally. It's been the change of scenery that we needed, and I think it's contributed to us even doing better work. From a business standpoint, the most obvious positive has been that we're now in the Central Time Zone, which means I'm now not needing to get up before the rooster does to work with most of our clients who are in the Eastern/Central time zone as was occurring when I was in L.A. And travel is a bit easier. Aside from that, we're still very much who we are and what we're known for.

**Can you share an example of a marketing campaign you've done in the past year for a client? What were the results, and why was it special?**

OK, if I have to choose one marketing campaign (and there's far more than one that I love for different reasons), it's the work that we did this past year for Arlington Memorial Gardens in Cincinnati. The wonderful clients who did not want to have their marketing sound, look, or be thought in the same way as competitors. They wanted all of their marketing messaging to be interesting, which meant saying things imaginatively, originally and freshly. Full of cleverness, surprise and being bold.

The campaign focus was the need to preplan in order to take the guesswork out of your funeral with the messaging centered around the idea of "If they don't know what to get you for your (insert: birthday, Christmas, etc.) then how will they know what to get you for your funeral?" In terms of results, while I wasn't privy to all the numbers, we were told on more than one occasion that their at-need business had noticeably increased but maybe even more importantly, that they set a record for preneed sales last year. We're happy to hear that the client is happy with what's being developed to help them be successful.

**Are funeral homes and cemeteries spending enough money on marketing? And if they are, do you think they are using those dollars wisely? Where do they most often go wrong?**

This is the second biggest roadblock to success for funeral homes, cemeteries and B2B firms, and I say that with the utmost confidence. Now, some people are going to view my response as the typical answer given what I do, but my experience with funeral homes and cemeteries confirms that they underbudget to the point that almost nothing they do will result in them boosting their market share or visibility. Not even a little change. If you see your marketing budget as an expense, the budget will be the lowest number possible and nothing good will come as a result of spending it. It's wasted money.  Now, if you see your marketing budget as an investment in growth (i.e., visibility, preference and sales) then you have a much better chance of succeeding – from growing both at-need and preneed business to even being in a better position to sell your firm at a good price or buy another one because you have money on hand. Or you will just have more better tomorrows for your staff and yourself.

Oh, and to answer your question about spending it wisely, it all depends on whether folks understand and are willing to think differently and step away from things that they're doing that don't have the same impact as other channel/media choices. Here's a story to this point: I had a nice Zoom call about two months ago with a gentleman that owns a number of funeral homes in the Midwest and is the runaway leader within a large business footprint. When I asked him what motivated him to want to speak with me, he said this: "The future depends on this mindset. You either see yourself as a funeral home owner that does marketing or begin to act like a marketer that's in the funeral profession." That owner gets it as do the larger firms and corporates.

**We all know you do incredible work, but is there an example of funeral home marketing that you were NOT involved in that you've seen recently that you'd like to highlight because it impressed you?**

So, Forest Lawn in the L.A. area had run a campaign (i.e., billboards, Facebook posts, etc.) that was geared to selling high-end cemetery property. If you know anything about Forest Lawn, you know that they have some of the most beautiful and well-maintained memorial parks in the country. So, they used their branding along with property beauty shots to attract wealthier folks (and families) to the idea of choosing a burial or cremation property location that reflected how they would like to be remembered. The marketing messaging revolved around the idea of *"Don't just leave your mark. Leave a landmark."* All the marketing materials showed beautiful property, views, and property options like estates. It was one of those times that I wished they were our firm's client and we had come up with the line.

**Do you have any final thoughts to share on funeral home marketing?**

In the spirt of wanting to be helpful, let me offer up five "Chicken Soup for the Marketer's Soul" thoughts:

- The most critical part of marketing is the message. In a competitive marketplace, like the one everyone is in, the most fascinating option always wins. Like always. End of story. Don't have a bland message or say what others could.

- While you may not be aware of what other firms (similar to yours) are doing to enrich their fortunes, there's a need to be open to new ideas. There are new approaches that are brimming with untapped potential to create new possibilities and produce results not thought possible.

- Your audience doesn't know what you really offer them or even know your name as much as you think they do. If you did any type of research on this, you'd be more than surprised at the results. Don't let your competitor be the better-known brand.

- Make the marketing about what the BENEFIT is to the audience. Or put another way, when a person walks into the Home Depot to buy a quarter-inch drill bit, it's not really the drill bit that the person wants. What that person wants is a quarter-inch hole. Make the marketing about the solution to your customers' needs and wants.

- A timid marketer comes across in the same way as a timid person. Timidity is associated with feelings of apprehension and lack of confidence. Timid folks (and firms) are afraid of drawing attention to themselves because they feel like they don't have anything different or fascinating to offer. Which is exactly the opposite of how a business like yours wants to be perceived. Don't be timid.

*Rolf Gutknecht is president and CEO of LA ads, a full-service marketing firm specializing in helping success-oriented funeral homes, cemeteries, manufacturers and service providers create compelling marketing messaging and develop impactful marketing programs to grow their business. Rolf can be reached at rolfg@laadsmarketing.com or 800-991-0625 ext. 2. Check out the LAads website by visiting www.laadsmarketing.com.*

# Mike Miller Shares Insights on Inspecting Crematories, Using Third Parties and More

*By Thomas A. Parmalee*

Mike Miller, chief operating officer of FT North America, knows a thing or two about cremation.

He started in the business more than 35 years ago at Stewart Enterprises, where he rubbed elbows with seasoned executives and learned life lessons from Frank B. Stewart Jr., who was its chairman and controlling shareholder before it was acquired by Service Corporation International.

After SCI acquired Stewart, it extended a very nice offer to Miller to stay on with the company. But Miller had been buying Stewart Enterprises stock for more than a decade, and he was in the enviable position of being able to try something new.

"I had an offer from InvoCare Limited," he said, referring to the Australian public company that mainly operates in Australia, New Zealand and Singapore. At the time, it was looking to expand into the United States." He took the job.

A little over a year ago, he was wooed out of semiretirement by FT, which put him to work growing its business in North America.

We recently caught up with Miller to get some of his insights on cremation operations – as well as why he thinks doing business with FT is a great option for funeral homes.

**Is FT growing?**

FT North America has been on a steady growth path since its first U.S. sale in 2008. As more and more people who understand the important metrics of a successful cremation business become familiar with how our focus on quality leads to reduced maintenance/downtime costs, our focus on efficiency shows up in reduced labor and gas costs. Our focus on safety ensures customers are doing everything possible to provide the best for their employees and community. Ultimately, our customers realize that FT is the only cremation equipment manufacturer that is aligned with their vision for serving cremation families.

**Beyond the United States, what areas of the world do you sell cremation units to? And what areas of the world do you focus on?**

FT is more than 100 years old. We have operated in many different countries throughout Europe since 1908 and have many clients all over the world in Asia, Australia and South America. That is at the heart of what makes us a unique provider, as our designs and equipment have been meeting the strictest of European standards, which far exceed U.S. standards.

My team focuses on North America, which is primarily the United States, with several locations in Canada, and interests in Mexico.

**What are the pros and cons of using a third-party crematory?**

That's an interesting question. As you know, I have experience running operations for half the country at Stewart Enterprises, where we owned all of our own crematories – and I was partial owner/operator of a large crematory in Los Angeles that performed about 4,000 cremations annually for only third parties, so I've lived both sides of that coin.

The biggest pro of owning your own crematory is complete control of the cremation process. You can always ensure you can meet the needs of the families you are serving because you have control over scheduling – witness cremations, rush cremations, casketed cremations, oversize … those requests that need special consideration don't need to involve a third party to "make it happen" on the timeline the family expects.

Additionally, costs like labor to drive cases back and forth to a third party should be considered when thinking about whether to own your own crematory. Some locations I know are driving two hours to the crematory and two hours back. If you are doing more than a couple hundred cremations a year, it doesn't take much for those costs to justify consideration for adding your own crematory.

On the other hand, third-party providers are the backbone of the industry in many ways. Barriers to entry for adding crematories can be overwhelming. Third parties can eliminate a lot of the red tape that some might experience with trying to open their own crematory operations.

For many operators, it's simply a matter of knowing their third-party provider is convenient, in compliance, in budget and trustworthy. Just like with start-ups, they offer longtime operators the opportunity to meet their customers' needs without the barriers that they may face in their current locations.

**What are some red flags you should be on the lookout for if you use a third party and conduct an inspection?**

I would say visit unexpectedly and visit often. In the corporate environment, we had compliance officers that held routine inspections, with detailed checklists that held us to a very high standard.

As a third-party provider, the best operators I worked for "showed up" at the crematory on a regular basis. One owner in particular would bring a case in on his own from time to time. You never knew when you'd look up and see him at your door. A good third-party provider should be welcoming and appreciative of that interest. It shows they operate at a high standard at all times, not just because they knew you were coming. Likewise, good owners know what they see. If you are uncomfortable, trust your gut and look for alternatives.

**Fill in the blank: When a firm is handling ___ cremation cases per year, it's time for them to think about investing in their own crematory. Explain.**

That is a hard one to answer because so many variables are at play. It could make sense for you to consider adding a crematory at 100 cases if you are having someone drive several hours a day to get there and back, 300 if you're in a growing market, or 1,000 if your business has achieved that level of success and you want complete control of your vision for serving those families. Everyone's journey to exploring the addition of cremation equipment and facilities is a unique path. Helping make those dreams and visions a reality are a big driver for us at FT. Check out a number of our projects at FTNorthAmerica.com. If you can dream it, we can most likely make it happen.

**Are there any new state regulations that funeral professionals should be aware of as it relates to emission standards, and how might this impact other states?**

The biggest concern for adding or updating cremation equipment is ever-changing state regulations. The new NOx standard in California, for example, reduced the acceptable levels of NOx emissions from 60ppm to 30ppm from one year to the next. Fortunately, since we completely build our machines and burners, we have been the only provider that I know of that has been able to redesign the FTIII to meet that standard in testing. We hope to have state verified tests this year with one of our scheduled new machine installs. Those kinds of potential future regulation changes are what crematory owners and potential owners need to take into consideration when choosing a provider. Is what you are buying today preparing you for whatever comes in the future?

We've also been designing and building the highest-quality filtration systems that meet the strictest European standards for decades. Any FT you buy today is already designed for additional filtration should future regulations require it. I know that was important to me as a crematory owner. I could sleep at night knowing I was prepared for whatever the future looked like.

**How often should you conduct routine maintenance on your crematory and who should conduct it?**

Like a car, boat or other significant investment, routine maintenance is the key to protecting it. You should always follow the guidelines of your manufacturer, as all machines are designed and built differently.

At FT for example, our MaxLife lining system is designed to double the time between routine maintenance by replacing traditional refractory with our own proprietary "blocks," which can save thousands of dollars over the life of the machine in maintenance and downtime costs.

**Are crematory operators paid enough in this business? Are they appreciated enough? How important are they to the funeral home?**

Crematory operators are your last line of defense against significant issues and mistakes: I repeat: Crematory operators are your last line of defense against significant issues and mistakes.

Never underestimate the role of a good crematory operator in your organization. You need someone in that role who can read, understand, notice red flags and make the call to STOP when there is a question. If you have created workarounds for the operator to *not* think on their own, you may want to consider upgrading that person at your location.

**What type of training should most funeral professionals get when it comes to cremation? Is there a particular course, program or conference you recommend they attend/go to?**

Both ICCFA and CANA have a good one-day operator training program that I think does a good job with the basics.

This last year, we were honored to partner with the Cincinnati College of Mortuary Science, providing the college with a brand new FTIII, loader, processor and ash transfer cabinet. That donation was an easy "yes" when we heard they were elevating the art of cremation in the same way as they elevated the art of embalming when I graduated in 1992. You can read a detailed article about FT's donation to CCMS here.

We're also in the process of creating our own in-depth training program for FT customers that will take place at the Cincinnati college twice a year. Stay tuned for more on that.

**What are some ways that a funeral home can assuage concerns from the community – or address those concerns – about a crematory being put into a residential area?**

As with any "not in my backyard" type business, rumor and misinformation can get far ahead of you if you don't get buy in from important stakeholders prior to announcing your intentions.

The best advice is to get ahead of it with local, county and community leaders. Provide education and information before you publicly announce your plans. Arming them with what they may hear and the answers for why much of that is simply not true before they hear it from constituents, as well as the value families will experience from a local and trusted provider after a loss is critical. Our info packet is available to you by logging into FTNorthAmerica.com and noting "Not In My Backyard info packet" in the notes.

**Do you think we'll ever see a method of disposition challenge cremation as the preferred choice of disposition? Why or why not?**

I am always intrigued by the new options that are offered to families after a loss. Only the future can say if they will exceed cremation as the preferred choice of disposition. People are people, and there will never be one option that is "better" than another in my opinion if it helps people grieve or honor their loved one in a way that provides peace.

*Visit https://www.ftnorthamerica.com/ to learn more about FT North America.*

# Finding His Destiny: Tony Kumming Takes the Not-So-Obvious Path

*By Thomas A. Parmalee*

Tony Kumming had just graduated from Ball State University with a degree in mathematical economics.

But he needed to find something to do before heading off to law school.

So, he got a job at the funeral home consolidator located in the Tampa Bay area, where he'd once lived, and which was near the law school he planned to attend.

"I had about nine months to do whatever I wanted," Kumming, now 40, explained about that period of transition in 2007. "And I got a job at the Keystone Group in downtown Tampa. And during that time, I quickly realized I enjoyed the people I worked with."

Those "people" are individuals that you may know quite well: They have names like Jim Price, Will Bischoff, Bob Horn, Steve Tidwell and Steve Shaffer.

Shaffer helped Kumming realize his destiny more than any other.

"I was just looking for jobs in the area, and ironically, Steve Shaffer and my mother are first cousins," he explained. "My uncle had recently passed away, and my parents and Steve were at the funeral together."

And that is how he learned that there might be an opportunity for him at Keystone, working in the corporate development department.

He interviewed with Bischoff and was offered an entry-level position, analyzing whether certain funeral homes might be good acquisition candidates.

"I was there for three years before the company was sold to SCI," he said.

Shaffer and Price ended up teaming up with Sterling Partners to launch Foundation Partners Group, which acquired some of the Keystone firms that SCI was required to sell as part of the deal. As a result, one day Kumming was working for Keystone and the next he was working for FPG in the exact same office as it simply took over the lease.

He did, in fact, go to law school – although only part time – earning his law degree from Stetson University College of Law in 2010 and passing the Florida bar exam.

"At the time, being young and with no family, and with nothing else to compare it to, it didn't seem crazy," he said of going to law school while working. "But looking back, it was really like doing two full-time jobs. Thankfully, Stetson has a part time program, so all my classes were at night. So, it never interfered with work."

Asked about Shaffer, he notes that although they are cousins, he never knew him before getting the job at Keystone. "My mom is one of five and Steve is one of nine, and they lived three houses down from each other growing up, but I didn't know Steve until I started working at Keystone," he said.

But Shaffer and those other titans of funeral service played a collective role in convincing him that a full-time job as a lawyer wasn't the path he was meant to walk down.

"A lot of things in life come down to people," Kumming said. "And the people in the profession and the people I worked with at Keystone were great."

He also sensed on a gut level that there were incredible opportunities in funeral service, just there for the taking for someone eager to grab them – someone like him.

"From the late 1990s to 2007, when I entered the profession, not many transactions had happened, and I had been told the baby boomers were coming – and lots of them would want to sell their business," he said. "I enjoyed the work and who I was working with … and the opportunity was compelling."

What was also compelling was Candice, who he met when he joined Keystone in 2007. She was a sales administrator at Keystone.

"We've known each other almost 20 years and have been married for eight," he said, joking that it took him awhile to convince her to go out with him – and then it took *her* awhile to convince him to get married.

"She was working at Keystone when I started," he said, noting that they went on their first date almost four years later. Asked if he liked her from the start, he said, "Yes, definitely. It was something that I knew immediately."

The two have a 6-year-old daughter and a 4-year-old son, and they live in Treasure Island, Florida. While Candice left the workforce for a time, she now serves as a consultant for Pinnacle's accounting team.

*Tony Kumming, his wife, and their two children.*

**Finding His Way**

At Keystone, Kumming says he "really developed a passion for the funeral profession," noting that it was not lost on him that he essentially "stumbled upon" a career while waiting to go to law school.

After FPG bought the collection of Keystone firms, Kumming worked for his new employer for about two years.

Asked about the executives at Keystone, he said they were all mentors, even if they were not trying to intentionally guide him to a career in the profession. "I think their passion came through with what they were sharing with me," he said. "I could tell that their careers were rewarding for them personally and professionally."

At FPG, it was the same office and a lot of the same people – and the same type of work. But there were real differences.

"It was funded by people without experience in the funeral profession – and it was eye opening to see different approaches to the same issue," he said. "It really made me realize the need to listen to people in the profession – not to say there is only one way to do something. But I think the fact I was at FPG only a couple of years until I left is a strong sign of which one I prefer."

In fact, listening is one of the best pieces of advice he said he can give others.

"I use the people I trust for guidance," he said. "I talk about anything with former owners or just to get business, leadership or management advice. I use the relationships I have built – and that is available to everyone. That is something that might be underutilized in today's world."

While he's not a licensed funeral director, Kumming would like to one day change that.

"I believe that will be in my future," he said, noting that he may be able to do a better job relating to staff if he becomes licensed. "I'm not afraid to roll up my sleeves, and I recently went out on my first removal," he said. "I think it is valuable for people who work at a funeral home to understand and believe everyone in the organization is marching to the same drum."

After figuring out that he did not want to stay at FPG, Kumming – for a time – considered leaving the profession.

"I was looking at different things … one that clearly made a lot of sense was looking at the law profession," he said. "I interviewed at a couple of law firms and had a job proposal, but during that time, we had worked on a couple of deals … and I got to know Jeff Boutwell, who started the NewBridge Group in the late 1990s after leaving Thomas Pierce."

It was a natural progression to go from a firm that focused on buying funeral homes to working for NewBridge, which, at the time, served as a broker for firms looking to sell.

"I used my experience on the buy side to succeed in my role at NewBridge," he explained.

As for teaming up with Boutwell, he's thankful to have had the chance.

"He's done and seen everything in funeral service from an ownership and management perspective and has an ability to see what's coming," Kumming said. "And he goes about his business in a fair and honest way."

*Tony Kumming with a combination of Pinnacle Funeral Service and Vineyard Capital Partners colleagues.*

### The Art of the Deal

Money, he observed, is – and should be – the biggest factor when selling a funeral home, but he thinks some other factors remain underappreciated.

That includes the connections owners have with the community as well as to individuals. "If you look at it from a 30,000-foot view, from the funeral home owner's perspective, they are essentially getting into a long-term relationship with whoever they sell to," he observed. "You have to feel confident that what you are signing up for is legitimate."

When he joined NewBridge Group in 2012 as a senior adviser, he knew the company was primed for growth.

"It was really focused on the Southeast, being based in Atlanta," he said. "I had some family in the Midwest, and I felt like over the years, that I had not seen as many opportunities there as you would anticipate."

Kumming had a theory: The Midwest was an underserved market, and NewBridge could gain market share by making it a priority.

"We ended up being very successful," he said.

When Boutwell shifted his focus to some other things, Kumming had the opportunity to become managing partner at NewBridge and eventually became its president. Along the way, NewBridge went through a metamorphosis.

"In 2019, we really started to shift our focus from the sell side to more of a buy-side representation," he said.

Asked why the company made the adjustment, he said, "We went through a process of looking back at all of our prior clients and did a deep dive to research what was successful and what wasn't. We learned that a lot of times a seller who sold for the last top dollar wasn't necessarily the happiest."

What often ended up happening is that since the "winning bidder" was usually the one who paid the most – and since most companies use the same valuation methodology – they would end up making decisions to rationalize paying more than others.

And that usually meant big changes, such as slashing staff or raising prices, which could alienate members of the community that the seller had served for so long.

"Former owners, a lot of times, see reducing staffing cost as reducing service to their families and — I'm speculating — see that as a reflection of themselves." He added, "The other side of the coin was that we found that the sellers who were the happiest were those that joined companies and leadership teams that they felt the most comfortable with and had commonalities. So, at NewBridge, we wanted to help sellers find their best-fit buyer for the most rewarding outcome."

In the process, the firm represented two main clients: Rollings Funeral Service and Pinnacle Funeral Service, which was founded in 2006 by a group of investors, Vineyard Capital Partners, which is led by Boutwell, who serves as the group's managing partner.

Kumming was intimately involved with the staff at Pinnacle over the years, and when the opportunity to lead the company as president presented itself, he was intrigued.

"I had a hand in the acquisition of those businesses," he explained. "So, it was somewhat of a homecoming. I probably knew half of the people who worked at Pinnacle through my interaction with them at NewBridge."

**Growing Pinnacle**

Last year, Pinnacle acquired about a half dozen firms, and it now owns 30 funeral homes and one cemetery in seven states: Georgia, North Carolina, Tennessee, Ohio, Indiana, Wisconsin and Illinois. Companywide, it has about a 70% cremation rate. Most of its rooftops operate their own crematory, but it has a handful of firms that work with a third party, Kumming said.

"This time last year, we had 25 funeral homes – and we have similar acquisition plans for the next year," he said.

In addition to serving as president of Pinnacle, Kumming is also one of the investors in Vineyard Capital partners, which owns the company.

Although Pinnacle is almost 20 years old, it still does not have much name recognition, Kumming said. But that is something he's seeking to rectify.

"Our plan is to remain privately owned in 20 years just like 20 years ago," Kumming vowed. "That is probably one of our biggest value propositions when considering succession. Our company, our team, has been stable and will *remain* stable for many more years. That is something that a lot of people are looking for in a transition."

What sellers have seen from some other companies, he noted, has given them a sense of unease.

"Sometimes, there have been promises that have not been delivered," he said sadly. "Plans to grow the market … and then those plans go away. Promising to get into new markets and then that does not happen. Or, bringing in a new business model for local operations that is inconsistent with what the seller anticipated."

The investor group behind Pinnacle, he said, has largely been the same throughout its lifetime. "Retired attorneys retired funeral directors, bankers and doctors – they see this as part of their retirement," he said. "Generally, it is a friends and family type environment. We are open to new investments, but usually the opportunities are gobbled up by the current investors. On occasion, when we see opportunity, we can bring in new people, but it's usually people already connected to me or someone else who is an investor … it's kind of a web of people."

As far as what types of firms Pinnacle seeks to acquire, it prefers businesses that are focused on cremation. "That is generally one of our biggest criteria," Kumming said.

The company also looks at whether a potential acquisition is close to any firms it already owns. "Just because of the relationships we have built in states where we already are, that is usually where our acquisitions would be, but we are open to anywhere else," he explained.

The type of firm Pinnacle acquires can vary greatly.

"As an example, last year we bought a business that did 70 calls, but we also bought one that did 500 cremations," Kumming said. "The spectrum can be quite vast in the call amounts. The one that was 70 calls was essentially next door to an existing location and made sense. A 70-call firm in South Dakota, however, wouldn't make much sense at all."

Perhaps the biggest factor, however, that determines whether Pinnacle bids on a business is the team that is in place at the firm. Even if an owner is retiring, if they have identified someone to take over and run the business, that can be a huge deal, he said.

"While there are some things we do change, there is still a lot of autonomy at the location level to run the business," he said.

Asked what he struggles with most in running Pinnacle, Kumming said "the people side of it."

He explained, "They are our greatest asset, but there are also a lot of individual personalities you have to manage. I put a lot of time and effort into it given how important it is. You have to get your people tools and resources to be the most successful."

Another tough task is making sure you are in compliance, with everything from keeping track of annual preneed reports, staying on top of licensing, responding to audits and filling out a tax return. "These things are necessary, but they are not something that necessarily adds value to us as a company or to the families we serve," he said.

Kumming is enjoying his role at Pinnacle.

"I went from doing a lot of work to relying on others to do analysis and look at opportunities … and now I I spend that time on operational stuff," he said.

Whether it's focusing on building a more robust preneed program or enhancing a funeral home's digital footprint, he says that he stays very busy at the helm of a company that serves about 6,000 families on an annual basis.

He's excited about the growth that lies ahead, even if the pipeline may not be as full as it was a couple of years ago.

"The fact is there are headwinds we've all faced," he said, referencing the pull-forward effect in the death rate as a result of COVID-19, higher interest rates and inflation.

He added, however, that we're in a part of the year when it is typically slower.

"People are still busy finishing their year-end finances from the prior year," he said. They want to get fresh, updated financials for projection purposes."

For those wanting to make a change, however, now is as good a time as ever, he said.

"We are kind of in this post-COVID world where a lot of things are normalizing, and it's little easier to see into the future and what that will look like," he said.

That means buyers can be more confident in their proposals, which can favor sellers.

*Visit https://www.pinnaclefunerals.com to learn more about Pinnacle Funeral Service.*

# Fortitude Research and Marketing: Taking A Holistic View to Bolstering Funeral Homes and Cemeteries

*By Thomas A. Parmalee*

George Owens, the president of Fortitude Research and Marketing, got his start at one of America's most iconic companies: J.D. Power & Associates, a global leader in consumer insights, advisory services and data and analytics.

The firm was only about 25 years old when he joined in 1995. He stayed for about 12 years, working on everything from building and managing proprietary measurements for brands, to conducting automotive studies and serving as a director of diversified industries.

Eventually, his work at J.D. Power brought him into the orbit of Service Corporation International, which is the largest death-care firm in the world.

SCI was increasingly looking at themes such as loyalty and customer engagement, and J.D. Power had a staff that could glean the type of insights it needed to boost market share and provide more value to families.

"The company has always had a great focus on how to build a great culture and enduring relationships, as well as how to engage customers – and that has come right from the top," Owens said of SCI.

By 2007, Owens found himself being invited to join SCI as a full-time employee, and the idea was so intriguing that he did what some thought was unthinkable: He left his job at J.D. Power and made the trek to Houston for what he thought would be a two- or three-year stint.

"But it turned into a fabulous 11 years in the SCI marketing department," he said. "I was able to work on customer engagement, customer loyalty and other marketing programs. It was a fabulous time for me and certainly a time of growth for SCI."

While in Houston, Owens prided himself on doing all he could to create great customer experiences, and just as importantly, to make sure those experiences were measured, so SCI could gauge what it was doing right and what it needed to improve.

"The main reason I went there is I wanted to take what I learned at J.D. Power and put it to work," Owens said. "SCI said if I had a good idea, they would fund it – and they were true to their word. We did all kinds of things that I think were game changing and that the industry still follows."

For instance, Owens was intimately involved in a customer engagement program that sent surveys to at-need families – a program that still exists today. Owens also helped develop a customer excellence program to recognize individuals in the field based on their performance. "All of the success that comes to any of these firms comes from those individuals caring for families at their worst time," he explained.

He worked with great mentors, such as Phil Jacobs, who he called "a visionary marketer." Others that stood out during his time at SCI include the late Steve Mack; Jay Waring (now the company's chief operating officer); Dan Garrison, a senior vice president; and of course, the late Robert L. Waltrip, the company's founder.

Waltrip provided Owens with lasting lessons that still resonate with him today.

"Mr. Waltrip talked to everyone, whether it was someone cutting grass at one of his locations or someone who was cleaning up the funeral home," Owens said. "He loved his funeral directors – he loved all of his employees. What I took away from him was that this is a business of people helping people – and he lived that every day."

Owens also has the utmost respect for Waring, who he says comes from a long line of funeral directors and from a family who operated firms that were a mainstay of Boston and the surrounding area. "Today, Jay runs SCI with the same principles that his father believed in, and that Mr. Waltrip and Mr. Mack instilled in him," Owens said.

Looking back at his time at SCI, Owens said he appreciates that the company always looked to the data in deciding what it needed to do next.

*George Owens*

**Launching SoCal Approach**

Owens launched SoCal Approach in 2018 with a former J.D. Power colleague, Michael Cooperman, who serves as the company's chief marketing officer. The two men launched the firm to bring a different style to measurement and engagement in the death-care space – one steeped in data.

In 2024, the company rebranded to become Fortitude Research and Marketing.

After 11 wonderful years in Houston and with his son going away to college, Owens said it was the right time to return home to Los Angeles and make a big move

When he teamed up with Owens to launch the company, he wanted to help those who wanted to help themselves, Cooperman said. "Whether it is improving operations or protecting and improving an online reputation, those are all things we are passionate about," he said.

Most other marketing firms that serve the profession tend to be specialists, Cooperman observed.

"But we are more like general practitioners," he said. "We are going to look at your business holistically and recommend strategies … sometimes digital, sometimes *not* digital." He added, "If you go to a surgeon, they are going to want to do surgery, and if you go to a digital marketing firm – and there are some fantastic digital marketing firms that specialize in the death-care space – they are going to tell you to do something digital. We want to help shape your success, and digital may be part of it, but it may be more traditional, or it may be doing events or more mailers. We are going to look at your business holistically."

No matter what approach they take, funeral homes should pay attention to customers, Cooperman said.

"They are what drives loyalty," he said. "We know if customers have an outstanding, top-notch experience, 90% of them are coming back. But if they have a slightly less-than-optimal experience, loyalty tumbles."

The bottom line is that customer experience drives new business, he said.

Owens agreed, adding that when a customer has a *negative* experience, the harm can be substantial.

"There is nothing scarier to a small business than a bad review on Yelp," Cooperman added. "You feel like you have no control … and it is really scary."

Today, the company has several other key team members, including:

- Andy Lopez, chief revenue officer.
- Lisa Gonzales Minnehan, chief operating officer.
- Chance Parker, chief research officer.
- Eric Germansky, creative director.

*Michael Cooperman*

Several other important employees round out the team.

One of the wider known projects that Fortitude Research and Marketing has worked on has been the annual "Funeral and Cemetery Consumer Behavior Study" that it has conducted on behalf of The Foresight Companies.

"Chris Cruger (also formerly with SCI and now the CEO of Foresight) has always been a personal mentor of mine," Owens said. "Foresight has been a fabulous adviser and partner and has given us really good advice."

## Listening to the Data

The new approach to data and measurement that Fortitude Research and Marketing takes is embodied in its CXP solution.

"It examines at-need and preneed," Owens said. "it is much more than a survey – it is a measurement tool."

On the at-need side, the tool explores everything from the initial communication a funeral home makes with a family as well as the process. It also looks at the preneed experience a family has with a firm.

One of the tool's selling points is that it looks at people a funeral home has touched who have *not* turned into customers, such as seniors who may go to a seminar or program. It can help funeral homes and cemeteries determine *why* those families didn't convert and whether they are still in the market for services.

When Owens and his team were developing CXP, they thought it was critical to gather data and information from more than just one person – the tool gleans insights from every single individual that may have sat in an arrangement conference.

"We send a survey to *everyone*," Owens said, noting that when his grandmother died, both he and his brother made arrangements, "so why only send one survey?" He added, "What if everyone had an opinion? With SoCal CXP, we allow them to touch other folks."

CXP includes calls to action via the survey that is sent to families, allowing a customer who may still be interested in making prearrangements to request more information. "We provide all that data, and all that advice and counsel," Owens said.

Specifically, CXP helps firms to:

- Know how your customers are responding to business operations and understand what they expect in the future.
- Assess your operational effectiveness and diagnose which business processes need immediate attention.
- Get ahead of negative reviews to prevent brand assassins and drive positive reviews to your preferred ratings platform.
- Uncover opportunities to drive incremental revenue and turn data into profit, with a customer experience program that generates positive return on investment.
- Understand which employees to reward and which employees to coach and train.

Fortitude launched the tool with NorthStar Memorial Group which it has worked with in introducing multiple solutions to the market. SoCal also has a great relationship with Carriage Services, Owens added. "Two of the largest funeral and cemetery companies are part of believing in our story," Owens said.

Funeral service has a tremendous opportunity in converting at-need families into customers that preplan, Owens said. "How do we approach these customers?" he asked, noting that "sales" should not be a dirty word.

"Protecting their family with a prearrangement is one of the most important things they can do," he added. Moreover, a funeral home that has a robust preneed program can sustain and boost market share by taking families that are fair game for competitors to serve *out* of the market.

Other than promoting preneed, the only other ways available to a firm to enhance their footprint is by growing through acquisition or by differentiating themselves in the marketplace, Owens said.

**Focusing on Death Care But Available to Help Others**

While the majority of Fortitude Research and Marketing's clients are funeral homes and cemeteries, it is happy to serve businesses in other verticals as well – and has done so – in areas such as hospitality, entertainment, government, transportation and logistics and even a beverage company.

"But we are very fortunate and proud to say that the *bulk* of our time is spent with firms that help people on their very worst day," Owens said, noting that customers in other industries typically hear about SoCal through word of mouth.

"We talk to everyone everywhere," Owens added. "I could be sitting on an airplane and start talking to someone, and it may turn into something. We are all about outreach and talking to people."

No matter what the industry, Fortitude prides itself on providing firms with the same type of expertise they'd love to get from a company like McKinsey or Boston Consulting Group but at a price they can afford. "Our specialty is underserved markets and verticals," Owens said.

The ideal SoCal client, Owens said, is anyone who believes in looking at data and understanding what it is customers have to say.

"If I learned anything from my time at JD Power, it is that customers will tell you – they will tell you when you are good or not, they will tell you what they want, and they will tell you what they *don't* want. They determine how strong your brand is," he said.

Fortitude's ideal client understands the value of measurement and looking at data to guide what they do – and those can be independent funeral homes, or they can be large businesses, Owens said. "There are visionary leaders that understand that who come from 50-call funeral homes, and they may be at SCI, at NorthStar and at Carriage … they exist everywhere," he said.

Cooperman said, "If you are looking to grow your business and improve operations, *those* are the clients we want. There are locations that are very satisfied with their business and don't want to rock the boat … but if you are looking at business and thinking you can do better, we can help you improve operations."

Owens added, "We *don't* do acquisitions and divestitures, we *don't* do valuations or advise you on pricing. We concentrate on teaching you to understand what your customers are saying … those other things are critical, but *this* is the area of our expertise."

*Visit [https://www.fortitudeinsights.com](https://www.fortitudeinsights.com) to learn more about Fortitude Research and Marketing.*

# Cadence Aims to Help Funeral Homes Provide Estate and Grief Services to Families

*By Thomas A. Parmalee*

A company that was founded in 2020 in Saskatchewan, Canada, to help streamline estate planning, giving families more time to focus on grieving and healing, is starting to gain traction in the United States.

Cadence works directly with funeral homes and crematories to support families after a loss, according to Hannah Mason, partnerships manager at Cadence.

The company was co-founded by Rachel Drew, who serves as CEO, along with Krystian Olszanski, chief technology officer; and Rachelle Perron, strategic adviser (all pictured at the top). According to the company's website, "After experiencing first-hand the difficulties of settling her mother's estate, Rachel Drew (at far left in the picture) founded Cadence with the mission to make this process easier for those in similar circumstances. Drawing on 8 years' worth of experience as a hospice volunteer and executor adviser, she understands how critical it is for families to take care of their estate settlement matters during what can be an especially vulnerable time."

The company's digital platform helps with "all the tasks required with closing out an estate – getting benefits and filing claims," Mason said.

Cadence has a support team to help families navigate the estate settlement process as "human support is essential," Mason said. "If a family has questions or gets stuck, or maybe it is more of a complex estate situation, they can connect with one of our support specialists." She added, "We also help with grief support as well."

Handling someone's estate and grieving a loss are "directly embedded in each other," Mason said. The platform helps with several common tasks, such as attaining Social Security benefits.

"There are some wild statistics, such as 82% of widowers have not received their full benefits," Mason said. "People often lose money, not knowing it is available."

Cadence also helps with identity theft protection, and it communicates with Equifax and TransUnion. "We can help make those notifications and protect their identity after death," Mason said.

Insurance claims and determining whether probate is needed is another area where Cadence can help. For instance, some family members do not know if they can do a small estate affidavit or if they need probate. "We are not lawyers and do not replace the need for an estate attorney," Mason said.

An overlooked task that often slips people's attention is closing out digital accounts, such as Netflix, Facebook and Amazon, which can tie into identify theft, Mason said. "We can help close out bank accounts and those digital accounts," she said. "For people on our platform, we can also send reminders on what forms will be required during tax season."

Asked about leveraging artificial intelligence, Mason said Cadence currently uses AI behind the scenes and prioritizes human interaction to ensure that families are treated with compassion.

**A Suite of Services and an Expanding Roster of Partners**

Mason joined Cadence over two years ago after it began doing business in the United States. She is based in California.

"My background is in grief support," she explained, adding that she experienced loss at a young age.

Right now, Cadence has several dozen partners throughout the United States and Canada, with about 60% hailing from Canada.

While Cadence is primarily focusing on the funeral home space, it also works with financial institutions and wealth managers.

It offers two main services.

Its Legacy Planner product helps people plan their affairs ahead of time, and its Executor Assistant product helps a family at the time of need. Both products "communicate with each other," Mason said, explaining that many at-need families use the Executor Assistant product before deciding to opt in to the Legacy Planner for prearrangements – or vice versa.

"The more that people have things in order ahead of time, the easier it makes the role of the executor," Mason said. "It makes it simpler, so they can sort through things more easily."

The Executor Assistant tool has a few opportunities for people to raise their hand about preplanning, Mason said. "Being able to generate those leads and provide those to our partners is important," she said, adding that while some partners may have previously provided families with articles about estate planning or directed them to a simple website, they appreciate the more robust solution Cadence offers.

The opportunity to ask about preplanning is a newer feature on the platform, but so far, Cadence has been surprised by how many customers opt in to being contacted with more information about preplanning, Mason said.

"When people are taking care of these types of things and seeing all the work involved in taking care of their loved one's affairs, it gets the wheels spinning as they think about their own future and other family members," she said. "While that was not why the company built this tool, we quickly realized this was relevant to funeral homes and their business, so it is nice to be able to offer a feature that helps them further their business and is not just an extension of care they offer to families."

*Hannah Mason*

**The Details**

Funeral homes that work with Cadence typically pay a monthly subscription fee based on annual call volume – and pricing is affordable, so firms can include it as an added service in package pricing, Mason said.

"Most funeral homes roll our solution into their administrative fees or embed it into current packages," she said. "They may include it in a top-tier package or use it as a differentiator between packages."

Some early partners have experimented with reselling the solution, buying it from Cadence on a per-user basis and adding it as a line item on the price list, she said.

The company prefers the subscription model, however, as its overarching goal is to help as many people as possible and make the solution available to everyone, Mason said.

"Some people with the smallest estates often have more complex situations in handling their affairs," she observed.

Cadence works with both small and large firms – any business that wants to think more about how it is providing aftercare to families, she said.

"There is a lot shifting right now in end-of-life and death care," Mason observed. "As cremation rates continue to rise and as new forms of body disposition take hold, younger families want different things than their parents. This is a prime opportunity for the profession to think outside the box and think about what their role is in supporting people at the time of death."

There are a few prompts throughout the Cadence platform where families can respond to a survey and leave a Google review, which can also help funeral homes, she said.

As for grief support, the company publishes a newsletter that families can opt in to receiving through the platform, and it also hosts a monthly virtual grief group that is run by certified grief educators and experts. Audio recordings to help families navigate grief are also built into the platform.

"The approach we take is very educational and is all about normalizing grief," Mason said.

She added that since coping with grief sometimes depends on faith practices, people can look at it and deal with it differently. "So, we stay a little bit more in the field of neuroscience, which looks at what is really happening, so people can understand what is normal," she said.

If a survivor needs more support, Cadence can provide a referral to a grief counselor or local grief group or work with the funeral home to provide further assistance to a family.

Sometimes, a funeral home has someone they work with in their community to help a family who may need a higher level of support, she noted. "We can embed referrals to the platform if there is grief support a funeral home is already using," she said.

When Cadence began in Canada, the company founders always intended to expand the solution to make it available throughout North America, Mason said.

Once the model was built and tested in Canada, it was adapted to comply with U.S. regulations and systems. For instance, Canada offers a Canada Pension Plan as opposed to Social Security in the United States.

The estate process in the United States tends to be more complicated than in Canada, Mason said, with total possible tasks to settle an estate in Canada being 800 to 1,000. In the United States, the platform typically projects possible tasks to be in the 1,800 to 2,000 range, she said.

As Cadence spreads the word about its solution, it is being proactive about attending conferences and sharing how it can help funeral homes. It is a preferred partner of Selected Independent Funeral Homes, Mason noted.

Mason hopes that more funeral homes will explore using Cadence to help their families.

"I talk with funeral professionals on a daily basis, and they want to guide families, but they feel like it is out of their scope to speak to the estate," she said. "They carry a fear of giving the wrong information to a family or directing them in the wrong way."

Being able to provide an added level of service but working with a partner to do so could be the perfect solution, she said.

"When families ask about the insurance piece or probate, instead of sending them to a Google search that may be a rabbit hole, you are able to say, 'We have a partner' and you can guide them through that," she said. "It can take stress away from families and give them a clear direction."

*Visit [https://www.cadenceco.com/funeral-homes](https://www.cadenceco.com/funeral-homes) to learn more about Cadence.*

# The Profession Gears Up to Honor Jim Price with the Lasting Impact Award

*By Thomas A. Parmalee*

On April 12, the International Cemetery, Cremation and Funeral Association's Educational Foundation will present its Lasting Impact Award to a man who is accustomed to being the one handing the award to others: Jim Price.

Price has made it his mission to give back to the future of the death-care profession and was president and chairman of the ICCFA Educational Foundation from 2015 to 2023.

"Under his leadership, the Foundation experienced incredible growth in donations received, scholarships awarded, and impactful initiatives established. Price's commitment to service remains unwavering as he continues to serve as a trustee for the ICCFA Educational Foundation, along with his membership in both the Government & Legal Affairs Committee and Veterans Committee. Additionally, he was inducted into the ICCFA Hall of Fame in 2022," the ICCFA states.

Price, 75, lives in the Valrico, Florida, a suburb of Tampa, and serves as the senior vice president of industry relations at Johnson Consulting Group – the same title he held when he worked at Park Lawn Corp., working alongside J. Bradley Green and Jay Dodds.

He's also worked at numerous other firms over the years, including Pierce Brothers Valley Oaks Memorial Park & Funeral Home in Westlake Village, California; Bonney-Watson Funeral Home in Washington State; and Midwest Memorial Group in Michigan. He co-founded Keystone Group Holdings (which became Keystone North America before it was bought by Service Corporation International) and Foundation Partners Group.

For years, Price was tasked with calling the winner of the Lasting Impact Award to personally let them know that their contributions to the profession were being recognized in a big way. Several months ago, he found himself in the strange situation of getting such a phone call himself.

"Well, I received that same call from current chairman of the ICCFA Educational Foundation and I was so surprised!" he said. "Particularly since we had an upcoming meeting at which this agenda was going to be discussed. Little did I know that there was a meeting before the meeting. I am very honored, appreciative, and grateful to have my work recognized and join the giants in our profession that have won it before."

The award was first presented in 2014 and has become known as one of the most prestigious honors in the profession.

"I recall that the idea was presented to me by Nancy Lohman coming out of an ICCFA Executive Committee meeting in California at the Fall Management Conference," Price said. "I supported the idea, particularly since there were so many individuals that had made significant contributions to education in our profession."

Gino Merendino, president of the ICCFA Educational Foundation, can't think of anyone more deserving to win the award than Price. "The scope of Jim's commitment and tireless service to the ICCFA and death-care profession has been nothing short inspirational," he said.

That Price would end up working in death care was almost a foregone conclusion when he was born: His three brothers and two sisters grew up above their mom and dad's funeral home, Price Funeral Home, in Lake City, South Carolina. "I began by helping my dad," he said.

He quickly found a place in the management ranks.

"Around 40 years ago, I moved into a general manager role of Pierce Brothers Mortuaries & Cemeteries in Southern California and then to a vice president of operations role," he said.

That meant he rarely had the chance to engage in the everyday tasks of being a funeral director with his dress shoes on the ground. "Yes, I did miss it," he said. "Assisting families often during the biggest challenge of their lives was incredibly rewarding as a funeral director." He added, "It has always been the same. I've always been in an operational position that required the recruitment and retention of great associates."

He has fond memories of working with the late Tom Johnson earlier in his career, and he considers it a privilege to now be working for his son, Jake.

"I knew Tom Johnson since the late 1970s as a location manager for International Funeral Services in Southern California," he said. "Shortly after Tom became president of Pierce Brothers Mortuaries & Cemeteries, I accepted the position of general manager of Pierce Brothers Valley Oaks Mortuary & Cemetery. That was 40 years ago. A few years later, Jake Johnson and my son, Jay, both worked summers at the cemetery when they were in high school. So, yes, the Johnson family and I go a long way back."

Asked about his tenure at Park Lawn, he said, "I appreciated and enjoyed my tenure with Park Lawn Corporation. I was afforded the opportunity to position the company very positively through North America in our profession. I am proud of what I accomplished and am excited about now doing the same for Johnson Consulting Group."

**Death-Care Professionals Cheer for Price**

As news spread about Price being the latest in a line of funeral service titans to win the Lasting Impact Award, people cheered.

Nadira Baddeliyanage, executive director of the ICCFA, called Price "one of the most selfless individuals I have had the privilege to meet in our profession." She added, "He cares deeply about the death-care profession and is committed to making a difference. His passion for his work is very evident in how he serves ICCFA's Educational Foundation. Jim has been instrumental in raising donations, which in turn has made it possible for the Educational Foundation to grant a record number of scholarships to our educational programs. As Nelson Mandela said, 'Education is the most powerful weapon which you can use to change the world,' and Jim Price is a true believer! I look forward to celebrating Jim being awarded the Lasting Impact Award at ICCFA's Annual Convention and Expo in Tampa."

Jake Johnson, president and CEO of Johnson Consulting Group, said he didn't have to think too hard when he had the opportunity to follow in the footsteps of his father and offer Price a job. He noted that he's known Price ever since he was a boy.

"He was always a presence in the room – he made you feel comfortable," he said. "I can reflect on that as a kid and also as a professional – he's still the same person."

Whenever you are trying to get something done or need some help with something, Price is the type of man who can help you mightily, Johnson said.

In fact, perhaps Price's primary concern when he joined Johnson Consulting Group is that he wanted to be sure his duties would not interfere with him giving back to the profession he loves so dearly, Johnson shared.

"I completely agreed with that," Johnson said. "We created a special position to have for Jim in the sense that we know he can be impactful in a lot of different ways." He added, "We just want Jim to keep doing what he is doing and give back in the profession – being involved and being out there."

He's also a huge asset to JCG clients as very few people can rival his experience and expertise, particularly on the cemetery side, Johnson said.

"I always did – and still do – look up to Jim," Johnson said, reflecting on his work alongside Price at Keystone all the way up to today.

Kim Price, regional vice president at National Guardian Life Insurance Co., said she is extremely proud of Jim's accomplishments.

"I have seen his dedication and creativity improve both the ways we serve families and the opportunities within the profession for personal growth," she said. "His passion has led to many innovative programs, my favorite of which is the Journey to Serve initiative to hire veterans into funeral service."

She observed that during his tenure as chairman of the ICCFA Educational Foundation, fundraising topped $1 million. "More importantly, it led to so many deserving people receiving scholarships to DeadTalks and the ICCFA University," she said. "He has mentored so many people throughout his career – both funeral directors and suppliers. I encourage all who have not had an opportunity to review the videos in his program, 'Honored to Be Asked to Share' to do so. These interviews of the movers and shakers of our profession are invaluable to the new field of funeral professionals coming up. The impact that he has made on our profession will truly be lasting. This is such a fitting award for Jim, and I congratulate him on this achievement."

*Anthony Kaniuk of the NFDA has been lucky enough to be able to call Jim Price a mentor for many years.*

Anthony Kaniuk, director of industry relations at the National Funeral Directors Association, has been proud to call Price a mentor for nearly a quarter of a century.

"I believe there are a few lions who are pride leaders in funeral service, and Jim Price is definitely one of them," he said. "He teaches you to observe, analyze and keep learning. Learning from other leaders is not just about copying their actions or words. It's about how you analyze how you think, communicate, make decisions, handle challenges, motivate others and achieve results."

By listening to Price, Kaniuk has mastered the art of setting goals – and he's much more willing to experiment, take risks and reflect on what he's learned. "Leadership is best learned from experience," Kaniuk said. "When I asked Jim 10 years ago about working for NFDA, he said, do it! You'll learn three things by doing so, 1) You'll learn what it means to work with a board. 2) You'll learn how to work with a board. 3) You'll work with a board."

Kaniuk concluded, "Being a great leader, Jim knows mentorship has always been the most successful way to succession; he has done this with and for so many in the funeral profession over the years. I am grateful to be just one of them."

Joe Weigel, owner of Weigel Strategic Marketing, admires Price's "uncanny" ability to get things done, which he attributes to his willingness to allow others to do what they do best.

"Jim's not a micro-manager; he identifies the people with the expertise to get the job done and then gets out of the way," Weigel said. "I witnessed this firsthand during the development of both the ICCFA Educational Foundation's 'Final Responders' PSA campaign and the National Alliance of Children's Grief's 'Faces of Grief' PSA campaign. He sets the vision and the rest of us deliver on this vision."

Price is not content to merely "sit" on a board, Weigel said. "He wants to be involved and make a difference, as he has with ICCFA's Educational Foundation and the National Alliance of Children's Grief," he said. "Jim is a *doer* who wants to give back and make a lasting impact however he can. He's done this his entire career, which is why he is so deserving of the ICCFA's Lasting Impact Award."

Steven A. Tidwell, special adviser to the CEO at Service Corporation International, co-founded Keystone with Price, Steve Shaffer and Bob Horn. He would serve as the company's president and CEO.

"Jim has a big heart and has always been someone you could count on," Tidwell said. "As a businessman, he knows and understands the funeral and cemetery business and draws on his lifetime of experience to make good decisions."

He also has an innovative mind and is adept at leveraging innovation to develop and deploy creative strategies, Tidwell said. "And while he takes his commitment to funeral service very seriously, Jim has a great sense of humor," he said. "I've seen his use of humor oftentimes break the ice is a tense situation. It typically works, and the topic of conversation or decision ends with a positive and fair outcome."

Price absolutely deserves this honor, Tidwell concluded. "Jim has not been just a card-carrying member of the various trade groups and other industry roundtable type of events – he has been very active in most all of them and over his career in the funeral profession and has contributed greatly … my congratulations to Jim!"

*Jake Johnson knew he was getting an all-star when he hired Jim Price.*

**A Passion for Education**

The award from ICCFA means a great deal to Price given how he's been so involved with the association over the years.

"Southern California has some of our profession's largest and most successful combination funeral home and cemeteries in the United States," Price said. "The Forest Lawns, Rose Hills, and Green Hills just to name a few. Even though I was a licensed funeral director embalmer, I received that opportunity as general manager of Pierce Brothers Valley Oaks in Westlake Village, California, and I got involved with what was at that time known as the Interment Association of California, now named CMAC (the Cemetery Mortuary Association of California) which provided me with the opportunity to attend my first ACA (American Cemetery Association) Conference, which eventually became known as ICCFA."

The focus of the ICCFA has always been on education, which squarely aligns with what Price is all about.

"In order to make education accessible to our profession's future leaders, I've always known that our ICCFA Educational Foundation needed to raise a lot of money," he said. "Partnering with our profession's suppliers and corporations, as well as individual donors has provided us with millions, which has positioned us on average to provide around 150 scholarships to ICCFA University and our annual DeadTalks conference."

Asked what tasks have stuck out to him over his career beyond the usual services provided to families, he singled out the purchasing of a mausoleum back from an L.A. family and selling it to Hugh Heffner, selling a private mausoleum to Gerald Cantor, the founder of Cantor Fitzgerald; and making funeral arrangements with JD Powers Jr. for his father.

As for the most meaningful mentors in his life, his dad – James Price – ranks at the top.

"He was the first mentor that I ever had … he was a wonderful example of a person who was dedicated, caring and committed to being of service to others," he said.

As for other mentors, he could list dozens, but two are at the very top: Bob Horn and the late "great" Tom Johnson.

"Their positive attitude and business acumen is only part of what set them apart," he said. "Yes, we were acquirers of many businesses – however, we were always an operational company and the highest title in our companies was always the former owners. Bob and Tom's example helped me to become a better leader and taught me how to offer the same type of leadership for my associates as my career advanced."

# Petra Lina Orloff, the Founder of Beloved, Brings Flair to Obituaries and Eulogies

*By Thomas A. Parmalee*

Petra Lina Orloff has never given a second thought to finding Prince Charming as she knows exactly where to find him – in the pages of a book.

The founder of Beloved, which offers professional writing services to funeral homes that want to provide families with the best obituaries and eulogies for deceased loved ones and animal companions, is happily single (with four cats) and closing in on 50 – although you'd be forgiven for thinking she's in her 20s if you follow her on Instagram.

The thought of settling down or starting a family never once crossed her mind.

"I have had 48 years of training, and I keep getting better at writing – and I have constructed my life without children or a family in order to do the things I love best," said the lifelong Detroit area resident. "While it may seem selfish, it allows me to give more to people in the ways I enjoy giving … that was a choice I made very early on in my life: no family, no kids."

But that doesn't mean Orloff doesn't have a soft spot for romance.

In fact, she's currently working on a historical romance novel, which she expects to make an entire saga. She'll publish it under her own name, which is a big deal given that much of her work has been as a ghostwriter.

"I've been able to ghostwrite because I'm very adept at different voices and styles," she said. "I can create very unique personalities and voices for the people who I write for, and that has kept me going as a ghostwriter."

*Petra Lina Orloff*

**Finding Her Passion**

Writing has always come naturally to Orloff, and so it should come as no surprise that she eventually discovered she had an unmatched talent to write obituaries and eulogies.

"I just fell in love with books as a child, and I was devouring books all the time," she said. "I remember very clearly going up to my first-grade teacher, and I remember saying that one day I would be a writer. I'm not even sure I knew it was a profession – I just knew it was something I wanted to do."

Her home, she said, was the library. It was a delightful treat to go there and be surrounded by cascading waterfalls of books.

She remembers books being expensive, but as a child, she could go to the library and get whatever stories she wanted. For her, books were a valuable commodity.

"And they still are. For me, nothing has changed," she said.

As a child, she would stay at home and write stories, filling up notebooks of devious tales. She began publishing professionally – writing and getting paid for it – at age 14.

"When I was 17, I began writing marketing and PR pieces for businesses, and I pursued that throughout college," she said. "Throughout my undergraduate and graduate school career, I was doing all this freelance work on the side as well as pursuing my studies."

While she was a freshman in college, there was a professor of Victorian literature who Orloff "absolutely adored." She became her model of what she wanted to be – a writer and a teacher.

"I knew I wanted to be a professor of English, so I proceeded in that route but still maintained my journalism and PR major," she said. The idea was to have something practical in her arsenal "just in case," she said.

Ultimately, however, Orloff earned her Ph.D. and began teaching right away, spending 14 years at the university level, including Wayne State University. She has also lectured in Canada, across the United States, Germany and Scotland.

**Founding Beloved**

Over the years, Orloff found herself being asked to write the occasional obituary for a client or friend. She received nice feedback on her work, but she kept herself plenty busy writing about a whole variety of topics – and so she didn't give obituaries per se much thought.

But then her father, Frederick Conrad Orloff, died at age 59, and suddenly writing his obituary took on a new meaning. She wrote a heartfelt tribute honoring her dad.

The obituary was published in her small-town newspaper, the *Cheboygan Daily Tribune*. "It was a long, creative piece," she said. "I don't think they had much news."

Two weeks after her father died, the memorial service was held.

Around that time, she found herself standing in line at a Walmart in northern Michigan. "A woman started talking about something she read in the newspaper to another woman right in line in front of me," she said. "Then, she pulled out my father's obituary and showed it to the other woman. It made me so happy, not to be the author of that particular piece, but that my father was being remembered and shared by strangers."

She found a whole new appreciation for the power of good writing. "People think that because they are literate, they can write," she said. "But the power of *good writing* is memorable – and it never leaves you."

After that experience, she continued to write about a variety of things but increasingly gravitated toward writing obituaries. "I just sort of opened up to it more, and they came in. And I wrote a lot of eulogies, too," she said.

It wasn't until 13 years after the death of her father, however, that Orloff founded Beloved in 2017, which provides professionally written obituaries and eulogies for a network of funeral homes.

It was simply time to serve funeral homes and grieving individuals at a higher level given how important they are to remembering a loved one, Orloff said.

"I was reading more and more about dying a good death, the good death movement and the celebratory life movement, and it just got me thinking that this is part of that," she said.

Spending quality time to write an obituary or a eulogy for a loved one "is part of the new way of looking at the way we remember and memorialize people," she said.

Orloff also had begun to discover that there were more like-minded people who were interested in remembering someone in a very positive way after their death. A great obituary, she said, can provide a jumping off point for family and friends to reconnect after someone's death as they move through grief. It should not simply be a biography of someone who has died, she stressed.

The bulk of the obituaries Orloff and her network of writers work on are through funeral homes, although some requests come directly from grieving family members, she said.

*Petra Lina Orloff, the founder of Beloved.*

**The Process**

In terms of crafting an obituary or eulogy, she has found that talking with two or so survivors or close friends of the deceased tends to be a good number. Or, she'll talk with the person who is planning their own funeral who may be thinking about what they want their obituary to read like ahead of time.

"I have a 20-minute phone call," she said. "I don't do Zoom because I feel like that might put a little more pressure on the family in terms of being camera read and so on."

After that conversation, she'll draft an obituary or eulogy and send it to the family. Based on their feedback, she may revise what she wrote, but those revisions are typically minimal, she said.

The turnover time varies.

"I've been called at 2 in the afternoon and have been told, 'We need this by 2:45 p.m. because we need to put it in the newspaper,'" she said. "So, I've been on those crunch deadlines and been able to produce. But generally, it will take me a few hours … I let the conversation sit with me for a while."

As far as how everything comes together in her mind and how it ends up on paper, it's a bit of a mystery even to Orloff.

"I can't describe how it happens, but everything comes together in my head and there it is … I write it in my imagination before I write it on paper," she said. "I never sit down to a blank screen, because in my head, it is already composed."

Such a supreme talent probably comes from a lifetime of "thinking in stories" and turning every experience she's ever had into one, she said.

"Whether I was telling it out loud or writing it down, to me, it always comes out as a story – even the smallest, most mundane moments are moments of storytelling for me," she said.

Sometimes, it can be challenging to write an obituary or eulogy.

"A family may be too aggrieved …. it may be a child who has died, and they cannot talk," she explained. "So, I may just get a few notes from the funeral director. At that time, my first and foremost thought about writing an obituary or eulogy is that it is not only about the person who died – it is about the people who remain. So, I am writing to the family, writing to the friends and thinking about what these people need to hear."

As to why more funeral homes don't leverage professional writers as families craft obituaries and eulogies, Orloff thinks it may be because funeral directors have prided themselves on doing it on their own for so many years.

"So, there's been a lot of resistance" and some firms have also struggled to determine how to fit it into their pricing, she said.

"My service sometimes has gotten placed into packages, and sometimes the option has done well and sometimes not," she said.

But she's found it telling that for the firms who have offered her services – even if they have not become a big seller on an itemized price list – they still call her when the loved one of a staff member dies.

In addition to helping celebrate the lives of those we've lost, Orloff also has enjoyed helping other writers – many of them academics – supplement their income. She knows many people who have left teaching simply because it does not pay enough, she said.

"I know people who are the heads of departments in liberal arts that need a second job because they cannot afford to pay their bills based on their salary," she said. "My idea was always to help keep them in the classroom or keep them doing what they love and find them something that could supplement their income."

While she may rely on other writers with all the obituary and eulogy requests that come in, she still personally looks over and edits every assignment Beloved is given, she said.

*Petra Lina Orloff.*

**Pricing**

Most of Orloff's business comes directly from funeral homes. Families are more likely to want and appreciate her services when it comes from a trusted recommendation from a funeral home rather than an online search, she explained.

"Funeral homes can buy in bulk from me, so they get lower pricing," she said.

For instance, they can buy a bundle of 20 obituaries and use Beloved's services for whichever families they want over the course of a quarter or a year. Or, they may decide to include it in certain packages or offer it to families as an itemized item. "Some may just pay for my services out of pocket if it is a very special situation or customer," she said. "I mostly get that when it is children that pass away … they want to give something to the family."

She encourages what she offers to be included in a package as she thinks it fits in nicely with that model. "This is a tribute … and people often get them printed and framed," she said. "They keep them forever. This is not just something I see shared on social media or read at a funeral and then it is done – this is something I see people really get behind."

If a funeral home is buying only a single professionally written obituary or eulogy, Orloff charges a $350 flat rate, she said.

"But if they buy more than that, the cost decreases incrementally," she said, noting that a package of 50 obituaries has been her maximum order, although she'd be happy to take on more.

In addition to writing obituaries and eulogies, Orloff also conducts workshops for funeral homes – either virtual or in person – about how they can write better obituaries on their own.

"I go in and tell them how I do it," she said. "Mostly, the questions I ask and the manner I go about it and the way I get information."

The questions she asks family members and friends are not always typical, she said.

"I care about diving deep," she said. "And I have developed a really good rapport with people … the more I speak to people, the better I get at it."

Some useful questions to ask include:

- *What did you think when you saw your husband (or wife) for the very first time?*
- *What was it like to hold your son (or daughter) for the first time?*

"What I like about those questions is it brings people back to a very happy spot, and they get to remember that moment and relive it," she said. "When people start smiling and stop crying, their tone gets a little softer … and that is the beauty of those kinds of questions."

She may also ask how a couple's parents took the news of their engagement. "You just want to go straight into the heart or into the soul," she said. "It elicits the best information – and people enjoy it."

These questions also tend to work well because often, when someone dies, the survivors are simply tired of dealing with an illness or all the struggles that go along with old age or failing health. "They want to remember that person differently, and I allow them to do that," she said.

Just as she trains funeral directors to ask questions and write obituaries, Orloff does the same with her stable of writers. "We have a grief counselor we work with who talks to us regularly about what people are going though as they grieve," she said. That type of wisdom helps her and the writers she employs ask better questions, she said.

Another area she's increasingly helping people with is how to leverage artificial intelligence in writing obituaries and eulogies, she said.

"I love AI and I hate AI," she said. "If you do not have 48 years of storytelling experience, you can coach AI to write well for you in a voice that is your own, and that is one of the things I go over when I talk to funeral directors," she said. "I teach them to use AI to write these things and to write them well. Not bland and oblique and stale and neutral, but '*Here is how you train this system to write something better than you can do – and do it quicker using the questions and interview template I'm giving you.*'"

That can be a game changer for funeral home owners who don't want to use her services for every single obituary but who aren't writers themselves. "They are pulled in so many different directions," she said. "If you are not a writer, you should be using AI, but you should be coaching it to write well," she said. "Don't just use it to spit out neutral, basic, bland content."

With all that said, Orloff knows that what she can provide to funeral homes is "head and tails above AI."

Moving forward, Orloff would like to continue to grow Beloved and work with more funeral homes.

"My ideal client is someone who values their families enough to provide this service," she said. "Someone who sees the worth of the obituary and eulogy as a special service."

She added. "There is only one *me* hiring writers and going over their work, so you can't get this service from anyone *but me*. I truly believe I write the best obituaries in the business."

*Visit https://www.beloved-press.com/ to learn more about Beloved.*

# Years Later, the Emotional Toll of COVID-19 Is Still Evident

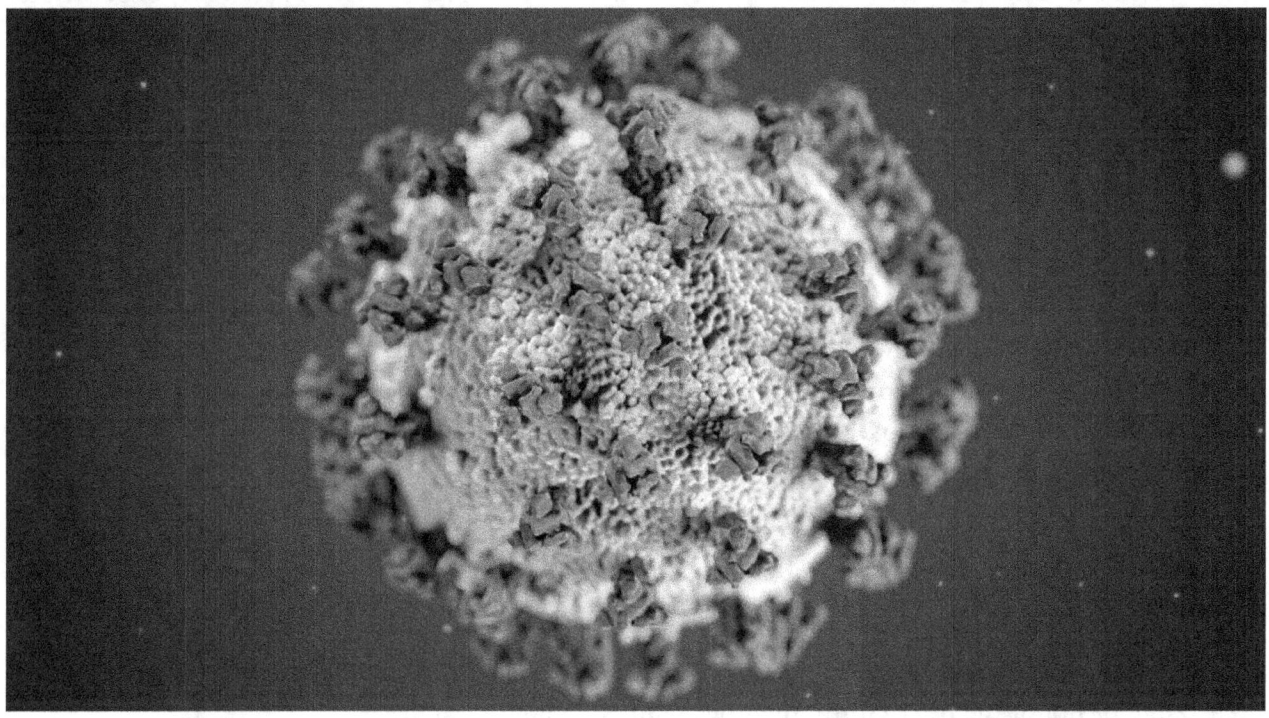

*By Thomas A. Parmalee*

Some days, it's hard to grasp the impact of everything we had to contend with during the COVID-19 pandemic.

Everything seems so *normal* now.

But then something will give me a jolt and help me appreciate how much everything has changed — particularly for funeral directors and everyone remembering lost loved ones — such as the below post a friend of mine recently shared on Facebook:

*Four years ago today we buried my dad. COVID had just begun to shut things down and his funeral was surreal. Just immediate family was allowed, so my brothers and I stood at the cemetery, six feet apart, and honored my father. When the graveside service was over, we all said our goodbyes and went our separate ways. The life he lived deserved a more dignified send-off. But hearing the soldier play taps and watching him hand the folded flag to my brother was among the proudest moments of my life.*

I'm sharing that message here lest any of us forget how important it is for us to remember those we have lost — and for as long as anyone can remember, we do that by holding a funeral, a memorial service or a gathering of some sort. And if you operate a funeral home, you're the expert on this and should be there to help families who need it.

For a time, after the pandemic, I recall there was lots of hope in funeral service that some of these families who had suffered such a massive loss during the pandemic would come back to the funeral home to hold a "real" service for their loved one.

With the "pull forward" effect that we have seen as a result of COVID-19 (death rates have been going down since people that would normally be dying now died sooner), such a response would have no doubt been welcome to funeral homes who are struggling with declining revenue.

But that response did not materialize on the scale that most had envisioned, but it seems to me that funeral homes should not abandon the idea of trying to reconnect with families who lost a loved one to explore how they might make up for NOT providing the level of service that both the family and the funeral home would have wanted to have been provided.

Whether it is holding a gathering on the birthday or anniversary of their loved one's death to share the memories and the hugs that they were forbidden to share during the pandemic, or if it is making it easy for a family to upgrade their urn or perhaps even buy cemetery space and hold a graveside service for the interment of cremated remains, there are services you can and SHOULD be providing to those who suffered a loss during that time.

Sometimes, in our haste to put the pandemic behind us, I think we have a tendency to forget how much it impacted us and those around us … over 1 million Americans died of the virus. Don't forget that these were *your* customers — these were *your* families.

At the very least, it's up to every firm that served a family affected by COVID-19 to let them know that they are there to support them — and that you will *still* be there to help them prearrange or honor the next family member who is taken too soon.

# The Death Deck Might Be Just What Your Funeral Home Needs to Get People Talking About Preplanning

*By Thomas A. Parmalee*

Lisa Pahl, a licensed clinical social worker, had no way of knowing that she was about to embark on an exciting business adventure when she met Lori LoCicero, whose husband was dying of pancreatic cancer at age 44.

While Pahl was accustomed to helping navigate the end of life in her role as hospice licensed clinical social worker, it was LoCicero's first experience going through such a traumatic ordeal. She had lots of questions, and the two women had much to talk about.

After her husband, Joe, died in 2008, the two women continued to talk, and their conversations increasingly gravitated toward how it was so hard for people to talk about the taboo topic of death – until it was too late.

Eventually, the two women (pictured at top with Pahl on the left and LoCicero on the right) launched The Death Deck, which they describe as both a game and a tool that allows friends and family members to open up and share thoughts and preferences about death in a nonthreatening and even fun way.

The deck consists of 112 cards – 80 that have multiple choice questions and 32 open-ended questions that urge players to "dig deep" before responding.

Numerous funeral homes have used the game to help families spark conversations about death – and Pahl and her co-creator also offer an abbreviated version of the game that can be branded to market individual funeral homes, which can be used to encourage families to proactively think about preplanning, Pahl said.

Just recently, Pahl delivered a presentation at Darling & Fischer Funeral Homes in the Bay Area of California.

"They hosted a day of gratitude for hospice and health care professionals," she explained. The funeral home gave attendees the Death Deck as well as a related game, called the EOL (which stands for End-of-Life) Deck.

"The Death Deck is for when death seems far away – it is meant to normalize conversations about death, and we weave a lot of humor into the cards," Pahl said. "The End-of-Life Deck is for people suffering from a serious illness or older adults."

She noted that the Death Deck is the more popular of the two games, perhaps because while talking about death in advance is hard, talking about it when it is imminent is even *harder*.

Pahl, who still works in hospice, uses the decks in her work. "There are lots of questions in both decks about disposition options and what people want for themselves," she said. "People get the chance to talk about their end-of-life preferences."

With the Death Deck, people will learn about cremation jewelry and new disposition options, such as composting. They will consider whether they want to be cremated or buried. About 20 of the 112 questions are disposition related, Pahl said.

Custom decks with 16 cards that can be branded with a funeral home's logo are a favorite with end-of-life providers, Pahl said. "They leave those behind with pens and that kind of thing," she said. "It is something with more intention to help families preplan."

Creating the games, which are available through the Death Deck website and at online stores such as Amazon.com, was no easy task, Pahl said.

But the games have proved to be a wonderful success, with the biggest hurdle continuing to be getting people to actually have conversations about death.

"People tell me this seems like a great idea, but they still avoid it," Pahl said. "They may purchase the deck, but they can't figure out how to get the family to play it. So, I think that remains our largest issue to tackle – this is a topic people don't want to talk about, and we have made it as fun as we can."

But they are definitely making inroads toward accomplishing their mission. "Our sales are great, and have grown every year," Pahl said.

Hospice care and end-of-life professionals as well of death doulas buy both the Death Deck and EOL deck regularly, but Pahl would still like to see the games in the hands of more "everyday people."

Funeral homes use the decks regularly in their community engagement activities, and Pahl has spoken at death and dying classes and at various venues in her capacity as a social worker. She's also been a podcast guest on numerous shows. "I worked as a hospice social worker for 17 years," she explained.

Along the way, she's met some incredible people.

"I was just the keynote speaker at a caregiver conference on how to have these important conversations," she said. "I've met the coolest people … people who work in death and dying tend to be great, compassionate and creative people."

All of her work advancing the games has helped her as a social worker, she said. "I get to introduce so many things to my team outside of the narrow hospice world because of the creativity in the death space," she said.

As to how funeral homes can incorporate the Death Deck into what they do, she said, "Preplanning is the way to go." An at-need situation is not the right time, she explained.

"We have had funeral homes that give families a Death Deck when doing their preneed arrangements, and we have gotten some great feedback on that," she said.

Pahl's goal remains to help people avoid complicating their grief by making final preparations ahead of time.

"Losing someone is hard, and it just gets harder when you haven't prepared ahead of time," Pahl said. "We are trying to help people prepare, so that the people left behind are not left with a mess."

## The Bridge Between Hospice and Funeral Homes

The hospice team has a "huge influence" on decisions that come at the end of life, Pahl said.

"Families look to us for guidance, and usually it is the social worker talking to the family about the arrangements they have in place," she said.

In the area of California where she works, Pahl estimates that about 80% of families with a loved one in hospice opt for a direct cremation.

"Recently, I have been finding myself really sad about that because I will talk to families about what their plans are for how they are going to honor their family member," she said. And many times, they don't have any plans, she said.

"So often, families are now saying maybe they will go to dinner and just choosing direct cremation," she said. "I think because so many are choosing cremation, it then become a race to see who can provide it cheapest – and we are losing the benefits of the funeral home and the collective grief experience."

As to what funeral homes can be doing to serve families being served by hospice better, Pahl said educating hospice care providers about the value funeral homes can provide, including the specific services they offer, is key. Show them how you can improve the grief experience, she advised.

"Direct cremation is leaving it in the hands of a bereaved family," she said. "I will reach out six months later, and they still haven't done anything because it takes someone to organize it."

**More Ahead**

If you thought that Pahl and LoCicero would be content with moving along the conversation about death with two games and that's it, well, you'd be wrong.

The two have a Grief Deck in the works, which will be rolled out next year.

"It will have the same design – some multiple-choice questions and some open-ended questions," Pahl said. "The idea is to give people an opportunity to share their grief. We designed it to be used as a tool for bereavement groups, as well as for grievers who want to find a way to express their grief with people."

You can buy the Death Deck on Amazon.com or on via the Death Deck website. Bulk pricing for funeral homes who want to purchase a large quantity of decks is available, as well as the option for a smaller deck with a funeral home's branding.

*The Death Deck website, which you can visit at https://thedeathdeck.com, has more than just a couple card games. On it, you can find some great blog posts about death and dying written by Pahl, as well as additional resources for families planning for the death of a loved one. You can also buy Death Deck merchandise, listen to podcasts about death and more.*

# From Tragedy to Triumph: How Jon Lefrandt's Incredible Loss Led Him to Serve Others

*By Thomas A. Parmalee*

Jon Lefrandt, 40, thought his destiny was to follow in his father's footsteps to enjoy a successful career in real estate, but life took a sudden turn when tragedy struck his family when he was in his mid-twenties.

That was when his father, Harold – only 46 at the time – died after a courageous three-and-a-half-year battle with brain cancer.

"Dad was a commercial real estate developer," Lefrandt explained, noting that he "found a lot of love in redevelopment" even though it may have seemed an odd career choice for someone who had majored in sculpture at Brigham Young University.

Harold Lefrandt took his creative energy and revitalized run-down commercial properties, transforming entire communities. "I thought I could channel my creativity in the same way," Lefrandt said.

But Lefrandt's dad – who himself was only 11 when *his* father died – was diagnosed in his early 40s.

The oldest of seven children, Lefrandt was in Japan completing the last week of a mission, and he was looking forward to having his father pick him up to bring him home. "Instead, I found myself rushing home for my father's brain surgery," he said.

After the surgery, his dad's cancer went into remission but only for one-and-half years before it returned with a vengeance.

**The Pivot**

After returning home from Japan, Lefrandt, who earned a bachelor's degree in advertising and marketing from Brigham Young University and a master's in real estate development from the University of Utah, David Eccles School of Business, threw himself into a career in real estate. It looked like a path he'd continue down. "I did a lot of work with residential and custom home builds," he said.

But with the death of his father and with the arrival of the 2008 recession, Lefrandt began to take a closer look at his future – and it didn't seem as clear anymore. At the same time, he realized that several of his friends – "really smart people" – were for some reason working for a preneed marketing company based in Portland, Oregon, which was then called Lincoln Heritage Funeral Planning.

Lefrandt flew to Oregon to see what it was all about.

"I thought I was just interested in the business side of it … I was intrigued by the numbers," Lefrandt said. "But when I went there, it hit me on a totally different level, probably because of my personal experience with loss."

Lefrandt had done some soul searching, and he'd come to realize that he needed to do "purpose-driven work." Not the type of work that was fixated on "making a buck."

So, he took a job at the company, which was in the process of rebranding itself as Precoa.

Reflecting on his experiences with loss, Lefrandt could immediately grasp the importance of the work he was doing.

"We didn't have a preneed policy for my dad because he was so young," he explained. But that did not stop him from thinking that his dad deserved "the greatest mahogany casket" they could find … right before he considered if, in fact, that would have been what his dad truly wanted.

"I fell in love with helping funeral home owners see the problems that multigeneration funeral homes have," he said, observing that in many cases, it may have been the founder of the business who was an entrepreneur, with future generations along for the ride without a guiding compass or a progressive mindset. "They would just keep doing things the way Grandpa told them to do … and I saw a huge need," he said.

He also saw that he could bridge the gap between grieving families and business owners, and at Precoa, he managed its appointment setting team, which was a critical component of the company's engine and model.

"When I started there, we had about 20 appointment setters and we grew it to 90," he said, noting it was a period of rapid growth in which he spent countless hours learning from funeral home owners and family service counselors. "It kind of changed the game for me," he said.

He marched up the ranks to become Precoa's director of marketing, opening up a satellite office that booked appointments for agents who produced $20 million in preneed in the first year the office was open. Lefrandt had become a man to be reckoned with.

Eventually, however, he wanted to reach families with more modern technology but with "human touch and human compassion at the heart of it," and so he struck out on his own.

Asked about how multiple companies were started by former Precoa employees – with Sepio Guard being one of the others – Lefrandt said Precoa has a knack for attracting talented people.

"The people who left were the ones who wanted to bring more innovation to Precoa," he said, noting that the company did a great job attracting purpose-driven staff. "The customer service side of it is world class … and they attracted a lot of good humans that maybe would not have been in this industry otherwise."

*Jon Lefrandt*

**Calling His Own Shots**

When Lefrandt struck out on his own, it was to start a company he and his business partners called the Domani Group, which has its roots in an Italian word – *domani* – that means "tomorrow."

"My business partners and I all served missions for church; I served in Japan, another in Italy and another in South America. We landed on '*domani*' and used that word and later combined it with the word aftercare."

While the company began with a focus on preneed marketing, it wasn't long before it developed Domanicare, which began as an aftercare solution that revolved around text messaging. Soon, that became Lefrandt's primary focus, and for a time, he got out of preneed marketing altogether. The Domani Group was shuttered in 2019.

Focusing strictly on Domanicare, which recently rebranded itself to become Elevia, went a long way in smoothing over the relationship with Precoa, which Lefrandt said initially viewed his undertaking as a threat. "But where we are today, I have countless clients that work with Precoa," Lefrandt said.

That early pivot to focusing on aftercare and text messaging has made all the difference for the company.

"We tested out text messaging super early," Lefrandt said, noting that when Domanicare (now Elevia, which he serves as its founder and CEO) sent out its first text message campaign, it immediately drew dozens of responses.

"I knew in that moment, there was something magical about it," he said.

But back then – and up until today – he has always believed that the text messages Elevia sends out and any follow-up responses should be sent by people – not an artificial intelligence or bot.

"We've always wanted it to be human centric," he said. "If it is not powered by humans, it becomes super informal, and it's just not great."

After seeing the initial response to the text messages, Lefrandt and his team began asking funeral homes what they were doing with aftercare. "Almost every one of them had an immediate guilty conscience because they knew they should be doing more but were not," he said. "For the most part, aftercare was the thing everyone neglected."

It was understandable because for many funeral home owners, the at-need business was what was demanding all their attention. "Aftercare was always the afterthought," he said.

He recognized a major pain point for funeral homes, and he realized families desperately wanted – *needed* – aftercare.

The proof of that lies in the data.

"The text message response rate is 50% on the initial campaign we do," he said. "That said to me that people wanted to hear from the funeral home and wanted the relationship to continue." He added, "I realized that we could grow and scale and help way more funeral homes if we were incredibly disciplined and if we narrowed down our product to focus on the aftercare world – and that proved to be true."

Today, Elevia serves about 1,500 funeral homes, cemeteries, pet loss centers and hospices in the United States and Canada, with its core business being funeral homes. "We would not be able to do that on the preneed side," Lefrandt said. "The model is very expensive, not to say that the Elevia model is *not* expensive – it is. Building technology platforms that can handle millions of contacts is a difficult beast, and we figured that out. Now, it is a well-oiled machine."

After about two years of focusing strictly on the entity now known as Elevia, Lefrandt and his team shifted some of their focus back to traditional preneed marketing, by relaunching its preneed marketing business as Domani Preneed in April 2021. Today, that company is run by Riley Facer, who serves as CEO. "It is a separate entity," Lefrandt said of Domani Preneed. "I hold equity in that business and helped launch it, built the model, etc., and sit on the board, but am not involved in the day to day."

At one point, Lefrandt thought the two companies could be synergistic, "but they are so drastically different," he said. "We realized what Domanicare (now Elevia) could do for growth and if was tied to preneed, it became more complicated."

Running what is now Elevia also allowed Lefrandt and his team to work with multiple preneed providers. Running it as a company that is separate from Domani Preneed was "100% the right move" and rebranding it as Elevia further distinguishes the two companies as being completely separate, he said.

*Jon Lefrandt is interviewed during a video shoot.*

### Elevia: Much More Than Just Aftercare

With the rebranding, Lefrandt wants to make it clear that Elevia offers much more than just aftercare solutions.

"We are not selling insurance, but we are able to do appointment setting," he said. "We can do surveys. We've started hosting events teaming up with For Grief (a separate company that Lefrandt started that focuses on helping families navigate their grief) and the speakers bureau that we created. We are driving crazy traffic in the cemetery world to Memorial Day events. We are able to do so much more than aftercare."

What Lefrandt wants death-care professionals to think of when they think of Elevia is a company that focuses on *the consumer experience*. "We are a consumer journey platform," he declared.

Elevia wants to know about all the touchpoints a funeral home, cremation business or cemetery has with consumers and how those interactions happen. "We want to educate them beyond their preneed and aftercare clients," he said. "Who are the people coming into services and how can we engage with them in a meaningful way?"

As a result of all the learning it has done in the space, the team at Elevia is well equipped to create customized customer journeys for funeral home clients.

**An Important Partner**

In November 2020, Domanicare (now Elevia) announced that it was joining forces with Homesteaders Life Company.

Homesteaders has made a significant investment in Elevia as well as Domani Preneed and For Grief. Their ownership stake for each business varies, said Lefrandt, who serves as Homesteaders' chief consumer experience officer – a position he took in January 2024 after more than two years as the company's senior vice president of consumer experience.

"Partnering with Homesteaders in 2020 was a great decision for us," Lefrandt said. "I really value the leadership and direction of Steve Shaffer (president, CEO and board chair of Homesteaders) in this profession. He and I are aligned in creating more meaningful experiences for funeral homes and the families they serve. At Homesteaders, the focus is 'to help families design a better farewell, benefiting those they love.' I am very much aligned and in support of that mission and am proud to work together with them to help make the profession better."

While Homesteaders' clients receive preferred pricing from Elevia, the company works with death-care professionals "across the board," Lefrandt emphasized.

Domani Preneed, however, exclusively sells Homesteaders Life products, he said, reiterating that rebranding to Elevia and distancing itself from the Domani name made sense to emphasize that distinct difference.

So far, the reaction to the rebranding has been "remarkably positive" from customers, competitors and prospects, Lefrandt said. "The biggest thing for me is to continue to convey that this is *not* just an aftercare solution," he said. "This is a consumer experience platform and offering. So, it is really about exploring what that looks like and partnering with us to enhance that experience. That is vital for any business — regardless of what business you are in."

That may be a challenge as businesses don't usually have "consumer experience" as a line item on the budget, but Lefrandt is soundly convinced that firms that make this a priority will trounce competitors.

Jumping on that bandwagon is crucial, he said – especially since everyone is so transient, and they usually don't rely on the funeral home their parents or grandparents looked to during a time of need.

"Now, we live in the world of Google and search," he said. "We have to think about death care with a very different mentality than ever before, and that presents an awesome opportunity. We know we can help educate consumers on the value of funeral service in a much more impactful way."

One of those impactful ways is by helping funeral homes do a better job generating positive online reviews, Lefrandt said.

"That is one of the biggest returns on investment we can offer, and I think we are the best in the business," he said. "We have generated over 80,000 five-star reviews across the country."

He appreciates the fact that getting online reviews can be tough for funeral homes as it can be an awkward ask.

"You are not going to ask at the arrangement conference or when people come to a viewing or the service itself," he said.

Elevia has found that when it includes the request in the follow up via text messaging, it's natural – and the positive reviews come freely and easily.

"Because people are on their mobile device, they don't need to do anything but click a link in a text message," he said. "That makes it seamless and easy for families."

The bottom line is that funeral homes should pay more attention to online reviews. "If you don't have positive reviews, the likelihood of you capturing new business is very slim," he said. "When I see a location with five total reviews, but it has been in business for five generations, it blows my mind."

Fortunately, Elevia "can absolutely help with that," Lefrandt said, and when it brings on a new client, it offers a "catch-up campaign" to collect positive reviews from families a firm has served over the past several months. "Generally, we give a free, 30-day trial with us," he said, noting that at a bare minimum, the offer can help a funeral home boost its positive online reviews.

Elevia can also help a funeral home recognize when a family is not happy. "Sometimes, they have no idea a family was as disgruntled as they were until they see their response and the dialogue," Lefrandt said. "And if a funeral home is trying to resolve a concern, we let that play out first before sending out a text message prompting a family to share a review."

*Jon Lefrandt*

## AI, Pricing and More

Asked about artificial intelligence, Lefrandt said he uses it every single day. "It's the future, and like anything, we have to lean into that a little bit."

But at the business level, Elevia is striving to use AI to make operations more efficient – and that's it. "My commitment today is still that every message is read and responded to by humans," he said. "When dealing with grieving families – as I look at those scenarios – I don't have any confidence in AI. You can almost feel that it is robotic," he said.

There are, however, ways that AI can help with scripting or prepopulating data that can save businesses and customers time, he said. "We are not afraid of it," he said. "We will look for any and all opportunities to use it where it makes sense without taking away from our core, which is to have this be a human experience."

The pricing for Elevia is simple and easy to understand: Funeral homes pay $399 per month for six campaigns per year for up to 600 contacts. There are no long-term contracts.

"The majority of locations fit into that 600-call range," Lefrandt observed.

If a firm needs something above that threshold, Elevia will consider what price to charge on a case-by-case basis.

"There are different variables that go into custom pricing," Lefrandt said. "If someone has 40 locations that they manage from one headquarters, that is a lot different for us, as we are not directly dealing with 40 rooftops."

If you are a Homesteaders Life Insurance Company customer, you are in luck: You'll pay only $329 per month for six campaigns per year for up to 600 contacts, according to Lefrandt. Customers that do business with Homesteaders may also enjoy some other limited perks, such as a longer trial period, which Elevia determines on a case-by-case basis.

Elevia also serves other markets that interface with death care, such as hospice and home health and pet loss and insurance. There are currently no plans to expand into new segments as Lefrandt still sees ample room for growth in established verticals.

The areas Elevia focuses on outside of death care are "synergistic with our core," Lefrandt said. "They go to the foundation of aftercare. For instance, with life insurance, we can focus on the beneficiary and the person grieving. And with pet loss, we often see even more engagement than with traditional funerals. The fact that we are validating grief is appreciated so much." But funeral homes, cemeteries and cremation businesses will always remain the foundation that Elevia is built on, he vowed.

What is common with all these verticals is that Elevia is generally communicating with a senior population, something it has gotten really good at, he said.

## Where Two Paths Diverge

The death of Lefrandt's father at such a young age is a tragedy, but there is no doubt about it: If he had not had to navigate such a profound loss, it is unlikely he would have ended up working in death care.

Moreover, as a result, about 10 million text messages that have been sent out to individuals who have recently lost a loved one and all the words of support that Elevia has lent to those struggling to cope have been sent.

On its own, each of those text messages might seem small. But when you combine all of them together and consider how many lives Elevia has changed, how many smiles it has created and how much help it has provided, it's clear that while Harold Lefrandt not only had an incredible impact on others during his life, but that his influence continues today though his son, Jon – and no doubt through all his children in their own ways.

Those two things – his father's death and the good that came after – may be hard to reconcile, but Lefrandt is now in a place where he can grasp what it all means.

"I think all things in life can be used for good," he said. "So, I look at it … and I think there is no way I would have ever created these solutions and helped all these people if it wasn't for the loss of my dad. It was because of that I was so intrigued and that I thought I could help this space."

The memory of the great times he had with his dad and the lessons he learned from him continue to be a driving force for Lefrandt.

"I am grateful that I have been able to use my creativity, entrepreneurial energy and enthusiasm – coupled with my personal experience – to make navigating the loss of a loved one better for other people," he said. "That is truly the motive behind all of this that has led to its success … I always felt the money would follow naturally if I did things for the right reasons, and that has been the case."

Through all the ups, downs and the pivots, Lefrandt's family and faith have been his rock, with his wife of almost eighteen years, Ashley, serving as his cheerleader-in-chief, never wavering in her belief in his ideas even when he may have doubted them himself. Through it all, she's teamed up with him to raise their four children – two boys and two girls – and make their home in Highland, Utah a happy place.

"She has been my confidante and friend," Lefrandt said.

From the outside looking in, it's evident that even though Lefrandt has had his share of challenges, he's a very blessed man.

*Visit https://www.elevia.com to learn more about Elevia.*

# Continuing Vision: Jeff Holcomb Is Committed to Helping Funeral Directors Earn CEUs

*By Thomas A. Parmalee*

Jeff Holcomb, 66, has been a funeral director for about 43 years, and he once dreamed of owning his own funeral home.

While the stars never aligned for him to do that, he scratched his itch of becoming a business owner in a different way: In 2006, he launched Continuing Vision, which hosts virtual and on-site events with the goal of helping funeral directors fulfill continuing education requirements.

"I did have aspirations at one time of owning my own funeral home, but the cost kind of put that on the side – and I started Continuing Vision in that respect of wanting to be an owner of something," he said.

A first-generation licensed funeral director, Holcomb became interested in the profession while his father was working on a part-time basis at James Funeral Home on Atlantic Avenue and LaPolla Funeral Home in Canarsie, a neighborhood in Brooklyn. "That is where we lived and that is where I started," Holcomb said. "I was actually in a Seminary College studying for the priesthood and saw funeral service as a vocation that was more my calling."

Today, he manages a firm owned by Service Corporation International on Staten Island – Harmon Funeral Home, where he has been for five years. The funeral home serves about 250 families per year.

The bulk of his career was spent at Aievoli Funeral Home in Brooklyn, where he worked for 25 years.

Over the course of his career in funeral service, the experience that stands out the most is the death of his son, Brian Holcomb, on July 1, 2022.

"That really changed my perspective," said Holcomb, who is married and also has a daughter. "I had always been on the other side of death, and now I was that person … it was a gut-wrenching change."

His son died after a battle with cancer, Holcomb said.

"He beat the original prognosis by a year," he said. "We fought hard and tried to give him any chance he could in fighting the cancer … until the end, I did not realize how much pain and suffering he went through."

His son continued to work right until the end, he said: He was also a funeral director, working at Aievoli Funeral Home in Brooklyn.

The ordeal has helped Holcomb connect with families, he said, noting that when someone dies, there may be massive medical debt and all sorts of other challenges left behind. "You try to have compassion for the family," he said.

As for Continuing Vision, he says he started the company because as a funeral director, he saw that it could be a struggle to earn the necessary CEUs to renew his license. "All the offerings were always through the associations at their meetings, and as a working funeral director, I always had to stay back at the funeral home while the owners went," he said. "There is not a lot of time to earn CEUs at a small firm if the owner is away and you have to man the store."

So, he got to thinking that he could not possibly be the only hardworking funeral director in such a situation. "I decided to create something," he said. "I would move around borough to borough, giving everyone opportunities on different days."

He knew he was on to something from the moment he held his first event in 2007.

"We did it at the 69th Regiment Armory in Manhattan on Lexington Avenue," he said. "We had a military presentation and about 75 people for that first event. It went very well, and it has *continued* to go very well."

He suspects that is largely because he's a funeral director and fairly well known in the profession. "I am one of them," he said.

When you come to a Continuing Vision seminar or workshop, there are absolutely no association fees or requirements to be part of any group, Holcomb said. "We opened it up to everyone, and it worked," he said.

When he started the company, virtual events were not even considered for CEU purposes, so Holcomb learned how to coordinate on-site events by going out and doing it. As a funeral director, however, it came naturally.

Today, the company hosts both on-site and virtual events that offer CEUs to licensees. "So, for New York, if you need 12 credits, six of which have to be attended and the others which can be completed online, you can do it all through Continuing Vision," he said.

It wasn't until the COVID-19 pandemic erupted, however, that Holcomb began to get serious about virtual events, he said.

For some time, Holcomb focused on offering CEUs and doing events only in New York, but it became apparent to him that funeral directors in other states also struggle with meeting CEU requirements and could benefit from Continuing Vision's events.

"I then branched out into New Jersey with the help of some speakers," he said, singling out Edith Churchman, owner of James E. Churchman Funeral Home in Newark, New Jersey, for her assistance.

Continuing Vision courses are also approved by the Academy of Professional Funeral Service Practice as well as in Georgia, Alabama, South Carolina, North Carolina and Indiana. The company recently began offering CEUs for Tennessee licensees as well, Holcomb said.

"You just have to navigate the waters with some of the states in terms of those that accept Academy approval – and find out the nuances of state notification, etc.," he said.

Asked about CEU requirements, Holcomb said he thinks that every state should have some type of minimum requirement.

"You don't go to a doctor or trust a nurse who doesn't continue their education," he said. "You want to keep up with new trends and procedures with embalming and with integrating different things into your services."

While each state should have some minimum requirements, he believes there should be some leeway for them to customize them as needed.

Over the years, Continuing Vision has made a clear impact on the profession, which is not lost on Holcomb. Over 7,500 people have attended a Continuing Vision program either virtually or on site over the years, he said.

The majority of his offerings continue to be an on-site format, he said.

"I tend to gravitate toward restaurants or catering halls, especially during the week as they have availability," he said. "They offer a nice setting, have nice rooms and the food is usually good." He added, "I don't like the idea of having a tray of cookies or paper cups for coffee – most of these places have porcelain cups, and there is not a cheap feel to it."

Typically, Holcomb designs a program so that it covers six hours, which usually translates into six CEUs. "Even with the inflation and different venues upping their cost, I try to keep the price at $210 for presales," he said. "The day of the event, it is normally a little higher – about $270. We offer a continental breakfast, lunch and coffee throughout the day – the whole nine yards."

As he's built Continuing Vision, Holcomb has gotten a great deal of help from various funeral professionals, including Regan Moreland, a funeral director from Alabama who serves as his digital marketing manager and web administrator.

He's also been blessed to work with some incredible speakers and instructors, including Kari Northey, also known as "Kari the Mortician," out of Michigan; John Hill, who works for James Funeral Home in Huntersville, North Carolina and is a funeral service education instructor at Fayetteville Technical Community College in Fayetteville, North Carolina; Dr. Jennifer Lares, a mortuary officer with the U.S. Army who also does consulting work with Larry Stuart Jr. and Raven Plume; and Kelley Romanowski out of Minnesota.

"The most impressive presentation I have seen in recent times was 'Are You Facing It or Fearing It? The Transformation of Death Care,' which was presented by Kari Northey and John Hill," Holcomb said.

As to what presenters can do to deliver a better experience to attendees, Holcomb has some wise words of advice. "Put a little personality into the presentation," he said. "Just reading from slides puts people to sleep. You have to mix it up. It's almost like you are an entertainer when you are performing."

While Holcomb has built an impressive business, he scoffs at the notion that he's getting rich running Continuing Vision.

"Everything has a cost," he pointed out. "This isn't a million-dollar business. Most events I have done have just broken even on covering costs. But it's not so much the monetary aspect – it's more about giving back to the profession and giving them the availability to earn their credits. And we have some nice social gatherings."

*Visit https://www.continuingvision.com to learn more about Continuing Vision.*

# Gail Rubin Continues to Blaze a Trail in Funeral Service

*By Thomas A. Parmalee*

Gail Rubin, 65, may be able to put a Before I Die Festival into a box, but you'd be hard pressed to put *her* into a box.

She's not a licensed funeral director, she's not a traditional supplier to the death-care profession and she's not a preneed salesperson.

But with that said, she knows as much about funeral service as almost anyone, she provides an array of services to funeral homes, crematories and cemeteries and her clients have handsomely boosted preneed sales.

If there *is* a word that describes her, it would have to be *pioneer*, which is fitting since you'll usually find her brightening one of her New Mexico haunts or strutting around a convention floor in flashy cowboy boots.

Rubin is that rare individual who has carved out a niche in death care that is entirely her own – one that will be very difficult if not impossible to fill if she ever makes a departure.

Fortunately, that day may be far into the future – if it ever comes at all – as we are talking about a woman who wrote a book for people who *don't* plan to die. Yes, we may be lucky enough to have Rubin with our death-care family for a long, *long* time.

FuneralVision.com recently caught up with Rubin, who shared how she went from enjoying a successful career in television to becoming the "Doyenne of Death," blazing a trail all her own amid Death Cafés, a flurry of books and a series of festivals that have informed the masses about funeral service and rituals surrounding death.

**You earned your degree in communications, worked at C-SPAN and then you worked at a communications firm for many years. What initially drew you to thanatology and the death-care field?**

In 2000, my husband David Bleicher and I got married in a very creative Jewish Western wedding in Albuquerque, New Mexico. Everyone had such a good time, I wanted to write a book about creative life cycle events and call it "Matchings, Hatchings and Dispatchings," about weddings, births and deaths. I got to write a monthly feature by that name in the *Albuquerque Tribune*. The stories about death and funerals got the most reader response. There are already plenty of creative wedding planning books, but 15 years ago, there wasn't much on creative funeral planning. So, I focused on funerals, and that changed the course of my career.

Thinking back to my college experience, I think I was meant to do what I'm doing now. I majored in film and communications at the University of Maryland, College Park. In a film production class, one assignment called for everyone to make a three-minute, black-and-white 8mm film project, titled "The Bubblegum Film."

My film was a satire of the opening of the classic 1957 Ingmar Bergman film, "The Seventh Seal." A medieval knight wakes up on a beach at dawn. Death has come for the knight, and to fend off his own demise, he challenges Death to a game of chess. As long as the knight wins, he gets to live. In "The Bubblegum Film," Death (played by Bob, my boyfriend and future ex-husband) doesn't know how to play chess, but he loves bubblegum. They agree to abide by the fortunes in the wrappers. At the end, Death wins. He puts his arm around the knight's shoulder, they walk down the beach, and Death starts skipping.

Considering what I do now, bringing a light touch to a dark topic using films and humor, I think I was always meant to be a thanatologist. By the way, "The Bubblegum Film" is available on YouTube.

**When did your interest in thanatology and death go from being a curiosity or interest to something that you decided you could pursue as a calling, career and livelihood? Was that realization sudden … or was it something gradual that occurred over time?**

It was a gradual transition. I realized my skills in public relations and event planning could be used to promote planning ahead for end-of-life issues. I became a licensed insurance agent, started my own publishing company, learned about getting sponsors for my projects, became a certified funeral celebrant and built the business up over time. It helped that my husband had a job as a schoolteacher, and I had paid off the mortgage on my house when I turned 50.

**How many funeral homes, crematories, cemeteries and suppliers do you directly work/consult with – what services do you provide and why should they work with you?**

Over the years, I've worked with many companies in the funeral field, including those that provide marketing and advertising to funeral homes, crematories and cemeteries. I can help with creative communications and outside-the-box activities that bring future customers into your facilities. I've done Movie Night at the Funeral Home, one-day Before I Die Festivals, The Newly-Dead Game in various settings, and I have been a featured speaker at on-site events. By using humor to break down resistance to discussing death far in advance of a death in the family, companies can fill their preneed pipelines.

**Do you have anyone else on your team, or do you rely on freelancers/contractors?**

It's mostly just me. My husband was my graphic designer, but I now use freelancers and volunteers to help with the Before I Die New Mexico Festival.

**What drives you in your daily work – what is your *why*?**

Every day, I find a way to use my creativity to expand the conversation about end-of-life issues and encourage people to act and plan. I'm not morbid, death is a fact of life. And especially since I personally experienced the benefits of having pre-planned, I want to get more people to do this.

**You were recently recognized by the Association for Death Education and Counseling with its prestigious Community Educator Award at the organization's annual conference in Houston on April 11, 2024. How gratifying is it to be recognized, and why was this award in particular so special?**

I joined ADEC 15 years ago when I was writing my first end-of-life planning book that changed the course of my career, *A Good Goodbye: Funeral Planning for Those Who Don't Plan to Die*. The people I have met through the organization are notable thought leaders in thanatology, the study of death, dying and bereavement. To be recognized for my innovations in community education about death by this prestigious group was incredibly gratifying. I'm not an academic, but this organization recognized that the kind of education I provide is meaningful and effective.

**You are the author of numerous books ... which one was the hardest for you to write, and why?**

So far, I have written *A Good Goodbye: Funeral Planning for Those Who Don't Plan to Die, Hail and Farewell: Cremation Ceremonies, Templates and Tips, Kicking the Bucket List: 100 Downsizing and Organizing Things to Do Before You Die,* and *The Before I Die Festival in a Box.* Probably the first one, *A Good Goodbye,* was the hardest, collecting information on a range of issues. While things have changed over 15 years since it came out, it has held up remarkably well. I included information on alkaline hydrolysis and other early funeral trends. I'm pondering a second edition with updates to include natural organic reduction, updated cremation statistics and other developments.

*In addition to being a pioneer, Gail Rubin has made her mark as one of death care's sharpest dressers. (Photos courtesy of Gail Rubin)*

**Which is your bestselling book? Why do you think that book is so popular?**

*A Good Goodbye* has won awards, and it's got great enduring information. It applies my event planning advice to the party no one wants to plan. It's also the only planning book out there that describes funeral traditions for various religions and cultures.

**Are you working on any future books – or what might you consider writing about next?**

I've been working on a book about my husband Dave's unexpected death from medical complications after prostate surgery, how planning ahead helped make a difficult time easier to bear, and the first year coping after his death. It will also include my 93-year-old father's death, how our choice of hospice for Dave influenced my dad, and my in-law's flirtation with medical aid-in-dying and hospice.

**When did you hold your first Before I Die festival – and how many have you held to date?**

I first found out about Before I Die festivals in 2016 and held my first one in Albuquerque in 2017. I have held six in New Mexico, working on the seventh in 2024. The 2018 festival was recognized with the International Cemetery, Cremation and Funeral Association's KIP Award for best event. I've also been involved with events with funeral homes and cemeteries in El Paso, Texas, Bakersfield, California, and Dayton, Ohio. There's more information about Before I Die festivals at www.BeforeIDieFestivals.com.

**Why would it make sense for a funeral home or cemetery to team up with you on a Before I Die festival … and if they do, what would that look like? What would you do and what would they do?**

Before I Die Festivals provide a range of activities and speakers at a funeral home or cemetery that get people to your locations without having to experience a death in the family. It's an upbeat educational opportunity to address people's curiosity. It's also a lead generating opportunity. One funeral home generated over $100,000 in preneed sales in the week after holding a festival. In addition to being a featured speaker at a festival, I can hold Death Cafes, legally show Mortality Movies, help plan the schedule of events, promote the event to my thousands of online followers and do media interviews to promote the event.

**For funeral homes that want to do it on their own without your involvement, what options are there for them?**

The Before I Die Festival in a Box includes the book that provides guidance for holding a festival, the Newly-Dead Game and Newly-Dead Bingo, guidance for holding Death Cafes, short and long planning forms and the 4-DVD set of the TV interview series, *A Good Goodbye*. The purchase also includes an hour of consulting time with me. To legally show movies at your location, you need an Umbrella license from the Motion Picture Licensing Corporation (www.MPLC.org). While I've never come across any movie license police, you don't want to mess with Hollywood attorneys.

**You recently lost your husband as well as your father. Has it been hard to continue working while coping with their deaths … or has it rather brought more meaning to your work?**

My husband's and father's deaths in April and August of 2023 were initially a blow. I suspended my podcast work for the year, but I still had a Before I Die New Mexico Festival in October. Sharing their stories has helped me and my audiences. We had preplanned and prepaid for their funeral arrangements. Telling about implementing those plans as The Doyenne of Death brings a deeper meaning and impact. I'll admit, I cry a little when I tell their stories.

**You are also a big participant in the Death Café movement. How many do you typically do a year – and are funeral homes involved? Do you think more funeral homes should participate in Death Cafés, and if so, how? And if they should NOT participate, what should they know about them?**

I was the first person in the U.S. west of the Mississippi to hold a Death Café, in Albuquerque in September 2012. I've done them monthly most of that time since, pivoting to online events during the pandemic. The reception centers in funeral homes are a great place to hold Death Cafes. I've held them in funeral homes during Before I Die festivals. Just know that the ground rules for holding an event and calling it a Death Café call for no selling or leading people to a specific course of action.

**People can buy all sorts of merchandise on your website, such as urns, cremation jewelry, etc. Is there a particular vendor you are working with – and how can others sell items on your store, if applicable?**

The cremation products online store is hosted by UPD Urns. I also offer my books, T-shirts, note cards, DVDs and The Newly-Dead Game in my Stuff to Die For online store. I'm open to working with folks who have interesting products they'd like to offer to the public through my site.

**You also have The Doyenne of Death Podcast, which features interviews about death, grief, funerals, and mortality. What has been your favorite episode?**

Since I revived the podcast, I did a three-part interview with speaker and author Greg Bennick. He is working on a biography of Ernest Becker, author of the Pulitzer Prize-winning book, *The Denial of Death*. We had an incredible wide-ranging conversation about humans' perception of self-esteem, mortality and immortality, the Pearls Before Swine cartoons of Stephan Pastis, and humor and death.

*Gail Rubin exhibiting at The Author's Fair at the Albuquerque Museum. (Photos courtesy of Gail Rubin)*

**What is one idea, offering or product you have introduced that you thought would be a slam dunk that did not resonate? And what did you learn from that?**

Years ago, I did a series of Mortality Minute audio spots for funeral homes to sponsor radio advertising. Each was a 60-second mini-program providing a light look at serious subjects related to death, funerals and developing trends in end-of-life issues. Each episode included a 10-second slot for a customized sponsor's message at the end. Only one funeral home bought into the program. I guess radio wasn't considered a good bet for funeral advertising. But I'm willing to revisit the program if someone wants to give it a try!

**What do you want your final goodbye to look like and how do you hope you will be remembered after you are gone?**

I will have a wicker basket casket from Passages International and a Jewish funeral. I would like the song "All Star" by Smash Mouth played: "Only shooting stars break the mold." I'd like to be remembered as a pioneer in helping people talk about death and plan for our 100% mortality. And hopefully they will say that I was a nice person and a snappy dresser.

**You are also working on an upcoming TV series, *Mortality Movies*. Tell us a little bit about it, when will it start and where can people watch it?**

*Mortality Movies* is a 30-minute program with three death educators discussing topics such as funerals, grief, and related end-of-life topics. During each episode, several film clips will be shown related to that episode's topic. The expert panel will discuss the film clips and share information that can help audiences understand end-of-life issues and plan for our 100% guaranteed mortality.

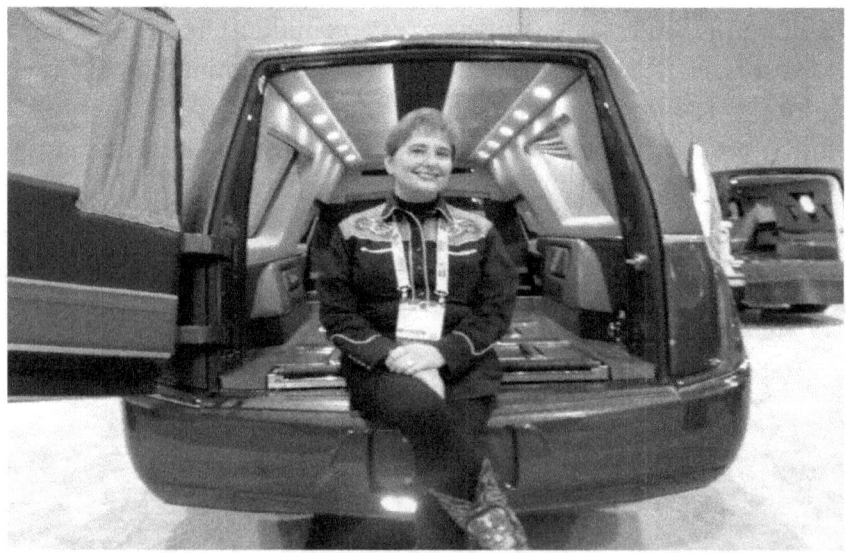

*Gail Rubin in a burgundy hearse at the 2017 NFDA convention.*

We are recording the series in Albuquerque's Studio 519 this summer. It will initially be available on cable access channels in Albuquerque and in other markets, and episodes will become available on YouTube. Subscribe to my YouTube channel, *@GailRubin*, to be alerted to new episodes!

**Do you have any final thoughts to share?**

My motto is, "Talking about sex won't make you pregnant, talking about funerals won't make you dead. Start a conversation today." I hope to speak with funeral homes, cemeteries, and crematories soon about ways we can fill your preneed pipeline!

*Visit https://agoodgoodbye.com to learn more about Gail Rubin and her work.*

# Sunset Software's CEO Aims to Help Funeral Homes Take a Burden Away from Families

"Great products like Sunset can help families when they need it the most."

Stephen Walter CEO    Kaela Worthen CTO

*By Thomas A. Parmalee*

Whether a death is expected or unexpected, the very last thing that most families want to do is think about closing bank accounts, reaching out to credit bureaus and paying their loved one's outstanding bills – some of which they may not have even known about.

After all, they have more important things to do: looking at old photographs, remembering the day they met that person who they had no way of knowing they'd marry and have children with and thinking about what charity would be the best one for friends and family to donate to in honor of their loved one's memory.

Fortunately, there are companies that can help the families that funeral homes serve with all the ornery details that they don't want to fret about during an emotional time. One of them that is taking away that burden is Sunset Software, which offers an estate app that funeral homes can offer to families – one that gives them the chance to earn commissions, so they can provide even better service to families.

We recently caught up with Stephen Walter, the company's CEO, who is helping funeral homes give families the tools they need, so they can stay laser-focused on what matters most.

*Stephen Walter*

**Tell us a little bit about yourself and how you started Sunset Software.**

While I was at college, I learned to program software, and my first job out of college was at a software company. Then I went to law school and practiced for a few years, before going back to software.

My co-founder, Kaela Worthen, is the real software genius of the team, but having a legal background in the estate/probate space is incredibly helpful as you can imagine.

After both Kaela's family and my family dealt with the estate settlement process, we realized there was an opportunity to help people streamline and speed up the process.

**What does your software do? Where can people find it?**

Our software is designed for estate executors, it automatically finds all the assets of an estate, then closes them out as it makes sense with a single click.

The app is not a tool for funeral professionals, but we've found that funeral professionals are a trusted point of connection with the executor as they begin the aftercare journey.

The app is available on both iPhone and Android.

**When did you start Sunset Software and how did you realize that teaming up with funeral homes might be a good idea?**

We started Sunset Software after we built a company called Paintbrush, which is in the small business lending area. While we were building that company, my mother was dealing with the estate settlement process after her mother passed away, and my co-founder Kaela's family was dealing with the same thing. After talking to each other about it, we realized that a lot of families go through this overwhelming process alone.

Teaming up with funeral homes is an obvious fit for us, and I wish we'd thought of it earlier. Unfortunately, we had to wait until a funeral home here in Salt Lake City reached out to us.

Funeral professionals are trusted partners for the families handling a death, however, they are not in a position to deal with the complicated legal and financial process of settling out an estate. We can help with that, and they can help families take off another stressful aspect of a passing as a partner.

**Other than funeral homes, what other businesses are you seeking to partner with? (i.e. hospice care organizations, etc.?)**

We also work with life insurance companies, funeral insurance companies, and software companies that help funeral homes manage their day-to-day tasks.

You charge a flat fee of $9,999 to settle an individual's estate. That is a sizeable expense for most people, so I'm wondering how you go about that sale. Are people able to speak with you or one of your customer service representatives before moving forward and using your services?

Pricing this software product was a challenge for us. Traditionally, estate executors have to deal with a number of billable hour partners, like lawyers and accountants, where the total bill is unknown. In addition, a lot of the online tools offered currently are little more than a guide, or a to-do list, which require the estate executor to personally handle all the hundreds of tasks, big and small on their own, between their own job, family, and personal responsibilities.

What we've learned, and our customers appreciate, is that we handle everything for them, without the looming threat of an unknown number of billable hours, or a requirement that they personally engage with financial institutions or complicated transactions.

Put simply, the time saved, the stress saved, and the legal/accounting bills that we save for an estate more than make up for our flat fee. We bill the estate directly, not the executor personally.

**What are the main tasks you take care of as part of that service, and how does your price compare to what someone would typically pay for what you provide?**

We aim to handle everything for an estate executor, using software to vastly speed up the process. First is everything financial. Instead of multiple meetings, and letters back and forth with an estate's bank, investment fund, retirement fund, etc., we simply integrate with their backend software to identify an estate's assets and close them out when the executor is ready. We can do this whether or not the executor has the username and password.

We also handle all of the notification tasks, including the government and financial entities like the credit bureaus, the DMV, the Social Security Administration, the State Department, credit card companies, insurance companies, etc. But that also includes the simpler process of shutting down all the recurring bills like utilities, cell phone, Netflix and other easy partners.

Finally, we handle the bills of the estate, close out any obligations including state and federal taxes, then we distribute the estate based on the guiding documents (probate, wills, trusts, etc.) to the beneficiaries.

By building direct software integrations with all of these services and organizations, we cut the settlement process from years to weeks.

**Can the services you provide replace or eliminate the need for someone to use an estate attorney – or will they typically still need an attorney to take care of certain tasks?**

Sunset cannot replace a great estate attorney to help a family plan and prepare or represent a family in probate court. However, after the death has occurred and the executor is properly empowered, we can take over the settlement process, including discovery of all bank accounts, retirement accounts, credit cards, property titles, etc. These are tasks that estate attorneys don't typically work on anyway.

**What if someone died without a will? Can you help?**

Yes absolutely, intestate estates can use our software just the same as an estate with a complicated will, trust, or some combination thereof.

**You recently started a partnership program for funeral homes … what research did you conduct before rolling out the program?**

We are excited to start helping funeral homes offer Sunset to their customers. In our experience, families aren't ready to start the estate settlement process until after they have finished with the funeral, but it's in the back of their mind much earlier. Letting the family know there is an easy tool to take care of the process is another wonderful way a funeral home can help take stress off of a family.

**Did you test it out with a funeral home or two before rolling it out on a larger scale? If so, what did you learn?**

Yes, and we learned a lot. The biggest takeaway was the distinction between hands-on and hands-off services. Funeral directors, and the staff at a funeral home, are experts at the sensitive and important hands-on process of taking care of the deceased and providing funeral or memorial services. They provide an incredible value to their communities. We fit better into the hands-off process of the sensitive financial and asset management process of estate settlement, after the deceased has been mourned and celebrated.

**How does the partnership program work? Do funeral homes earn a commission for referring business to you, and how is that tracked, etc.?**

We provide funeral homes with whatever setup that makes the most sense for them, to fit smoothly in their process. Whether that's printed material, email links, text messages, or even a phone call or Zoom conference to hand off. We track and attribute all of our customers, even those that don't use a tracking system and work with our partners to make sure every connection is accounted for.

Our commissions are paid out monthly, as a thank you honorarium to our valued partners. The referral structure is also tiered, allowing top-performing partners to generate more revenue through the model. On top of the financial connection, we love the feedback and open communication with our partners, and we hope that the additive revenue is helpful as they navigate their own operations.

**How many funeral homes are you currently working with, and what's the potential for growth?**

We work directly with only a dozen funeral homes today, but we work indirectly with hundreds through our software partnerships. Our growth comes from customers with great experiences, and if we keep that up, I think we could work with every funeral home.

**What are some of the main pain points you can ease for funeral homes?**

Outside of the financial component for the referral program, I think our biggest help for funeral homes is we are another tool in their toolbag to help their families. Estate financials are a huge stress point after a death. With our Sunset partnership program, funeral homes can communicate to stressed out families that there is a simple, software approach to estate discovery and settlement.

**If funeral homes want to learn more, who can they reach out to get more information about your partnership program?**

Please schedule a time to chat with us. I personally handle all of our partnership discussions, so you can also just email me *Stephen@SunsetApp.com*, and I'm happy to answer any questions.

*Visit https://www.sunsetapp.com to learn more about Sunset Software.*

# Has Rehan Choudhry Created 'the YouTube for Memorialization?'

*By Thomas A. Parmalee*

Rehan Choudhry, 44, might not be a household name … but if his app, Chptr, takes off the way he hopes, he'll bring the stories of thousands of deceased loved ones to homes throughout the United States – and create an entirely new revenue stream for funeral homes and their television station partners.

Already, the company has raised $3.6 million in funding as it has rolled out the app, which is designed to give users the opportunity to share and hold onto the memories of lost loved ones. The app has more than 6,000 users who have created more than 3,000 videos – and it has the *potential* to transform how funeral homes, families and media companies think about obituaries.

The revolutionary aspect of Chptr is that for the first time, television stations have allocated dedicated air time to run the local stories of community members who have died, Choudhry said. "And the reason they have done that is because the cost to produce those videos have gone down so much … we have created an inventory to memorialize a person on TV, and we have done it in a way that everyone benefits without gouging the customer," he said.

The app is free, but users can add on services for a fee, such as having a video professionally produced and paying to have service details aired on television – or to air the entire video on TV.

A few dozen funeral homes in three different markets – Binghamton, New York; Springfield, Missouri; and Burlington, Vermont are working directly with Chptr, which recently announced a partnership with Gray Television.

Choudhry is hoping to multiply the number of funeral homes he's working with substantially in the coming months. "If a funeral home is interested in starting right away (regardless of whether there's a TV station in-market or not), we can get them up and running in less than 30 minutes. It's super easy," he said.

As funeral homes sign on to offer Chptr to families, the company plans to develop new partnerships with additional television stations and networks, creating "a direct pipeline for funeral homes to be able to send customers and their content to their local station," Choudhry said.

While funeral homes that use Chptr are not given market exclusivity, the first firms to become customers will get "a ton of support" and receive "all the benefits of being first in line," he said.

*Rehan Choudhry, founder and CEO of Chptr, aims to bring a new obituary model to funeral service.*

## An Unlikely Entrepreneur

Choudhry, the founder and CEO of Chptr, may seem like an unlikely candidate to introduce a new obituary model to the death-care profession, having honed his professional skills in the casino industry. From there, he leveraged what he'd learned to launch a music festival.

In fact, those who knew Choudhry earlier in life may be surprised that he's enjoyed any success in business at all.

"I had chronic sleep apnea, and it wasn't diagnosed until I was 35," he said. "It destroys your short-term memory, and it destroys your attention. So, when you are not diagnosed, it looks like you have a learning disability."

As a result, for the longest time, Choudhry could not focus or perform well in school, he said. "At one point, a college counselor said instead of going to college, I should drop out and become a plumber," he said.

Looking back at that experience, he said, "I think when you're dealt a hand like that when you are really young, you train yourself to be able to overcome quite a bit, and you develop a level of resilience that helps in entrepreneurship."

As the father of a 3-year-old and 5-year-old, he hopes to use what he overcame to help them as they encounter their own challenges, he said. "When I grew up, the assumption was that I was lazy or dumb," he said.

But as a first-generation American whose parents – both doctors — came here from Pakistan, Choudhry, who was born in Chicago and raised in Iowa and Virginia, had a chip on his shoulder. "I wanted to prove something," he said. "When I believe in something, there is nothing that will stop me from seeing it come to fruition."

Despite the challenges he faced, Choudhry pushed through and graduated from the University of Tampa with a degree in computer information systems.

As far as how his mind works Choudhry calls himself a "generalist at my core," which has helped him throughout his career as he's passionate about solving problems – especially those that impact communities.

"I started my career as a systems developer for the Department of Homeland Security as a contractor right after 9/11," he said. "We developed emergency response systems, and it was some of the most meaningful work I have ever done."

But "sitting around in a bunker" wasn't the future he saw for himself, and left something to be desired, and so he ended up going to Vanderbilt Owen Graduate School of Management in Nashville, completing his MBA in 2007. Then Caesars Entertainment Corp. came knocking on his door.

"The CEO had created an incubator of sorts," Choudhry said. "There was a leadership development program … the focus I really wanted to pursue was analytical marketing."

Although he'd never set foot on a casino floor, he was deeply interested in the company's loyalty program. He joined eager to push that forward, but the Great Recession of 2008 hit shortly thereafter, changing everything.

He quickly realized that he needed to pivot or become one of the hundreds of people his company was laying off. "And I realized that nobody really invested in the local Atlantic City community anymore. Many casinos were just raking in cash, and no one had created community programming – and I thought it was desperately needed," he said.

He also knew that during a recession, people do not gamble as much – nor do they buy homes or as much clothing. Purchasing overall declines, but the one expenditure that tends not to be hit as hard is spending on entertainment. "People still spend money on movies and theatrical shows," he said.

So, Choudhry got to work designing programming that was more lifestyle focused and that had nothing to do with gambling in the casino. Through that work, he sought to bring value to the community.

"We wanted to create a new narrative for the company," he said.

As a result, he introduced Caesars first arts festival in Atlantic City as well as its first LGBTQ festival. Fashion shows and other events rounded out the programming.

While the initiatives did not save the company from the devastation of the recession, they did "make a dent," Choudhry said. And his work got noticed.

The owners of the Cosmopolitan in Las Vegas were opening a resort, and they decided they had to have Choudhry on their team no matter the cost.

They wanted someone untraditional "and I accidentally became that person," Choudhry said. He was hired and moved to Vegas in 2010, becoming head of entertainment for the property.

Chptr can offer funeral homes and television station partners a new revenue stream.

**A New Beginning**

Once in Vegas, Choudhry was somewhat appalled by the focus on Cirque du Soleil shows at the expense of everything else.

A touring band had not played in Vegas in ages. "I built an entertainment strategy that brought in touring bands," he said.

Eventually, however, Choudhry retired from the casino industry and in 2013 founded a music festival called "Life Is Beautiful," which was eventually acquired by Rolling Stone.

The three-day music, arts and culture festival was born as part of a major transformation of downtown Las Vegas, a historically underserved neighborhood.

"I wanted to create a festival that had an impact theme," Choudhry said. "I wanted to create an environment that was supportive."

The festival hosted 44 nonprofit organizations that focused on a wide range of health topics, and it became one of the top five music festivals in the world, he said.

A few years later – in 2017 – he founded Emerge Impact + Music, which became Las Vegas's largest live music event, spanning three days. The event reimagined the conference and festival experience by blending a progressive lineup of top next-generation musicians with inspired speakers and relevant social impact themes.

"It was a great idea and a fun event for everyone who attended, but it was really hard to build a large-scale event around emerging talent," Choudhry said in reflecting on why he stepped away from the venture.

When the COVID-19 pandemic broke out, however, he found himself in a different place, which was the result of going on a blind date a few years earlier with a television anchor.

After six months of dating, she ended up moving to New York city after receiving an incredible job offer.

"Basically, I faced a decision," he said. "Stay in Vegas and continue to live there … or chase this girl," he said.

So … he packed his bags and went chasing.

As a result, when everything started to get locked down, he didn't only find himself married but with a child on the way as well.

And there he was, someone in the entertainment industry, which was completely shuttered.

"My wife was doing news shows live from our living room," he said. "I rethought my life … I knew I didn't want to spend my life running festivals."

With time on his hands – after all, people could hardly leave their homes – Choudhry indulged his pensive mood. "I was trying to come up with something new," he said.

He started a blog about modern-day fatherhood. He considered writing a book. He was grasping at straws, pretty much, trying to find something that would spark his attention.

And then he found it … right in his living room.

It was his wife, who began making 60-second videos of neighborhood residents who had lost their lives in the pandemic.

"The approach that she took to tell these stories was different – I had never seen it before," he said.

She tracked down all the friends of colleagues of the person who had died and treated them the same, whether it was the person's mother, father, spouse, best friend … or their baseball teammate from high school or the colleague who may have only worked with them for six months.

"Historically, we thought of them as being on the outskirts, but she saw the memories that they had about a person were incredibly strong," he said. Moreover, the narratives she created about those who had died by looking at their lives through such a lens ended up being incredibly powerful.

In some cases, the loved ones of those who had died learned about a side of the deceased that they had never known about.

"I thought, 'Why can't everyone on the planet have these experiences?'" Choudhry said.

Not everyone could be interviewed by a news anchor, but he reasoned that they *could* tell these unknown stories and record their memories.

He'd finally found that spark he'd been seeking … and so, he rolled up his sleeves and threw himself into the fire.

In 2022, he launched the Chptr app.

**Shaking It Up**

In creating an app that allows everyone to record their memories of someone who has died, Choudhry hopes to shake up the written obituary space and replace it with a living memorial of digital content – content that can be packaged into short videos and shared with the world through partnerships he's been inking with television stations. Along the way, he's sharing revenue with funeral home and television station allies.

He's also working with newspapers, but taking a slightly different path there, focusing on different milestone-type events.

"Ultimately, we want Chptr to be a celebrations company," he said. "So, for newspapers, we are working with a newspaper group in the D.C. area – InsideNOVA (which is owned by Rappahannock Media, a multimedia company that publishes a number of newspapers, magazines, websites and niche products throughout Northern and Piedmont Virginia). They launched graduation celebrations, and we are doing that with them." In the future, Choudhry envisions doing more in the wedding, retirement and birth arenas, he said.

But it's the obituary space, which accounts for 95% of Chptr's business, where he thinks he can make the biggest impact. One day, he hopes that his work will pave the way for videos and television stations to replace written obituaries and newspapers as what he calls "the default solution" of announcing someone's death.

Unlike an obituary, the stories shared via the app are not meant to be a summary of someone's life and achievements, he said. Rather, they allow someone to look back at the time they may have gotten stuck in the rain with the person who died, or to relive the day they were cut from the basketball team with the deceased when they were in middle school.

"It's not about posting, liking or commenting … the platform is about engaging with the community that you normally lose after 90 days," he said.

**Making Funeral Homes and Television Partners the Priority**

As far as how Chptr will make its money, television stations and funeral homes are at the center of it all.

"We are the only ones working with TV stations," he said. "We are not trying to take away newspapers from the existing guys – they still have value, and there is an art to that. We would love to see the existing companies that are out there continue to do well despite the declines in obituary sales."

Already, Chptr has captured the attention of media companies across the country, which are seeing a decline in obituary sales, he said. "The industry is destabilizing," he said. "However, the demand for memorials has not waned – it's just shifting. And not to social media, but to video."

The problem, however, has always been that television stations simply cannot produce memorial content at scale, and so they have been shut out of even thinking about sharing individual stories of everyday people with a larger audience.

"We are the solution to be able to do it," he said. "We can help people through the toughest time of their life in a way that feels natural … that feels like a community conversation."

The Chptr app is free for people to download and use, and advertising will *never* appear via the app, he said. "We will never sell user data, ever," he vowed. "That is a hard line we will not cross, and it's built in to every deal we strike." He added, "There is nothing more offensive than someone stumbling across their person's obituary on a website five years after they passed not knowing it was placed on a website with dog food ads and flower ads – it's just awful … and the benefit of being on the outside of this is I get to see some things kind of clearly because I am not tied to a business model that was designed 25 years ago."

Choudhry's dream, he said is to build "a global storytelling platform," so that every single person's story gets captured not just when they die but for years later in the same way stories were told orally when we lived in smaller communities.

As far as turning a profit, that's not at the forefront of his mind, he said. "We're building an *enterprise*," he said. "If I can build a company that the public trusts to be able to share these memories, then I have done something."

*Rehan Choudhry has raised millions as he's rolled out Chptr.*

**Breaking Down the Business Side**

Since no advertising is shown and since the app is free, however, the revenue has to come from somewhere.

And that's where an optional suite of services comes in, which can be sold through the funeral home in many cases and create an additional stream of revenue.

"We are not selling the ability to memorialize," he said. "But we *are* enabling brands to be able to able to sell inventory on the air and on their website to promote the lives of people they want to promote," he said. "We have the ability to make sure everyone's story gets told. We are able to create memorial videos at *scale* – and we price them incredibly low."

How low?

A one-minute video professionally produced with audio, a voiceover and music costs $250, which includes basic service details being aired on a television partner's website. A family can also opt *not* to have a video produced but to air basic service details on a TV station for $99.

As for what a funeral home can earn from selling such a video to families, it is significant: The funeral home and television station would split $218.75, which comes out to $109.38 cents each, Choudhry said.

The funeral home realizes an additional benefit through the branding that goes along with the video, which includes the funeral home's logo, Choudhry said.

As a result, instead of a one-time notice being listed in a newspaper at a substantial cost to the family (and one that results in no or little revenue for the funeral home), the family can end up getting the service details of their loved one aired multiple times by their local television station (and the funeral home earns some revenue, too). "If it posts a week out, you will get air time several times a day with the listing," he explained.

As to how Chptr can take such a small cut – 12.5% — Choudhry explained that the platform he's built is based on artificial intelligence that compiles content from user-generated material, allowing it to be cost effective.

"We've built the YouTube for memorialization," he declared. "When YouTube came out, companies were spending billions of dollars on servers to host their video content, and they had to purge their content. But YouTube came along and said, 'We will hold it all for you and charge nothing.' All we are doing is introducing a modern model. We will charge what we can reasonably ask for … if we sell a $250 video, we are not sending camera crews out. We have a system that does all of this and produces broadcast quality content, which is why television stations are willing to run it."

Funeral homes can reap larger rewards, however, if they sell more than the one-minute video or the basic listing.

For $850, the family can have the one-minute video *aired in its entirety* on television instead of simply airing basic service details. Again, the funeral home would split that fee with the TV station after Chptr takes its 12.5% cut.

So, in this example, Chptr would earn 12.5% of $850, or $106.25.

The funeral home and television station would split the remaining $743.75 or earn about $371.87 each.

Families could also opt for a three-minute video that would be aired in its entirety on a local television station, which costs $2,500.

In this example, Chptr would receive $312.50, and the funeral home and television station would split the remaining $2,187.50, which would be $1,093.75 each.

"We are a platform, and we take a small percentage at the point of purchase, and there are no other fees," Choudhry said. "Almost 90% of the revenue goes to the partners." He added, "The idea that 350 words in a newspaper will cost you $500 is insane. With us, for $250, you get a beautiful video that you can share, and the memorial lives forever and can include an unlimited amount of content."

Whether you invite two people to share content about your loved one on the Chptr app or 2,000 people, it's free, he said. "You can share, and you can continue to share – you can connect with people and make those connections," he said.

The videos have been selling well, and in ways that might be surprising to some funeral home owners. "What we are seeing is that instead of two people spending $400 on flowers, they may come together and buy the three-minute video for the family," he said. "A lot of what we sell is gifted to the family."

If a family only buys a one- or three-minute video through the funeral home and there is not a television station in the market, then Chptr gets its 12.5% and the funeral home gets the rest, as no television station is involved. A television station could also sell a video and air it without the involvement of a funeral home, in which case it would keep almost 90% of the revenue. Choudhry, however, anticipates that about 90% of sales will involve revenue sharing between funeral homes and television stations.

"This is the first time that television stations have offered this ... funeral homes have access to television for the first time," he said. "There is no real conversation going on about how we make money without the other because there is upside for both – this is a new revenue stream for the television station and the funeral home, and everyone is happy."

As of now, Choudhry believes that traditional newspapers are only serving about 25% of people who die each year through the printed newspaper. "The other 75% are thought to be price sensitive," he said.

Through his app and with his model, however, he hopes to help a huge segment of people who've lost loved ones share their stories with the larger community at an affordable price – one that can help him grow and sustain a viable enterprise while also helping funeral homes and their television station partners breathe new life into their businesses.

*Visit [https://www.chptr.com](https://www.chptr.com) to learn more about Chptr.*

# Cairn Partners: Not Just Preneed Marketing

*By Thomas A. Parmalee*

Chris Rose, founder and president of Cairn Partners, wants to make one thing clear: He does not run a preneed marketing company.

"We work in the death-care profession and work with independent, family-owned funeral homes and cemeteries to help them defend, grow and protect market share," he said.

That involves outreach on both the preneed and at-need marketing sides of the business, and in some cases, it means working with funeral homes to enhance their sales development process.

"It's not just the marketing side, but the processes that allow you to be sure the marketing is properly executed," said Rose (pictured at top). "It doesn't do any good to do a Facebook advertisement or conduct a direct mail campaign if you don't have a process on the back end to capture that information and follow up with those people to turn it into more than just an activity – there has to be a follow-up process, even if it's not sales oriented."

So, who is Chris Rose and how is Cairn Partners helping funeral homes succeed? We reached out to him for some answers. Edited excerpts follow.

**When and how did you start Cairn Partners?**

I founded the company back in 2009 after buying a company that was essentially a shell corporation. What it had, however, was a commission schedule with insurance companies based on the volume it had previously done. There was no revenue stream, but the fact that it had a commission schedule was a very valuable thing, as I could earn commissions from other companies that were higher than if I had started a company from scratch. The first year in business, we worked with only a handful of funeral homes and generated $700,000 in preneed volume. Within three years, we were at over $25 million in volume.

I was previously a regional director at Forethought Life Insurance (Now Global Atlantic). The company was founded because after serving at Forethought for eight years, it was clear that independent funeral homes really needed more assistance in marketing strategy and outreach. At the time, there were marketers that were focused on the preneed aspect of the funeral profession and there were consultants that provided marketing services on the at-need side of the business, but there did not seem to be a model that focused on both as well as general business development.

We have over 20 full-time employees and a significant number of contractors. Our organization is built on a co-op model, which gives our partners skin in the game. Our partners have the opportunity to buy into the cooperative, so they are their own organization and use our services, but they can be independent, as long as it's not detrimental to Cairn.

**Where does the name Cairn Partners come from?**

Originally the company's name (the shell corporation Rose acquired) was Northwest Planning Partners, and the company was formed in 2002. It was a small insurance agency servicing funeral homes in Washington State. After purchasing it in 2009, we focused on building the business and found quickly that the name was not consistent with our footprint or our focus. While attending ICCFA events, I ran across a small boutique brand development company that was a married couple. I talked with them about my company and brand, and they convinced me that utilizing their services to rebrand the company was the right path to take. It was a very impactful decision that changed the trajectory of the organization. We locked ourselves up in an Airbnb in Northern Kentucky, and they put me through quite the interrogation process. Through that experience, we defined our customer base, our services, our focus, our mission and of course the brand that would reflect those aspects of our company culture.

A cairn is a simple stack of rocks. Which is reflected in our icon visible on our website. Cairns are some of the oldest monuments known to man. Historically, cairns have been placed to mark the location of a significant event like a battle, or celebration or a burial site.

If you have ever spent time hiking outdoors in the backcountry you may have noticed that cairns often mark a path that is difficult to see, and these waypoints guide us through rocky and dangerous ground.

We use this theme throughout our organization, including the process with our client BASE, CAMP, Trailhead Training, Gide Training, Waypoints, Stepping Stones and Trail Markers.

It seems to fit our company culture and add a little excitement to an otherwise relatively boring process built of programs, processes and standard operating procedures.

**How many funeral homes and/or cemeteries do you work with? Are you strongest in a particular area of the country?**

We work with over 250 rooftops in 20+ states. We literally rose from the ashes of the cremation trend on the West Coast. And that is the epicenter of our business. Because of our experience with cremation and what works and does not work, we have a particular advantage as we work with firms in the Midwest and the East. We work with standalone funeral homes, clusters of funeral homes, combos and standalone cemeteries. We only work with independent firms. Our goal is to keep independent funeral homes independent.

**How much preneed are you responsible for writing in a given year? How has that number been tracking over time?**

The amount of preneed we write per year is only one metric of many by which we define our company because we have services that are not directly related to preneed sales.

Preneed volume is akin to asking a funeral home their case count. Although that is the metric that most use to identify the success of a firm, I have found that this metric is a falsity. A more discernable metric is the net profit per call or earnings before interest, taxes, depreciation and amortization of the firm. Or perhaps the rating of the firm by its customers. Lots of firms have big case counts, are not very profitable and have poor reviews from their customers.

Although we do not consider ourselves to be a "third-party marketer," which is where we are commonly pigeonholed due to our focus on marketing and outreach, we are a medium-sized player in the third-party marketer realm. We spend a significant amount of our time on consultative activities in relation to at-need marketing, customer experience and training. We also have a cemetery division that works with stand-alone cemeteries and combos. Over the last 10 years or so, we have had a steady growth rate of between 5 and 10% per year either by helping existing firms grow or adding new clients to the Cairn Network.

**Do you work with multiple preneed insurance companies or are you exclusive to one or two? Explain.**

We do work with multiple preneed insurance firms as well as trust providers. We have found over the years that clients have a certain proclivity toward a specific insurance or trust provider. Often, it is based on the avoidance of change. Other times, it is a relationship with a person or an entity and other times those decisions are based on events or circumstantial information. It is our contention that preneed insurance products have become commoditized. We have little interest in spending an excess of time convincing the client to use blue ink rather than black ink. We educate them on the attributes of the different offerings by insurance companies and let them make an educated decision. We try to focus on the services Cairn provides that fill the gap between what the insurance company provides and what the funeral home needs to maximize the customer experience and attain their goals, which usually are to defend, grow and protect their market share. We would not be able to provide our services and value to many firms if we did not use the financial vehicle of their preference.

**What makes you different from your competitors?**

I think that any marketing company can claim to have the basic tools that we have at Cairn Partners. The tools are very important to fulfill the needs of the client. And by "tools" I mean, direct mail programs, digital marketing programs, aftercare programs, training programs, recruiting, etc.

One way we are different is in the consultative approach we take and the customization that occurs to serve our client. We do not just focus on preneed. I don't agree with separating out the preneed program as a different entity. I think that is a short-term solution to a long-term problem. A symbiotic relationship is preferred.

I am convinced that the best retail customer experience occurs when the at-need and outreach teams work together. That is also true when working with a combo. The customer can tell the difference when a combo tries to separate their services into "the cemetery side" and "the funeral side." It seems like an obvious goal to strive for and yet it is rarely achieved. Although most combos are set up as separate business entities, it does not mean that the customer sees them in that fashion.

In addition to that difference in strategy and approach, we also have several proprietary tools that allow our firms to meet remotely with the consumer and still provide the very best experience. These tools are available to all arrangers – preneed or at-need. Our goal is to help the firm be better.

There are sales and marketing companies that have some of these tools, all these tools or what I would call "better than nothing" tools. What differentiates us at Cairn is that we take a holistic consultative approach to provide what the firm NEEDS based on what it would like to accomplish. We have a process we call our Business Approach and Strength Evaluation (BASE) by which we identify the gaps in an outreach program. After discussing our findings with our client, we then provide our Client Assessment and Marketing Program (CAMP). This is focused on the action items we plan to execute with the firm. We can then identify the firm's willingness to collaborate in achieving the goals that have been mutually determined.

We are very focused on market segmentation and strategy based on that segmentation. We spend time focusing on the market that is being targeted: traditional, alternative or low cost. This is imperative in terms of the marketing approach. Each segment should be differentiated. For example, if a traditional funeral home client has an outreach program that is price focused like a low-cost provider, that model will fail. Conversely if a low-cost provider markets like a traditional provider, they will not be successful because their marketing budget will exceed their profitability. This natural business model concept is often lost on owners because they are very focused on case count rather than net profit per call.

For new firms to the market or alternative disposition firms (alkaline hydrolysis or natural organic reduction), we follow a similar process, but we must be cognizant that their model is not a traditional funeral home model. That means our goals derived from the BASE process may be very different and often more assertive.

**How have your clients' needs changed in the past 36 months?**

That is an interesting question. Their needs are relatively the same as they have always been, but the tools we use to accomplish their goals have changed. For example, the need to have a focused succession plan has always been there, but only recently has it become imperative.

It has been said before, but the funeral profession is slow to change for *many* reasons. Change itself is difficult, but if an operator is financially successful with relatively low execution expectations, this diminishes the incentive to get better. That has been the story for as long as I have been in the profession and before. The nature of the business, the barriers to entry and the family focused generational business mindset of independent firms in this profession ensures that sweeping technological and ideological progress in this space has been stunted and likely will continue to be unless massive change occurs.

There certainly seems to be more independent firms looking to sell rather than pass the torch to the next generation within the family. There is also the phenomenon of simply letting the business dissolve over time without taking a succession plan into consideration.

**How did the COVID-19 pandemic affect your business, and did you make any lasting pivots as a result of the pandemic?**

There are two phenomena that we have witnessed. Rapid adoption of technology and burnout.

The pandemic changed so much in terms of how funeral homes work with their clients. It required many of them to adopt technology and made them reassess how they serve clients and their market position. Some firms were inundated with both at-need cases and preneed opportunities and were simply treading water. Others did not have the capacity to assist everyone and sent at-need cases to their competition, which ultimately changed the landscape in some geographic locations. Still, other firms took the opportunity to expand and help more families by ramping up. Some small firms continue to embrace the technology they adopted due to the pandemic while others have abandoned it, which is unfortunate.

Post-pandemic, I see more funeral homeowners looking for an opportunity to slow down or transition.

Prior to the pandemic, Cairn had already adopted a business model that operated almost exclusively remotely. Except for our yearly sales meeting, we operated in the cloud with Zoom meetings and a cloud-based business culture. When the pandemic hit, we didn't see much of a change to our operations other than our ability to meet with our customers in person. We had been working on a remote-visit platform for our advance planners that would allow them to meet with clients remotely or in person regardless of an internet connection and complete the arrangement process with more efficiency and higher customer satisfaction. We launched that tool immediately and then started to train advance planners how to use the AP Dashboard in conjunction with Zoom.

**How do you think the pandemic affected preneed in general/overall? Are there any opportunities as they relate specifically to preneed that you believe came out of the pandemic?**

Preneed certainly saw a spike during the COVID crisis. For some, there was an immediate drop in preneed, because they didn't know how to work with the preneed customer. After they figured it out, there were years of increases. This occurred, of course, for preneed and at-need business. I think both have normalized a bit now, and we are seeing regular numbers return. I suppose that preneed will continue to be relevant in that people conclude that life is fragile and any of us could die at any time from any ailment.

Post-pandemic, some funeral homes are simply less accessible. Some are no longer fully staffed, and others are by appointment only and still others simply lock their doors and only let in customers. For those firms that have adopted this closed-minded approach, I think long term it will stunt their business and the growth of their business because they will be even more isolated from the knowledge that vendors and peers in the professional can provide.

For the profession, the opportunity is to realize that change can be positive, and that technology is not something to fear, rather it can free up time for the small mom and pop firms. It can be liberating and can provide better customer experiences while freeing up time for the owner and staff. Technology, if utilized properly, can reduce paperwork, double data entry and enhance the customer experience. Consumers want a better experience in a shorter amount of time. That is the trend. They want it their way and they want it now. Independent funeral homes can accommodate consumers if they embrace technology. If they do not, corporate entities and consolidators will continue to grow, and the independent funeral homes will become a less desirable option for consumers.

**What is one big thing you wish more funeral homes and cemeteries would understand about preneed?**

Funeral homes are a business. Yes, they provide a much-needed service to the community and most independent funeral home owners are empathetic and caring individuals. Most funeral directors are as well. But if you do not run your business with the intention of creating a net profit of which a portion will be put back into the business, negative consequences will ensue. Customer satisfaction will erode. It is equally damaging to take all the profits out of a funeral home and disperse them to the owners as it is to undercharge consumers for services provided and let your funeral home erode into shabbiness with cookie cutter services. There is a sweet spot. That is to use proper business tools to establish a budget and set aside profits for deferred maintenance and technological upgrades or better customer experiences. Preneed is a key component of this concept.

Preneed should not be an afterthought or treated as its own separate entity. Just like a small specialty food manufacturer is focused on manufacturing their specialty food products and getting them to consumers' needs to have a marketing budget and go to trade shows and work with distributors and customers and the community, the funeral home should also pay attention to similar aspects of community and top-of-mind awareness. That outreach should include educating the customer about the benefits of planning ahead. Preneed is often treated as a necessary evil. It may have arrived on the scene that way and probably ruined many marketing plans upon its arrival. But that was so long ago … it is time to embrace the necessary evil and make it part of the business plan, the marketing budget and the cost structure. It is not a necessary evil anymore; it is an opportunity to serve more customers. And if executed properly, it can feed itself as the engine to defend, grow and protect the business.

**How has the interest rate environment affected preneed and or your business in particular, if at all?**

The interest rates are what they are. We work with multiple insurance and trust providers with multiple products, so that the customer can see what the differences are and the implications of their product decisions. Ten percent of our funeral home customers do not guarantee their preneed funeral arrangements. They have decided that they do not want to manage their shortfall exposure and prefer to simply not guarantee. We are OK with that decision if the funeral home understands the competitive implications.

Our funeral home clients can be very sensitive to interest rates as they see growth rates as the main culprit of preneed shortfalls. Funeral home owners who see shortfalls tend to complain about growth rates, the fact is that shortfalls may be mitigated in many ways, one of which is through choosing a product that has a reasonable growth rate. We have a very thorough Stepping-Stone that includes a shortfall analysis that walks our clients through the reasons why shortfalls occur and their options to mitigate them. The shortfall analysis that we have performed clearly shows that growth rates are not the main culprit for shortfalls.

At the top of the list for reasons for shortfalls include:

- Preneed discounts.
- At-need discounts.
- Uncharged at-need upgrades.
- Inflationary increase management.

- Errors on the preneed Contract.

Interest rates will fluctuate, and of course, inflation typically has a direct correlation with interest rates. These are economic market structures that we do not control. The other reasons for shortfalls, a firm *can* control and just needs to take responsibility to do so.

**Tell me about the Cairn Coin and why Russell and Kelley Weeks, the owners of Weeks' Funeral Homes in Washington, were this year's honorees.**

The winner for 2023 was the first time that a married couple has been honored. In 2023, we honored Russ and Kelley Weeks as co-owners and employees of Weeks Funeral Homes. The details about the Cairn Coin are on our website.

The Cairn Coin was born from a weekly team meeting wherein we were looking for the opportunity to thank specific individuals in the profession that had an impact on one or more of our team. We identified several individuals who had been mentors or just outstanding people that exemplified the traits that we aspired to gain. We worked on that project for far too long trying to identify how to show certain professionals how inspiring they are to our organization. We did not limit the nominations to funeral professionals, in fact we encourage nominating individuals outside the profession or on the fringe of the profession. It took us such a long time to develop HOW we wanted to honor them that we had three winners in the first year based on the time we had taken to make those decisions.

Our team nominates individuals and then presented why their nominees should receive the honor. We then vote and present the award at our annual reception at the ICCFA Dead Talks in January.

Russ and Kelley were honored because of their commitment to the profession and how passionate they both are about the funeral profession and the customer experience. Russ purchased the funeral homes from his father and could have easily made a living on that legacy, but instead they decided to build a larger legacy and acquired multiple funeral homes and manage or own multiple cemeteries. Together, they built a business that not only serves the community but also employs a significant number of professionals in funeral service. Russ and Kelley's passion for serving others and doing so in an ethical and unselfish way is the cornerstone of why they were selected. Russ is very intentional about what he would like to achieve and how to achieve it.

**What is a book you have read that you'd recommend others read and why?**

I read way too many trade magazines as opposed to books. That is a bad habit of mine. I like to know what is going on in the now.

There are a few books over the last couple of years that I have chosen to purchase and physically read as opposed to "listening" to them through Audible or Spotify. The one that has been most impactful and that I have purchased and sent to others in the profession is "Staying Alive in the Funeral and Cemetery Profession: Building a Business, Weathering Change and Finding Growth" by Jake Johnson, the president and CEO of Johnson Consulting Group.

*Jake Johnson's book gets two big thumbs up from Chris Rose.*

When I first started reading the book, I thought that Jake was simply stating the obvious. But I found that his insights are brilliant in their simplicity. This is a "back to business basics" book that needed to be written and should be read by all in the profession. So much is missed by the funeral home professional who is just doing things the way they have always done them. Or perhaps the firm is on the cutting edge of marketing but is not paying attention to the look and feel of their funeral home or chapel. Or the funeral professional does not listen to the client. In some cases, they choose not to *ask* the client for feedback in fear of having to change.

What makes Jake uniquely qualified to write this book and simplify the business process is his experience in the profession. One *could* look at Jakes's success and attribute it to Tom Johnson's legacy and Tom's efforts to build a business in the funeral profession. That assumption would be a mistake. Jake took the opportunity to learn the profession from inside out and then reinvented Johnson Consulting Group to provide services that Tom originally intended, in addition to services that filled a gap in accounting and customer experience among other service fields. It is an easy read, and I think it should be mandatory reading for all funeral and cemetery professionals.

*Visit https://www.cairn.partners to learn more about Cairn Partners.*

# That Guy with the Glorious Beard from Tukios

*By Thomas A. Parmalee*

If you had to select the most iconic beard in funeral service – one that rivals Gandalf from Lord of the Rings, Billy Gibbons from ZZ Top or even Santa Claus himself, there really is only one person who can lay claim to the title.

The Tukios guy, of course.

But there is much more to Kevin Young than just his beard.

A licensed funeral director in California, he has been working in funeral service since the early 1980s and could not see himself doing anything else.

"The loss part is what really got me into it," he said. "I witnessed my brother's death. It was a death by drowning, and I could not save him."

His brother, Danny, was 16 at the time. Young was two years younger.

The tragedy unfolded at a reservoir in Ogden, Utah, during a Fourth of July campout, Young said.

"He and I were swimming in a beach area, and our mom and dad were out fishing," he said. "I swam out to these buoys that were out there."

That's when Danny tried to follow him and "went down," Young said.

His body was found about four hours later, and the family was absolutely crushed.

"All these years later … it is still vivid in my mind," said Young, now 65. "My mom never recovered from his death."

The topic of death and grief, however, were always with the family. Even before his brother died, they had dealt with tragedy, as Young had a sister who died at 10 days old.

As a teenager, he found himself working as a teller in a bank, where he'd often see George Larkin, the owner of Larkin Mortuary, which was eventually purchased by Lindquist Mortuaries & Cemeteries.

He was impressed by how Larkin dressed and carried himself, and also knew that the funeral home had served his family well in times of crisis. He had heard the business provided free rent to removal staff.

Although the funeral home had generally hired married couples for that job, it made an exception and gave Young the job, giving him his start in funeral service.

"I worked for him a couple of years and decided that was the path I wanted to take," Young said. "The whole thing fascinated me – working with Mr. Larkin and having the opportunity to see the embalming process. They were very much into the presentation of the deceased and how they looked. I learned a lot from him … it intrigued me and sucked me in."

He's thankful that Larkin is the one who gave him a chance.

"This was back in the day when people were very committed to a mortuary – and that is where your family went," he said. "It seems like that kind of loyalty does not exist anymore, but back then it did, especially in Ogden."

**An Ambitious Young Man Treks Further West**

After getting married, Young attended Cypress College in Cypress, California, where he earned his degree in mortuary science, so he could pursue his passion as a bona fide career.

In the 1980s, he worked at Westminster Memorial Park and Mortuary in Westminster, California, which was purchased by Service Corporation International.

"I started off as their night guy, working every third night and I was going to school, so I slept there," he said. "Once I graduated, my wife and I returned to Utah, but it really didn't work out for me, so we returned to California, and I got my old job back at Westminster, where I was hired as a funeral director and embalmer. We were doing 1,200 calls back in the 1980s, so I worked funerals and embalmed and then moved into the role of making arrangements and selling preneed. It was an all-inclusive place, where I could learn a lot about funeral service."

After that, Young worked for the Loewen Group, managing a firm in central California from 1991 to 1996 that served a farming community. "We had a high suicide rate for a small town," he said, reflecting on that experience. "I worked there for five years, and then took an assignment in Nebraska, where I worked from 1996 to 1999."

Each step of the way, his lovely wife, Jody (they dated for three months before getting married and have been a couple for more than 41 years, raising three children along the way), was there helping and keeping him on track, he said.

"She would come over to a funeral home and help lift a casket, or do whatever needed to be done," he said. "Back in the early days, I could not get a hairdresser, so I asked her for help."

At first, she was reluctant, and when she first did it, he saw tears running down her face. When he asked her what was wrong, "She said she just felt like this is someone's mom or grandmom, so why was she so worried about it? And from there, she started helping me out with hair and getting involved with helping out with the day-to-day duties of a secretary."

Eventually, Loewen found itself in financial trouble: Its stock began to dive, and its entire business began to unravel.

Young knew the gravy train was coming to a screeching halt, so he got off the tracks on his own terms in the late 1990s.

"I had a good friend calling on mortuaries for the Aurora Casket Company," he explained, adding that he'd heard a job was about to open up in Utah.

"And something my wife and I wanted to do was return to Utah," he said.

So, he interviewed for the post and was hired. He spent 15 years at the company.

While he enjoyed his time at Aurora, he admits he sorely missed being a funeral director.

"I think the biggest thing I missed was meeting with families," he said. "I felt like I was wired to help people through one of the most difficult times of their life … and there is a lot to the embalming process I missed." He added, "I did *not* miss having to work nights or weekends or getting up at 3 a.m. and working a Saturday funeral, and everything in between, but the love of funeral service is what I missed."

He had numerous mentors to learn from at Aurora, however, including Bob Jenkins and the great Roger Coomer. One area he delved into was how to ask good open-ended questions, he said. He also had the privilege of learning from Chip Ray, who seemed to know everyone. "It is hard to find someone who *doesn't* like Chip Ray," he said. "It was really awesome to be able to travel with him and learn from him. And Bob Jenkins was really customer centric."

He also singled out David Bowman, who he called "a classic gentleman" who was respected by everyone.

When Aurora was acquired by a private equity firm before transitioning over to Matthews and becoming Matthews Aurora, things started to change, however, Young said.

Meanwhile, offshore products were starting to flood the market, which was becoming much more of a factor as Young sought to build his territory. Crafty competitors started painting offshore caskets or putting new interiors or head panels into them, so you could hardly tell the difference from a higher-end option, he said.

Once again, Young felt as though it was time for a change, although he treasures the time he spent at Aurora. "It was a very good job, and it gave me the opportunity to meet lots of funeral directors, he said" – particularly in Idaho, Nevada, Colorado, New Mexico, Utah and Arizona.

*Kevin Young and his wife of more than 41 years, Jody.*

### The Next Chapter

For a short while, Young landed a job as a salesperson for Tributes.com, the company launched by Dave McComb, John Heald and Monster.com founder Jeff Taylor. Tributes.com was eventually acquired by Legacy.com.

It was then that he began running into Curtis Funk, the founder of Tukios, on a regular basis. He'd actually met him years earlier, however, when Funk was in high school and had launched FuneralRecording.com.

Invariably, he'd end up going to the same meetings and conventions as Funk as they both tried to sell their wares to funeral directors. More often than not, he found that Funk would outdo him when it came to getting customers to say "yes."

"But the blessing of it is that it gave me my first real introduction to Curtis," he said. "I felt like they took something from FuneralOne and put it on steroids – it was amazing to see."

He ended up having some deep discussions with Funk about salesmanship and gradually came to respect him and Tukios more and more.

When his job at Tributes.com ended, he worked at Coldspring for a stretch, but it was not the right fit.

It was a rough time for Young … nothing was working out.

"I could not see at the time that when a window closes, a door opens," he said. "It was so devastating for me to lose that job at Coldspring."

Amid the turmoil, however, he made a smart decision: He picked up the phone and called Curtis Funk.

After making that phone call, he was told he could start at Tukios on Monday – and he'd have six months to reach a certain goal.

And if he did so, he'd be taken off a probationary status of sorts and made a full-time employee, with benefits and all the rewards that go along with being a true member of the team.

"Curtis has kept every promise made to me," Young said, noting that he hit his target and Funk proved to be a man of his word. "He has never been interested in what he can take from me when I grow a territory but rather with what he can reward me with for growing a territory."

That's been a welcome change from what he's seen from some past employers, who always seemed to want to take as much money away as they could from the little guy to add to their own coffers, Young said.

"There is a lot about Curtis that makes me loyal to him and loyal to the company," Young said. "Curtis is the best boss I have ever worked for." He added, "For a person his age to have the kind of influence he does in the funeral space, with the contacts he has … and growing Tukios to be the largest tribute video player is a testament to the type of people he cultivates and to Curtis himself."

As to what he enjoys most about working at Tukios, Young noted that it's not the same company it was eight years ago – for one, Pamplona Capital Management, the same company that owns a majority stake in Legacy.com, bought a majority stake in Tukios in 2020. Today, Tukios has about three times as many employees as it did when he joined.

"But the culture has not changed," he said. "Curtis has not changed. And while the number of employees has grown, the same core group is here. The fact that it is led by Curtis is the reason."

As long as Funk is at the helm, Young, who once again calls Utah home, said he doesn't plan to go anywhere and will keep his head down and continue focus on growing Tukios's business in North Carolina, Louisiana, Texas, Wyoming, British Columbia – and anywhere else his hard work is required as a senior account executive with the company.

Of course, it helps that Funk allows him to have that glorious beard.

"I have always had some form of facial hair," Young said. "When I first worked at a mortuary, they did not allow a beard of any type, but I had a mustache for several years." He continued, "At one point the Loewen Group decided it was OK to have a beard, but it had to be neat and short and groomed, and I started a beard then."

One day, he approached Funk and mentioned that he wanted to grow his beard out ... *really* out. And Funk said he didn't have a problem with it as long as he kept it groomed.

"That is one of the things I really like about Curtis – he allows people to be themselves," he said. "We've had a few people with long hair, and Curtis had a mullet for a hot minute, although he probably does not want to admit it."

Young's beard has brought him a certain amount of notoriety, and it often helps break the ice in conversations with customers. The reactions his beard generates makes him smile while living everyday life as well.

"In fact, I went to a ZZ Top concert last year, and someone asked if they could take their picture with me," he said. "I said, 'You know I'm not in the band, right?' And they still wanted my picture."

He has even found himself being the model for a company that sells beard products, which Young still finds unbelievable. On top of that, he won "best all-around beard" in a beard competition.

And of course, he's taken up playing Santa Clause at various events, even selling his wife on the idea of playing Mrs. Clause.

"My wife is not the person to be on show and hates it, but it is well received," he said of playing Mr. and Mrs. Clause.

When he goes to various conventions, some people aren't shy about asking if they can touch his beard, which his co-workers find hilarious, he said.

"There was a lady from China, and she could not leave it alone," he said of one convention. "She wanted to braid it ... it has turned into this cult thing."

The beard, he said, has paved the way for him to have conversations he would have never otherwise had, and has helped him become a better salesperson – all because he was given the chance to be his authentic self.

As for other beards in the profession he admires, Young singled out David Nixon, president and CEO of Nixon Consulting; and John Feher, senior director of business development at Precoa, as two individuals with stellar beards that deserve the utmost respect.

Moving forward, Young aims to help Tukios continue breaking barriers.

"I am really proud of what we have put together," he said. "We are working on a lead generation tool to drive business to funeral homes, and I am excited to see that come out pretty soon. We are also working on an AI tool for image enhancements … I am excited about the growth we have ahead of us."

*Visit [https://www.tukios.com](https://www.tukios.com) to learn more about Tukios.*

# A Look Behind the Deal to Take Park Lawn Private: A Conversation with the Chief of Homesteaders

*By Thomas A. Parmalee*

When you get a chance to make three to four times the typical rate of return compared with a traditional investment, you take a good look at it.

At least, that's what you do if you're Steve Shaffer, president, CEO and board chair at Homesteaders Life Company, which has been serving the funeral profession since it was founded in 1906.

Then again, Shaffer has always been a numbers guy, having earned his accounting degree at Indiana University Bloomington and starting his career as a certified public accountant and auditor at the prestigious Ernst & Young in Indianapolis.

After that, he co-founded Keystone Group, which he served as chief financial officer and executive vice president before going on to become a co-founder of Foundation Partners Group, which he served as president and CEO.

So, when the opportunity came to take a major equity stake in Park Lawn Corp., one of the best-known funeral home operators in the profession, he was intrigued. The fact that he became convinced that he could consummate the deal and actually double down on Homesteaders' commitment to funeral service was likely the cherry on top of the sundae.

"Creative investments like this one position us to offer added value to all of our customers through things like higher policy growth and new tools and innovations that help them connect with more families," Shaffer told FuneralVision.com.

In short, in creating an affiliate to make an investment in Park Lawn, he saw benefits not only to Homesteaders but to funeral homes everywhere – current customers and prospective customers.

We recently caught up with Shaffer to get some more details on how the deal materialized and what he envisions for the future.

**Viridian Acquisition Inc. (an affiliate of Homesteaders) and Birch Hill Equity Partners Management are teaming up to take Park Lawn private. How much is Homesteaders investing?**

Homesteaders (by way of Viridian Acquisition) will make a $250 million investment in Park Lawn alongside Birch Hill Equity Partners. This investment, while significant, places us in a minority position in the company. Actual percentages will be determined at closing.

**The press release Park Lawn issued announcing the deal noted the all-cash transaction is valued at approximately $1.2 billion, including Park Lawn's net debt. Will Viridian assume any of Park Lawn's debt?**

The press release issued by Park Lawn detailed the transaction in Canadian dollars. In U.S. dollars, the total amount is closer to $970 million. Of that, Homesteaders is investing $250 million.

Homesteaders will not have any obligation on the debt. There will be a standalone entity that is both obligated to and servicing the debt. This is simply an investment for Homesteaders.

**Did Viridian Acquisition exist before this transaction?**

Viridian Acquisition was created solely in anticipation of the Park Lawn transaction which, for confidentiality purposes, was code named "Project Viridian" throughout the process. Its formation was made possible by the work we did early in 2024 to reorganize as a mutual holding company.

**What is your relationship with Birch Hill Equity Partners and how did you find each other and decide to agree to team up on this deal?**

BMO Capital Markets introduced us to Birch Hill in early 2024. We knew we wanted a like-minded partner to help facilitate the transaction. Birch Hill was selected carefully and specifically from a variety of potential partners because they fit so well from a cultural standpoint with both Park Lawn and Homesteaders, and they agreed with our long-term strategy and view of the opportunity.

**Does Birch Hill own other companies tied to funeral service? Or is this a new space for the company?**

Birch Hill has investments in adjacent spaces, including a natural stone business that supplies monument makers, but they have not previously invested in funeral service directly.

**What were the challenges, if any, of buying a company based in Canada but with significant U.S. operations?**

This was a complex transaction involving several parties, including a public company and a regulated insurance company, but Park Lawn's status as a Canadian company with cross border operations did not make it more challenging.

**How do you foresee this affecting the footprint of Homesteaders in Canada moving forward?**

Homesteaders is always exploring new markets and opportunities, but we do not have immediate plans to sell our products in Canada.

**How – if at all – do you feel this transaction will affect your relationship with firms not owned by Park Lawn?**

This partnership with Park Lawn provides us with a path to infuse capital into the profession at a time when it is difficult for operators to find informed, long-term, secure, reliable financing partners. It deepens our commitment to the funeral profession in a significant way, which should be attractive to any funeral provider who is looking for a partner that is committed to the space for the long term.

This investment will also place Homesteaders in an even stronger financial position, with returns 3-4 times higher than traditional investment yields. That's money we can reinvest in higher policy growth and new tools to help funeral providers connect with more families.

**Have you talked about any targets in terms of the number of acquisitions you'd like Park Lawn to make on an annual basis moving forward, in terms of EBITDA, families served, number of rooftops, etc.?**

We have not discussed any specific changes to Park Lawn's annual acquisition targets with the Park Lawn team. Those decisions and strategies will continue to be managed by Park Lawn's management team and the board of directors following the closing of the transaction. Homesteaders will not direct those decisions.

**Do Park Lawn firms use Homesteaders as a preneed provider currently – and what about moving forward?**

A number of Park Lawn's U.S. locations have used Homesteaders in the past, but Park Lawn as a whole does not currently write business with us. We anticipate many synergies moving forward, and the potential of using Homesteaders to fund their preneed program will likely be one of them; however, we have not yet determined how or when this transition will occur. We are committed as an investor in Park Lawn to allow them to make the best operational and strategic decisions for their company.

*Steve Shaffer of Homesteaders Life Company.*

**How have your customers reacted to this news? What concerns have you heard, if any, and how have you addressed them?**

A transformational transaction like this is always going to invite extraordinary interest, and that has certainly been the case here.

We've been pleased, but not surprised, that the feedback we've received from funeral providers has been largely positive. Our customers understand that this is a creative, smart way to step up our financial support for the profession, and they can see how their funeral homes and policy owners will benefit from higher returns we'll see from this investment.

Our customers also understand that Homesteaders is committed to providing an exceptional service experience to every funeral home, regardless of their location, size or ownership structure. We've been proactive in ensuring our funeral home customers understand the benefits of this transaction for Homesteaders and why it's a positive move for the funeral profession, and that's been a big factor in the positive response we're seeing in the marketplace.

**What did you see as the biggest risk in consummating this transaction. What opportunities did you see?**

My goal as CEO is to help ensure Homesteaders will be around for the next 100 years. As such, we make decisions today that will drive our growth five, 10 and 20 years down the road. There's a short-term risk in making big moves that are this complex, but it's one we can navigate with clear, crisp, proactive communication and consistent commitments in our actions for all of our customers in both the long and short term.

While this move may cause some short-term waves, we would not be pursuing this strategy if we didn't have high confidence in the long-term opportunity for Homesteaders.

**Were other firms competing to provide capital to take Park Lawn private – or was this a rather closed process?**

Our discussions with Park Lawn began as a friendly exploration of our mutual desire, as two strong, forward-looking organizations, to do something really positive for the profession. It was the right opportunity at the right time for Homesteaders and Park Lawn, and there were a lot of synergies between our cultures and strategic mindsets that made it immediately clear that this was the right direction for both companies.

**How much of a factor was it that leaders at Homesteaders, including yourself, have had a long history with Park Lawn's executives? How did that type of familiarity with people such as J. Bradley Green, the CEO of Park Lawn; and Jay Dodds, the company's chief strategy officer, help move things along?**

Our relationship with the leaders at Park Lawn certainly played a role in bringing both parties together for those initial conversations from a strong basis of trust. This is a relationship business, and we make a point to stay connected with stakeholders across the profession. Homesteaders has a deep commitment to the funeral space, so there's a real benefit for us in all aspects of our business to maintain connections with the key players and creatively exploring ways to leverage our strengths to complement partnerships like this. There was a similar mindset at Park Lawn that resonated with both teams from the very beginning.

**Once private, will Park Lawn continue to have a board of directors, and if so, what changes do you foresee to the board?**

Yes; as with most all organizations, once private, Park Lawn will continue to be governed by a board of directors. Homesteaders, Birch Hill and Park Lawn will all have representation on the board of directors, though the makeup of the board won't be finalized until the transaction closes, which we expect will be sometime in August.

**What else would you like the profession to know?**

This is a really positive thing for the profession.

We're bringing hundreds of funeral homes and cemeteries back into private ownership where they'll be managed by a team committed to the funeral profession for the long term. We're doubling down on our commitment to be a reliable capital partner in the space, both through this transaction and through continued growth and investment in our funeral home lending program. And we're doing this for the long-term. This is something that will position our 118-year-old mutual company to be here and remain strong for the next 100 years.

*Visit https://www.homesteaderslife.com to learn more about Homesteaders Life Company.*

# Mark Davis: Offering Cremation with Care and a Whole Lot More with ValMark+

*By Thomas A. Parmalee*

Mark Davis, 66, grew up in New Jersey, but it wasn't until he moved to Fort Lauderdale, Florida a couple of weeks before his sixteenth birthday that he found himself thinking about funeral service.

At Piper High School in Sunrise, Florida in the mid-1970s, he and some fellow classmates took a field trip to a local family-owned funeral home in Southeast Florida as part of a health services class.

"On the second floor was the casket selection room," he said. "I was 17 or 18 years old, and I see the price tag on top of the casket. And I had never been in a funeral home before and had no idea what a casket or funeral cost."

It was the days before itemized pricing, so the price on the casket – over $10,000 – included services.

"I said, 'Oh My God, that is a lot of money," he said.

After graduating from high school, he attended the University of South Florida in Tampa. When his parents went on vacation, he kept an eye on their shoe store, which is where he struck up a conversation with his father's car insurance agent, who asked him a lot of pointed questions about what he was going to do with his life.

"And I said I really don't know," he said,

"This gentleman was Jewish and knows my father is Jewish and he said to me, 'Have you ever thought about the funeral business?' And I said, 'Not really.' But when he said that, it took a minute, but I thought about the casket with the price," Davis said.

**A Passion for Business**

While it took some time, in the late 1970s, Davis eventually reconnected with his father's insurance agent, who introduced him to the executive vice president of Riverside Memorial Chapel in Miami Beach, which was looking for good people to work with him in the business. The firm is owned by Service Corporation International.

"I met with Al Golden, the executive vice president, and he explained to me about the funeral business," Davis said. "I was hired on the spot."

The Riverside business was by far the largest-volume funeral home in the Miami area back then, serving more than 3,000 families per year, Davis said. "Everything was centralized out of one location," he said.

Davis earned his associate degree at Miami Dade College while serving as an apprentice at Riverside, doing "everything you could think of at a funeral home," he said.

"I was working my ass off 50 or 60 hours a week," he said. "I remember going to work at Riverside at Sunday night at 6 p.m. and then working through the night and going to an 8 a.m. class in the morning at Miami Dade and doing a full day of school. My days and nights were running into each other, and it was crazy."

While he foresaw a career for himself in the profession, he did not want to own or operate a traditional funeral home.

"At the end of the day, I am kind of a PR and marketing guy who happens to be in the funeral industry," he said.

Still, after college, he managed a few funeral homes, starting a few operations for firms in the North looking to expand into Florida.

Along the way, he met his wife of more than 34 years, Valerie, while working at a firm owned by Gibraltar Corp., where he was a preneed sales manager, and she was an executive assistant. They met in 1987. While not a licensed funeral director, she has helped him with all of his businesses, mainly in a marketing capacity.

Eventually, the couple moved to Sanibel Island on the west coast of Florida, where they started The Cemetery Exchange, which enabled people to buy, sell and trade cemetery property.

"We were the only cemetery lot brokers in the state of Florida at the time," he said. "People wanted to sell cemetery property, but there was no other resource other than the classifieds section of newspapers, and who was really looking at classifieds to buy cemetery property?" he said. "So, we developed listings and worked with several family-owned funeral homes in the Miami area that were reselling graves and crypts."

He did "extremely well" with the business for a few years before ultimately selling it, he said. "And then, I was kind of looking for something to do," he said.

That is when the couple found themselves on a drive on Colonial Boulevard in Fort Myers, where they passed Fort Myers Memorial Gardens and Funeral Home & Cemetery, which is owned by SCI.

"There was a freestanding building sitting directly next to the cemetery, and the only thing separating them was a chain link fence," he said. "At the time, it was a daycare center, but it originally was a single-family home. And I said, 'If that building ever become available, it would make a great little funeral home.' And a month later, there was a For Rent sign in front of the building."

Davis rented the building and opened Horizon Funeral Home and Cremation Center in 1998.

"And across the street was another funeral home that was and is still owned by Carriage Services, Harvey-Englehart Metz," he said. "So, you could stand in the parking lot and throw a rock and hit three different funeral homes."

When he set up a competing business, Davis was intent on offering families a more affordable option – especially with cremation. "Within three years, we owned about 36% of the market," he said. After 10 years, he sold the business to two former SCI employees, who eventually sold it to Foundation Partners Group.

"And after FPG bought Horizon, in short order, they changed the name to Baldwin Brothers, which was a chain they had bought in Florida a few years earlier," he said.

At the end of the day, Davis pulls no punches about why he entered funeral service.

"It's a *business,* and when you are in business, you are in it to make money," he said. "Your number one obligation for yourself and your family is *to make money.* Money is a great motivator." He added, "I'm not a person who got into the funeral business as a calling – it's not who I am. I didn't get in it because my great-granddad or dad were in it. I got into it because I saw an opportunity to make a living, but in addition to that, I saw it as an opportunity to do something different."

He also realized early on that he was not a corporate guy and was not going to move up the ranks at SCI. "I said, 'I need to do my own thing,'" he said. "And shortly after that, I was able to do that and have been self-employed for more than 30 years."

*Mark Davis says he has always been deeply in love with his wife, Valerie, who has helped him with his numerous business ventures.*

**Launching ValMark Memorial Group**

Davis could have counted his winnings after selling Horizon and called it a day, but that's not the man he is.

"I am a guy who has to be doing stuff," he said. "But I was looking for something to do that was less stressful than operating a funeral home, so I started ValMark Memorial Group in 2009."

He developed various brands that funeral homes throughout the country could join as affiliates, starting with Veterans and Family Memorial Care.

"We worked with independently owned funeral homes across the country, doing some really great community engagement programs and public relations work. We set our funeral home providers apart from the competition – holding them up as experts in working with veterans and families when it comes to benefits, burial in national cemeteries and other things," he said. "The funeral homes that participated had tremendous results.:

Affiliates paid an annual membership fee for the services that ValMark provided, which included a Veterans and Family Memorial Care website that appeared on page one of Google search results.

"Our idea was to provide funeral homes with more exposure on Google than they could get organically through their own website," Davis said. "So, when someone in the area googles 'veteran' or 'cremation' and 'funeral home' in their area, they would show up because the special pages for veterans and their family members were delivering a differentiated message. This way, they were the experts working with the families of veterans."

As time went on, Davis added additional affiliations: America's Best Funeral Homes and Cremation with Care.

"All three brands are designed to help independently owned funeral homes gain that independent advantage," he said, noting that the American Marketing Association observed years ago that the number one way for a business to differentiate itself from competitors is through brand affiliation.

"So, why not the funeral industry? Why not death care?" he asked.

In addition to distinct webpages, ValMark provided tips on holding a variety of community engagement programs as well as Facebook posts. "A lot of the posts were geared around preplanning, as Facebook is predominantly best for preneed," he said.

Eventually, however, ValMark hit a plateau and while he continued operating it, he decided to launch his own cremation-oriented funeral home "because I saw an opening there," he said.

He put his head down and got to work.

**A Cascade of Surprising Events**

Davis found the perfect place to open his new business, and he already had the perfect name: He leveraged the Cremation with Care brand he'd started as part of the ValMark network and turned it into his very own Florida funeral home.

He located the perfect building two doors from his first funeral home, Horizon – an area that still housed three funeral homes within a stone's throw of each other.

"So, now it would be four instead of three," he said.

He chose the location because of its exposure on the street and its proximity to other funeral homes in the area, he said. "I was getting ready to sign a lease and the landlord had agreed to make some fixes and update the building, because it was not in a condition for us to move into. He agreed to spend over $60,000 to get the building up to snuff."

Right around the same time, however, COVID-19 started to really take hold.

"We were about a week from signing the lease … and I got a phone call from the owner saying he was not going to put a dime into the business. He was a foot doctor, and his business had slowed down."

Davis, of course, thought he was getting a raw deal.

"I said, 'We have all this money invested in starting this business and utilizing this business.' But what are we going to do? We continued down our course, and we kept looking for a location and an office to rent, but everywhere we looked, it was more money than we wanted to pay for a lot less exposure and visibility."

Eventually, he went back to the landlord and cut a deal, agreeing to rent the building with some minimal improvements that would allow a certificate of occupancy to be granted.

"So, I signed a lease and we applied for the funeral home license," he said. "We are not a direct disposal service – we are a licensed funeral home."

When a state inspector came, all he saw was a desk and chair. "There is nothing in the rules or regulations that says you must have furniture in the funeral home," Davis pointed out.

The license was approved, and with the building serving as what he needed to get up and running, he began operating out of his home office on Sanibel Island for an entire year before "even setting foot into that building."

Right after actually starting to use the office, however, Hurricane Ian hit Florida, triggering a mandatory evacuation of Sanibel Island in September 2022.

"Business was going well, and we were in 18 Florida counties, all out of one location," Davis said.

Davis moved his home office into a hotel in Aventura, Florida, not knowing at the time that he'd never live in his home again.

"Southwest Florida was devastated," he said. "There was no internet or power at the funeral home, but we were continuing to get calls. The phone was still ringing."

Somehow, he continued operating, even though the hurricane caused a massive upheaval on a professional and personal level. "We still had to get permits, dispatch and transport," he said. "It became increasingly difficult."

His home office at his Sanibel Island home was "wiped out," and he took three or four different trips there by boat to oversee the remediation of mold damage. "To make a long story short we never were able to return, he said. "We got it into good enough shape where we were able to sell it."

He found himself jumping between vacation rentals on an almost-monthly basis, so he could have a base from which to operate. Finally, he scored a two-year lease on a condominium in Naples.

"But adversity makes you stronger," Davis said. "We continued to plow ahead with the business and do what we do best. In just over three years, we have come out on top in a way I never expected with Cremation with Care."

This year, he expects to serve more than 2,000 families out of his single location in Fort Myers, which serves 18 counties. The business only does direct cremation. The price is $1,190 and $995 for hospice deaths.

"We are growing at such a phenomenal rate," he said.

Cremation with Care does not own its own crematory.

"There is no reason for us to own a crematory when there are cremation services and crematories that provide these services to other funeral homes," Davis said. "Right now, we work with regional crematories. So, for example in the Central Florida area, we serve four or five counties serving the Orlando area, so we use one transport service and one crematory that serves that Central Florida area. And we have one crematory and transport service for Southwest Florida. And so on, for the East Coast of Florida and north of us in the Sarasota area." He added, "I don't see a reason to go through the expense and to incur the liability and have to provide training to own my own crematory – as well as the maintenance and all of the things that go along with owning one if it is not necessary to do."

The members of his team, however, inspect the crematories they use multiple times per week because they are always going there to pick up cremated remains. "Our people know what to look for," he said.

When Cremation with Care gets a death call, it relies on transport partners.

"They hold that body until we provide them with the cremation authorization and burial transit permit approved by the county medical staff," he said. "We email or fax the paperwork to the crematory, and they schedule the cremation and let us know when it is completed."

Once that is done, Davis and his team coordinate the hand delivery of the cremated remains to the family.

"That is a big job," he said, observing that it must do that for about 150 families per month across 18 counties in Florida.

"So, we have individuals that work for us in these different regions who go to the crematory and pick up the cremated remains whether in a temporary box or urn, and they physically deliver the cremated remains to the family," he said. "It is all part and parcel of our service charge."

**Putting the Care in Cremation**

No other funeral home that he knows of hand delivers cremated remains, Davis said.

The reason he began doing so stems from his experiences running Horizon, he said.

"Back then, families would come to us and make the arrangements, not like now when it is over the phone and such," he said. "They signed the papers, and when the cremation was completed, we called them, and they came to the funeral home to pick up their loved one's cremated remains. They would come into the building, and we would do the handoff. And they would walk out, and we would watch from the window."

And what Davis and his team members saw was telling.

"We would watch these people walk to their car in tears," he said. "And they would just stand there for a minute … they didn't know whether to put it in the front seat or in the backset, to put a seatbelt on it or in the trunk. They had no idea what to do. And this was something that was repeated over and over again."

So, toward the end when he was operating Horizon, he began to have the cremated remains hand delivered, which has continued over with Cremation with Care.

"The idea that a human is coming to their door with their loved one leads to a lot of hugs, relief and tears," he said. "They invite us in, and they want to talk … the communication and the personal touch and the humanity … *that* is what we are selling."

The hand delivery of cremated remains has become one of Cremation with Care's calling cards responsible for its success, he said. "At the end of the day, every single funeral home or cremation service does the exact same thing. Why would a family choose ABC funeral home over XYZ funeral home if the mechanics of what we do is *exactly* the same?"

Another differentiator is that Cremation with Care has someone answering the phone – someone who actually works for the company – 24 hours a day, Davis said.

"They give us the credit card info over the phone, not online," he said. "They love what we do and talking to a human being that is providing them with kindness, compassion and sensitivity at the most difficult time of their life."

You have to provide families with a comforting message, and you also *must answer the phone*, Davis said.

"How many times have myself, Valerie or any of my people answered the phone only to hear, 'Oh my God, I'm actually talking to a person,'" he said.

When he worked at Horizon, he'd often get calls from price shoppers who told him they opted to use his business simply because he answered the phone, he said.

"If you are going to be in business, be in business," he advised. "People have questions, and they want answers. They don't want to wait 30 minutes for someone to call them back or to get a voicemail … *answering the phone is key*. Answer your telephone and you will win more business that way than any other way – it's not all about price."

While some may classify Cremation with Care as an online cremation company, Davis balks at that suggestion.

"There is no such thing," he said. "You cannot cremate a body online. You can't pick up a body online. The only thing you can do online is fill out forms, and people have been filling out forms online for years. There is nothing new and innovative about that."

Davis admits that he's unconventional.

"People thought I was crazy when I opened Horizon, and people thought I was crazier for opening up Cremation with Care in the most price sensitive and competitive market in the country," he said. "I just dove in. Why? Because I understand the consumer. I understand the marketplace."

**Reactivating ValMark as ValMark+ Memorial Group**

During the COVID-19 pandemic, Davis hit pause on everything related to the ValMark network. He stopped charging renewal fees to members in January 2021 but is gearing up to reactivate the network under a slightly different name: ValMark+ Memorial Group – the + signifies the more robust services he'll be offering members.

"We could no longer do community engagement, which was a big factor in our brand affiliated strategy ... so we had to shut that down," he said of the difficult decision to pause everything about two-and-a-half years ago when the pandemic erupted.

As a result, he did not ask about 500 rooftops around the country (consisting of a few hundred firms) to pay their annual renewal fees, even though their ValMark pages continued to rank on page one of Google, he said.

So, how does it all work?

ValMark affiliates get an exclusive designated territory to align their funeral home with the Veterans and Family Memorial Care, America's Best and the Cremation with Care brands.

Before he paused the network, territories were exclusive by county but moving forward, it will be exclusive by city, Davis said.

Existing members will have the first right of refusal to renew their memberships before Davis reaches out to their competitors, he said. It will cost $1,995 to reactivate the membership, and the annual renewal from that point on will be $1,495, Davis said.

That is a bit of an increase from the $1,200 members paid previously, but everyone who reactivated their membership or joins for the first time will also be eligible to send one staff member take an online program that will certify them as a remembrance planner, he said. Additional funeral directors and arrangers can become certified for an additional $395, he said. "I strongly believe that this certification is long overdue," Davis said.

"It will be an online training" he said. "We will provide them with a training manual or handbook, and they will then be able to take the training online and become certified."

He continued, "What we would like be able to do is market Cremation with Care on the state or even a national level." He explained that members would not be obligated to charge the same price for cremation as many funeral homes simply do not want to be locked down on price.

"If I were to provide you with an at-need case for $1,500 and we asked you to pay a marketing fee of $500, would you do that?" he asked. The answer should be 'yes' – because this is business you would never have had, and your competition is already at that level. Even if you made $10 in profit after paying us a fee, isn't it worthwhile to get the case in your door? Those cases represent opportunity."

Aligning with Cremation with Care does not have to be about direct cremation, even though that is the model in Florida, Davis said.

"In other parts of country, it will be more about the gathering," he said. "And we have a program that we have put out to our funeral home affiliates to help them convert the families coming in saying they just want a direct cremation into some type of remembrance or gathering" he said. "At the end of the day, when a direct cremation family leaves the funeral home, they are planning to do something to honor their loved ones – they are just not telling the funeral home what it is."

Even though the ValMark network has been on a hiatus for some time, Davis has no doubt that it will be a tremendous success as it gears up to become a force once again with a relaunch.

"When someone joins or renews, they are not going to pick from Column A or Column B – when you are part of ValMark+, you'll be part of all three brands," he said.

In the future, even more benefits will be offered to members, including a hospice collaboration program that's under development, he said.

"Every funeral home in the country has sent someone out to local hospices to make an introduction and hand out a brochure," he said. "Often, they get tossed in the wastebasket or put in a drawer, and everyone moves on with their day. But what we've been able to do is work with hospice organizations from the top-down, meaning leadership opens up doors for us at the local level."

The members of ValMark+ will find out how Davis and his team have done it, step by step, he promised.

*Visit https://valmarkmemorialgroup.com to learn more about the ValMark+ network.*

# Catching Up with the Founder of The Foresight Companies: A Conversation with Daniel M. Isard

*By Thomas A. Parmalee*

Daniel M. Isard, the founder of The Foresight Companies, is pretty much retired these days and no longer has an equity stake in the company he built.

But when it comes to individuals who helped get funeral home owners to start thinking like business owners – to focus on the numbers – he has to rank right up there at the top.

FuneralVision.com recently took notice when Isard posted on social media about having perhaps given his last talk ever to a group of death-care professionals.

For decades – at least a 30-year span – Isard was an absolute force in the profession, writing several books, numerous pamphlets and handbooks, hosting all sorts of webinars and experimenting with various business ventures along the way. If you're channel surfing cable TV, you may even see him sharing his wisdom on *American Greed,* an American documentary television series that focuses on white collar crime. (Isard was interviewed as an expert on the National Prearranged Services preneed insurance scandal.)

We recently caught up with Isard to learn what he's been doing, what he sees as his legacy and more. Edited excerpts follow.

**Tell us a little bit about yourself and what you've been doing since settling into retirement. Do you have kids in funeral service?**

I have completed 70 trips around the sun and look forward to more! I am not married but have been in a committed relationship for about a dozen years. I am proud of the two children I have fathered, Phillip (the owner of a company that is the manufacturer of high-end French Fries that are distributed around the country) and Risa (who earned a Ph.D. in sports management and is an assistant professor at UConn) as well as having raised my partner's two girls, Olivia and Sophia, both working in the medical world. I did not want to push or influence my children and stepchildren to go into the business. If they wanted summer employment, that was one thing, but they did not exhibit the skillset to work in the business.

**We heard you may have you given your last speech to a group of death-care professionals. Where was it, what did you talk about … and is it true?**

I have nothing lined up beyond the speech I recently gave to the New England Cemetery Association, so I guess I will be ending that chapter of my career. It felt melancholy and proper, going out on a high note. Education was my ministry to this profession. Between the speaking and writing, I hope I influenced many to be better business operators.

**You are the author of several books for the death-care profession. Which book do you think is your best and why? Can people still buy them?**

I have written four books. They were on business succession, business operations, cremation business practices and preneed. They are not now in print, but the preneed book ("The Complete Preneed Perspective") is being updated as part of a new mortuary college curricula. It should be available in the next 90 days or so. I will keep you posted when it is available. I liked the process of writing each of the books. They took a lot of effort. None is a favorite – they are all so different in subject matter.

**When did you start The Foresight Companies and what was the biggest change you went through as its owner? Did you ever think Foresight would last as long as it has or become as successful as it has?**

My background in financial services led me to Phoenix in 1984. The firm that hired me wanted me to help grow the company, so I had to discover a path toward marketing this company. In my first weekend there, I took every corporate client file out of the file cabinets and read through them.

Ironically, they had three funeral homes as clients. Two of the three were making money and the third was not. In contrasting the companies, I could clearly see why the third firm was losing money and the path they needed to take toward profitability. I ultimately began working with this third firm, and they implemented my recommendations for immediate success.

So, I decided this was an underserved market. I reached out to the National Funeral Directors Association and did a seminar for them, which led to a convention address, which led to an encore of the convention address. At the end of the convention, we had almost 100 funeral homes that wanted our help, which led to the death of the firm I had joined, as we grew too fast. So, I created my own company with five clients, and the rest is history.

My vision was always to build Foresight into a company and not a practice. The difference being a practice is generally a one-person enterprise, with some support help but a business had services provided by many following a corporate theme.

The theme was, in 1987, High Technology but High Touch, which resonated with funeral home owners and cemeterians. Fast forward to 2021, we had served more than 3,000 funeral home and 800 cemetery clients and built our staff to about 20. The company evolved during the last 10 years to create a continuity if something happened to me. The culmination of that was the merger with Doug Gober and bringing Chris Cruger on to be the next generation of leadership.

**What is the biggest regret of your career?**

In the late 1990s, if a private funeral home owner wanted to go out and acquire another firm (or build a new location), there were limited options for financing. The only provider of "goodwill" financing was a company that was a wholly owned company of SCI. Not to be anti-SCI but borrowing from a company that could acquire you if you default, I thought was like getting a mortgage from your mother-in-law.

I worked to create a lending company with another well-established person, and we raised the money in equity and debt to form Allegiance Capital. In our first year of lending, we issued many loans. Our equity partners were a NASDAQ company that bought out life insurance contracts from those with incurable diseases. The company was located in San Francisco and the bulk of its purchases were from HIV-stricken consumers. That is where the regret set it.

Shortly after we successfully launched Allegiance Capital, the combination cocktail of drugs was discovered to prolong the life of HIV patients. Therefore, their immense portfolio of viatical settlement contracts was now in an unknown status of when they might cash in on these policies. Our investor was suddenly on a path toward bankruptcy. They decided that they were going to "run" Allegiance Capital and made terrible decisions. So, this was my biggest regret in business.

But I converted a lifetime of failures into successes. I failed as a manager of bands, as a stand-up comedienne, I survived two large embezzlements and learned from each failure. Ultimately, my resiliency was the path toward my successes.

**What do you consider your biggest career accomplishment?**

I think that is raising the idea that funeral homes are a commercialized business that should have key performance indicators. I don't think anyone spoke of EBITDA (earnings before interest, taxes, depreciation and amortization) before me. The profession was still bragging about bronze caskets and adult calls.

**How tough was it to find the right people to transition the ownership and operation of Foresight?**

I began my personal plan for transition of Foresight about 10 years before the actual transition date. My goal was to take my job description and find who on my staff can do each of the many tasks I did. When there was no one on staff, that was part of the recruiting plan for additional staff.

The big issue was marketing, and Doug Gober is an energy force like no other. He filled that gap. As my partner, he was also instrumental in identifying the chance to bring Chris Cruger on board. I saw Chris's strong leadership ability immediately, but he has also excelled in marketing Foresight. The growth of Foresight has been through the efforts of them both, but also by Chris setting a paradigm by our professional staff to follow. This guarantees solid service to our clients.

The lesson to any of your readers is this:

1). **Know the value of your business**. Know the actual value number but also know what brings value to your business. Know what makes you different. Then find the people to promote these points of value.

2) **Don't be afraid to talk with your staff about the owner's lifetime.** If you are afraid to talk about it in advance, and acknowledge it, you are risking your succession and maybe your family's well-being if you die before a transfer. Everyone in your building should know what your funeral plans are and what the business continuity plan is.

3) **If possible, retire early.** I always calculated how much a client needed to have before they retired. If you can accumulate that amount before the magical date of retirement, retire early.

In my own case, due to the COVID-19 outbreak, I was planning on retiring at the end of 2021. Chris came to me in December of 2020 and asked if I would move that date up a year, and I said "yes!" I don't look back one bit.

**What has impressed you the most about how Chris and Doug have run the business since you stepped away?**

Chris's vision for Foresight was more transaction focused. He implemented that plan, worked with the existing staff to provide for our clients and marketed successfully to new clients. Doug and he along with all staff have done an exceptional job helping existing and new clients meet their goals. Chris and Doug have also done a fabulous job keeping Foresight's vision as a thought leader within the profession. Frankly, they have taken Foresight to a level I could not have taken it. I am very proud of their success and accomplishments.

*Dan Isard and Chris Cruger.*

**What is the biggest trend or development that more people in funeral service need to pay attention to but are largely ignoring?**

I think there are several trends (in no particular order):

1) **Focus on what families need you to do.** You are a service company not a merchandise selling company.

2) **Technology is more important than ever.** For internal purposes, communication and paperwork, it is critical. For marketing, it has never been more essential. All funeral homes are not the same. Show consumers how you are different.

3) **Staffing and licensure.** I am not anti-licensure, but we cannot as a profession focus on the wrong things. We cannot have one combined license for a funeral director and embalmer. These are two different skills. We need people that can talk with consumers and bond with them. More than half of all dead bodies are not embalmed. We need to make it easier to be a funeral professional, not harder.

4) **State laws that are outdated.** We have state laws that limit who can own a funeral home or how many funeral homes they can own. We have state laws limiting receptions within a funeral home. We have state laws that limit the combination of cemetery and funeral businesses in their states. Funeral homes should be allowed to own crematories.

**Do you have any thoughts on Homesteaders Life Company agreeing to take an ownership interest in Park Lawn through an affiliate and Park Lawn's plan to go private?**

I only know what I read on FuneralVision.com and the press in general about the Homesteaders/Park Lawn alliance. However, I would say that we will see more of it. I would also say that it is natural that the money and the operators should be one and the same. I remember when SCI in the 1980s/1990s not only owned funeral homes and cemeteries, but they owned an insurer and a manufacturer. It can confuse the stock markets when that happens. But it makes sense. I think this is common in Mexico and Japan to have these groups.

**What do you think your legacy in the funeral profession will be – and does that match what you *think* it should be?**

I have thought much about my legacy with the help of Chris and Doug and my life partner. I have no expectations of a statue in front of NFDA's headquarters or of being buried in Yankee Stadium. I love my career. It elapsed so quickly!

*Visit https://www.theforesightcompanies.com to learn more about The Foresight Companies.*

# Quilt Aims to Make it Easier for Families to Collect and Share Memories

*By Thomas A. Parmalee*

When Chris McDowell's older sister died of an aneurism at age 45, his entire family was crushed.

"As part of the process, I was the one who raised their hand and said I'd put together a slideshow for her service," said the 38-year-old McDowell (pictured at top), who grew up on Long Island and lives in Connecticut.

So, despite his heartache, McDowell began collecting photos from Facebook, and family members asked everyone to "email photos to Chris," so they could celebrate the life of Laura. Soon, it seemed as though he was drowning in pictures.

"I spent three or four hours at night before the service from 10 p.m. to 1 a.m. putting it all together," he said. "I was curating photos, editing, cropping and removing duplicates – only to put it all onto Google Drive for the funeral home, which burned it onto a DVD for the day of the service."

At the time, McDowell was only doing what the funeral home asked and wasn't necessarily in the frame of mind to consider how to do it more efficiently – and it was stressful.

"A few months later, I realized that if I spent three or four hours the night before the service gathering photos – and I am a reasonably tech-savvy person – then there had to be other people facing a similar if not more challenging problem if they are *not* tech savvy," he said. "I felt there had to be a better way."

And so, he began researching the various options available to funeral homes and families, and when he was not impressed with what he saw, he created a solution of his own – Quilt.

The name for the company came to him without effort.

"I thought about a family as a quilt with all these memories sewn together and handed down," he explained. "And what we have built allows memories to come together from different family members and friends from all across the world – and we pull it together digitally."

*Honoring the memory of his sister, Laura Pullar, remains a driving force for Chris McDowell.*

**What Is Quilt?**

Quilt was founded in July 2023 but only began introducing itself to funeral homes on a large scale last month. It's everything McDowell wished he had when he was gathering photos for a tribute video honoring the life of his sister.

He "bootstrapped it" with a former colleague that he worked with at a previous technology company. "It's been sweat equity up to this point, and we've called in some favors," he said. "That forces us to work scrappy … it gets us right in front of the funeral homes, so we can understand their pain points. And as we've talked to more funeral homes, we see a lot of opportunities to build more products. At the end of the day, we want to help funeral homes deliver the best experience possible for families. And we want to free up their time, so they can spend time with families and not in front of a computer editing videos."

He added, "The funeral home's expertise is taking care of families during their most difficult time. We want to take the technology burden off of them and allow them to do what they do best – and hopefully give them a way to generate more revenue for themselves."

Other solutions exist that are great at creating standard videos, but he wanted to design something that provided a more robust solution.

Through the Quilt platform, users can log in, add photos and comment on photos. And they can keep doing so even after a funeral or memorial service. "You spend all this time creating a memorial service that lasts two to four hours, but this lives beyond the service," he said. "It makes it more interactive and turns it into an ongoing memorial versus a point-in-time DVD."

With Quilt, McDowell said he's striving to add functionality and usability for both funeral homes and families.

"The way we interact with photos today and with social media is just very different than when some of these other companies started," he observed.

As someone who has worked with early-stage technology companies for about 15 years, McDowell knew he was up to the task of trying to shake up the space. He's hoping to duplicate some of the incredible successes he's enjoyed elsewhere.

"It has been exciting seeing a lot of companies grow from nothing to $100 million companies – and all the experience that comes along with that," said McDowell, who is focusing strictly on Quilt, other than a little consulting work on the side. "A lot of mistakes can be made along the way, and I've gotten to learn from that – and I've also seen some great execution, which I've been able to learn from as well."

With some other vendors that specialize in photos and videos, the end product is usually a video file that is streamed.

"With Quilt, think of a Facebook page, where a family can go and scroll through all the photos and see what is available, and then turn it into a slideshow," McDowell said. "The difference is in the way we present it to the family – you can go in and click on what photos you want to appear in the video, you can print photos at home. You can't do that with a video file."

In a nutshell, with Quilt, families get the ability to create a slideshow on demand.

"When researching this, I heard about families that would come in the morning of a service with a USB drive with 20 more photos they wanted to be put into the slideshow that would be played at the service," McDowell said.

That, however, typically poses a problem for funeral homes. By that time, they would have had a vendor edit the video, the photos would have been cropped and already burned to a DVD. "So, it makes it nearly impossible to add those 20 photos a family wants," McDowell said.

But with Quilt, a family can upload those pictures directly to the Quilt platform from their phone five minutes before the service – and those pictures can be included in the slideshow when it's time for the service.

Moreover, with Quilt, you can also include a QR code that is at the bottom of a tribute video as it plays at the service, which attendees can scan. That way, depending on the privacy settings the family selects, they can scroll through the photos on their phone, download them and even print them at home if they wish.

Even more exciting is this: Attendees or anyone who is given access to log in to Quilt can share photos of the deceased with the family. "An attendee can upload photos from their phone to Quilt on the spot – and depending on the privacy settings the family has selected, that picture could be automatically inserted into the slideshow on the next loop or it could be put into what I call 'purgatory' – where a family has to approve it, as we all may have that crazy relative we do not want sharing photos directly to the slideshow."

Asked how the video gets from the Quilt platform to play on the screens that may be on a funeral home's wall at a service, McDowell said there are two ways that happens.

"Either the funeral home plugs a computer into one of those televisions with an HDMI cord and they log into Quilt and press play – or we have similar devices that we have set up that they can plug right into the back of the TV, which is effectively a mini-PC that allows it to play directly into the TV."

Of course, he has also thought about different scenarios, such as what happens if the power or internet goes out.

So, you have the ability to put it onto a USB drive as a backup, he said.

Families can easily share the memorial video on social media – directly from the platform, McDowell said. "That is encouraged in many cases, because you may share it and say, 'Here is our Quilt for our sister, if you have photos, please log in and add them.' That broadens the group of folks who can upload and contribute."

One feature that a lot of funeral homes may appreciate is the ability to place a link to the Quilt memorial on the obituary page for the deceased, McDowell said. "So, when folks visit the funeral home and read the obituary, they can also go the Quilt memorial and add additional photos from right there," he said.

Of course, there are ways to password protect a Quilt memorial so it cannot be shared via social media, he said.

| Name | Person | Date |
|---|---|---|
| Jeremy's Memorial | Jeremy Lanvin | 07/31/2024 |
| In Loving Memory of Susan | Susan James | 07/29/2024 |
| Roger's Celebration of Life | Roger Barry | 07/18/2024 |
| We Miss You Meredith | Meredith Holmes | 07/09/2024 |
| Rest in Peace Sarah | Sarah Hannon | 07/08/2024 |
| Laura's Celebration of Life | Laura Pullar | 07/24/2024 |

*Quilt offers funeral homes an easy-to-navigate dashboard.*

**A Preneed and Marketing Engine**

What may be the most intriguing aspect of Quilt for funeral homes, however, is that it can be leveraged as a way to boost preneed efforts – and to generate positive reviews that may pull weight when families are searching for a firm to work with in an at-need situation.

That's because the platform collects the email addresses of anyone who logs in to look at photos, review them, or to add photos of their own.

"So, in conjunction with the funeral home, we can use that information to generate surveys and send them to people who have attended the service," he said. And based on what is learned via those survey responses, attendees can then be invited to share their feedback in the form of a Google review.

Or, the contact information of those who have attended a service that has been gathered by Quilt can simply be passed on to the funeral home, McDowell said. "That can be incredibly valuable to the funeral home," he said.

Quilt can handle that process of reaching out to families, McDowell said. But it would craft the email in conjunction with the funeral home, making sure it could approve whatever is sent out. "It is a sensitive time to reach out to the family," McDowell said. "We want to be sure we are being compassionate and representing the funeral home well in the email."

The email would consist of a survey, and a follow up email would thank families for taking the time to provide their feedback. If positive feedback were received, the family would be invited to share their thoughts on Google Reviews. Emails could be branded with the funeral home logo in tandem with the Quilt logo, based on a firm's preference.

"If the feedback is neutral to negative, we would share that with the funeral home, so they can take it and process it and adapt as necessary," McDowell said.

**Pricing**

Funeral homes pay Quilt $99 per service in which the platform is used, McDowell said, which includes the Google review component.

"If you can effectively take all the time and effort off your plate to produce the video and if you can generate four of five Google reviews from a funeral service, we feel that is good outcome," he said.

Funeral homes can charge families whatever they wish for the service, keeping the difference as profit. Most funeral homes working with Quilt who go this route are charging in the $200 to $400 range, McDowell said. Others are providing it to families at no charge, and simply building it into the service fee and using it as a way to differentiate themselves from competitors, McDowell said.

As far as what amount of time the funeral home will spend using Quilt, McDowell said it's "15 minutes max" compared with what may be four or five hours of work if they were doing it themselves with tools such as Apple Photo or Google Drive.

"You can add a little extra margin, but you can also save hours per service on the backend – and if you think of that over the course of a week, it may save you six to 10 hours," he said. "We see a lot of benefit to that. This saves so much time and is a much better process for the family."

It's also a process with lasting benefits – as Quilt introduces itself to the marketplace, it plans to give its early customers access to its platform forever, meaning they'll always be able to log in, add photos to a slideshow or look at photos that others have added. "We may fine tune that in the future, but right now, we do not want to do anything punitive to the family," McDowell said.

While the general public would no doubt find Quilt useful – and not just for funeral services but think of weddings, graduations and other occasions – McDowell's intent is to only offer the solution through funeral homes and to focus on the end of life.

So far, McDowell is pleased with the feedback he's been getting on Quilt from funeral homes.

"We are happy in the sense that the feedback we are getting is this is going to be really valuable for funeral homes – and therefore really valuable for families," he said. "Once we start talking to funeral homes, they become very excited about what we have to offer. This also allows the traditional, family-owned business compete with larger firms on an affordable level – and we are excited about that, too."

McDowell also has a sense of satisfaction that he was able to take something tragic – the death of his sister – and turn it into something positive.

"I want to help other families, so they don't have to experience what we went through … at the end of the day, this creates a beautiful legacy for my sister."

*Visit https://ourquilt.co to learn more about Quilt.*

# A Conversation with the Co-Founder of Holy Land Wood & Stone

*By Thomas A. Parmalee*

After spending a long stint out of the workplace, Jennifer Colonna Gesek knew it was time to step out of her comfort zone.

Fortunately, she knew just who to do it with — her husband of more than 30 years Andy. In 2019, they started Holy Land Wood & Stone, which sells Christian crosses, keepsakes and decor items handcrafted from authentic olive wood and Jerusalem stone sourced from the holy land.

We recently caught up with Gesek (pictured at the beginning of this chapter with her husband) to learn more about her, her company and how it serves funeral homes and cemeteries.

**Tell me a little bit about yourself.**

My husband Andy and I have been married for 30 years, and we have four children. I began my career in retail but took a 25-year hiatus to raise our family. As I return to work, I am eager to pursue my passion for helping others, particularly during their times of deep sorrow.

**When did you start Holy Land Wood and Stone?**

Although some of our products have been around for years, my husband and I started the company in 2019, right before COVID-19. Along the way, we've been fortunate to acquire several high-quality product lines that align with our mission of meeting the spiritual and emotional needs of our customers.

**What does the company provide, and how does it work with funeral professionals?**

Our company provides a unique bereavement line featuring two-piece keepsakes made of stone imported from the Holy Land and manufactured in Pennsylvania. These keepsakes offer comfort, peace and connection by placing one piece in the casket or urn and keeping the other with the family. We offer the Comfort Cross, the Forever in My Heart, the Star of David, and the Angel of My Heart, which can also be used for children. Funeral directors can use these keepsakes to comfort families with this unique gift and increase their revenue through repeat business. They can also be used during preneed planning.

**What did you do before you were the owner of Holy Land Wood And Stone?**

I was a merchandise manager for JC Penney and an assistant buyer for Anne Klein. For 25 years, I was a stay-at-home mom to my four children, during which I held various volunteer positions.

**What are your tips for others who may be in business with a spouse or family member?**

My husband Andy and I run the business together. We enjoy working together, but it can be challenging at times. We find it helpful to have assigned roles and try not to cross into each other's areas. Respecting each other, listening to ideas, and not always assuming you are right are all crucial. It's also essential for us to take non-work-related time together and to have individual time.

**How many funeral homes do you currently work with? Do they get discounted pricing and then mark the item up? If so, what is the typical markup?**

We work with many cemeteries and funeral homes throughout the U.S., and the number grows every week. Our customers tell us that our keepsakes allow them to minister to their families, providing comfort during times of sorrow and keeping families connected with their loved ones. Often, they use our products as beautiful, heartfelt gestures from the funeral director after all financial matters are settled.

Our customers use our products in several different ways. Our volume-based pricing allows them to consider giving the keepsakes as gifts from the funeral director. The volume pricing for the Comfort Cross starts at $17, and the Heart, Angel, and Star of David start at $14 each. Some customers absorb this cost in their budget, while others increase their package price to keep their program cost neutral.

Other funeral homes offer the keepsakes for sale to families. Our volume pricing allows customers to purchase our products at more than 50% off the manufacturer's suggested retail price, enabling a markup of greater than 100%.

These are just two ways our customers use our products, but they have found other creative uses as well. We would be happy to share other potential programs with those interested.

*The Forever in My Heart keepsake from Holy Wood & Stone.*

**Does the bulk of your business come from cemeteries and funeral homes? How do people typically hear about your business?**

Most of our orders come from cemeteries and funeral homes. People typically hear about our business through social media, word of mouth, and relationships with funeral directors at conventions. I also receive many referrals from people in the industry and spend time making outbound calls and talking to people directly.

**What are some of those most popular items you sell?**

Our number one seller in our bereavement keepsake line is the Comfort Cross. The cross is split into two mirrored pieces, each with deep significance. One side of each piece is smooth, and the other is rough.

The top piece, which the family keeps, has both a rough side and a smooth side. The rough side represents the life we are living here on earth, while the smooth side symbolizes the peace that we will one day have with our loved ones. The piece placed in the casket is smooth on both sides, representing the deceased resting peacefully with the Heavenly Father.

**What do you find so meaningful about operating your business?**

My husband and I are both practicing Christians. It's incredibly humbling to hear how our customers use our products to minister to others.

We've found that regardless of individual religious beliefs, what unites us is the love for our families and the shared sorrow of losing a loved one. We believe and hope that the connection our products provide can offer some comfort during a family's time of need, regardless of their religious beliefs or non-beliefs.

**Are there any other products that you plan to offer on the horizon?**

We are developing a line of products designed for situations involving cremation. These items will include rosaries with compartments to hold ashes, and we are also modifying our existing keepsakes to incorporate ash-holding features. As we manage our own manufacturing, we have the flexibility to swiftly test and adjust ideas. We welcome any suggestions or ideas from your readers to enhance our product offerings.

**Do you have any final thoughts?**

In the few short years we've been in the funeral industry, we have met some amazing people and learned so much from them. We feel truly blessed by how our company has evolved and by the many wonderful individuals we've had the opportunity to meet. It's been inspiring to witness so many people ministering to others and to have our own chance to do the same.

*Visit https://holylandwoodandstone.com to learn more about Holy Land Wood & Stone.*

# A Conversation with the Publisher of Executorium.com

*By Thomas A. Parmalee*

If you've ever suddenly found yourself as the executor of an estate, you know that it can be a real chore.

As one of several heirs to a small estate that was recently "created" so to speak when multiple family members of mine died around the same time without a will, I know how complicated it can be firsthand ... not as an executor but as someone who has simply been there to listen to an executor *complain* about the process.

As someone on the periphery, I've had to sign various things or give my opinion on how things should proceed, so I can only imagine what the executor has gone through trying to move things along.

And of course, I've also gotten dozens of mailers from companies looking to offer me an advance of whatever I may eventually receive once probate settles.

I know how this works ... they'll send me a $3,000 check and end up staking claim to five times that much two or three years down the line when everything gets settled. Sure, the $3,000 now would be nice, and whatever I receive will by no means be life changing, but no thanks.

These are issues George Robert Compton III (pictured at the beginning of this chapter) is all too familiar with as the publisher of Executorium.com, which aims to serve as a starting point for executors trying to navigate what is often an overwhelming process that they never saw coming.

He thinks his site can serve as a resource for funeral professionals who want to help families get the lay of the land of estate settlement after a loved one dies.

"Initially, I see Executorium.com of value to funeral homes as a good heads-up to pass along to clients," he said. "We endeavor to be a site worth mentioning to people who have experienced a loss and now have work to do."

He added, "Our mission to build estate administration awareness and improve the executor experience aligns with practical after-loss care without any barriers."

FuneralVision.com recently caught up with Compton to learn more about the Executorium.com platform and the mission he's embarked on. Edited excerpts follow.

**Tell us a little bit about yourself.**

I am the publisher of Executorium.com. I am also a dad and husband, which involves baseball, Boy Scouts and driving endless loops through Northern New Jersey.

**When did you start Executorium.com – and what is it?**

The experiences I collected at a 501(c)(3) organization, DFI, shape Executorium.com. Dissemination of information, involving many interrelated disciplines, which are not commercial in scope. I've added a clear mission – "Be a Resource for Executors and Estates." That is what Executorium.com is all about.

**Do you do this full time? If not, what's your day job?**

I started Executorium.com while I was the full-time principal at Construct Marketing, LLC, which is now sunsetting. I will be operating Executorium.com moving forward. The Executorium.com logo is an arrow pointing forward to remind executors and families to move forward … the logo is also a house turned over.

**I'm guessing that you had some experience as an executor that led you to start the site … what surprised you the most about being an executor?**

Good guess. Ex-executor here. I was surprised by how complicated it could get. I was surprised in retrospect that the executor had to invest as much time as they do. The executor is basically the 'new guy' everywhere he or she goes, with a significant learning curve, even if things go smoothly. We want to flatten it.

**How does someone typically become or end up an executor?**

*Poof! You're an executor!* No seriously, an individual may be named an executor in a will or appointed an executor by the courts. Beyond that, every state is going to have different laws.

**What are some of the biggest pain points of being an executor – and how can your site help?**

There's a big difference between, "I'm the executor on Mom's and Dad's will" and when it gets real, "I'm the executor of the estate."

I picture Executorium.com as a big newspaper that an executor can page through and get some context, get a view of the landscape, maybe view some code, some statutes, at least know where to find them. Maybe see a page where estate service providers are listed by county. Seeing what estate services are out there educates them like an exhibit hall. You can be a better executor if you know what resources are out there.

In addition, executor-facing content, original and curated, covers practical and fundamental estate issues and challenges: liquidation, grief support, donation, alternative dispute resolution, appraisal, valuation, cleanout, real estate, etc.

**Why was it so important for you to create an open-access resource available to everyone?**

Paywalls drive me nuts. If you have to register to view content, it limits views. The best way is wide open, shared and fed.

**What is your main driver in operating Executorium.com? What do you hope to achieve?**

All estates are different. Some very simple, some gut-wrenching. If Executorium.com can hold the light over some information, share resources, or be a resource, so an estate moves forward, we've achieved our mission.

**How much do things vary for an executor depending on what state they live in … and how challenging is it for you to provide resources that cater to everyone?**

Executorium.com is an organism, but it is not a "how-to." We can put information on peoples' radars, but we can't cater to everyone. As a growing organism, we continually update and populate the site.

Also, we don't seek to recreate what's done well somewhere else. Dissemination of information includes sending visitors to sites like NOLO and Justia because it's laid out well for executors. We direct visitors to EstateExec because its excellent resources shouldn't be missed. This strategy probably isn't great for our SEO, but the Mission is "Be a Resource for Executors and Estates" not, Win the SEO Game.

**Why should funeral homes be aware of this resource – and how can they work Executorium into conversations with families?**

The funeral home makes a big difference from my personal experience.

I do have this vision of exiting the graveside, with a briefcase, because I was the executor. I had no idea what was ahead. So, I keep that guy in mind.

Executorium.com is built to educate an executor and expand his or her awareness of the landscape they now find themselves in.

**You recently announced some advertising options for companies that provide services to executors. Can you tell us how that works and the cost?**

Because so much of estate administration and probate is county based, both the Government Pages Directory and the Estate Services Provider Directory are organized by county. So, county ads are displayed in both. This gives small service providers a venue to reach executors. Monthly county ad prices are $5 and up depending on the size of the county. State and sitewide ads offer reach for national companies and products to reach up to the full demographic at $50 and up.

**Beyond advertising, how do you earn revenue?**

Advertising is the primary revenue source.

Estate Service Providers Directory: Service Providers list 1 location in 1 county, in 1 category in the directory. There is a fee if the company wants additional counties or categories.

We do have an Estate Wanted page, so executors can find direct buyers and resellers of personal property – i.e. *"Wanted: Horatio Alger Collections"* etc.

We have avoided affiliate marketing because we prefer adverting to be advertising, and editorial to be editorial.

We are not in the referral business or in the selling information business.

**Are there any profit sharing/commission opportunities that funeral homes can participate in now or possibly in the future?**

Not currently, but the current Executorium.com resembles the original Executorium idea only partially, so I assume more adjustments are ahead as well. I have only just begun to explore the possibilities related to the funeral industry, as our early focus has been, *Be a Resource to Executors*. I am open to ideas.

# Embracing His Destiny: Charles "Chad" Snyder III Breathes New Life into the Family Business

*By Thomas A. Parmalee*

Charles "Chad" Snyder III, 42, a third-generation funeral director and the owner of Charles F. Snyder Funeral Homes & Crematory, which serves Lancaster County, Pennsylvania, remembers what convinced him to join the family business.

He'd just graduated from Lynn University in Boca Raton, Florida, where he'd earned a bachelor's degree in business administration and management and had moved back home.

"And I was watching Dad," he said. "At some point, your career can plateau – and I think my dad was hitting that plateau in his career. And I thought he needed some new energy … and that maybe my energy could help him."

But his father, Charles F. "Chip" Snyder Jr., never once asked him to join the business — nor did he push the idea when Snyder was growing up.

"He never said, 'I need help, son' – I could just kind of read it," he said. "And I think his skillset and my skillset … we are different people, but they are very complementary to each other."

Snyder's decision to join his dad has paid off for the firm, which has quadrupled the number of families served since Snyder joined as a full timer in 2004 after earning a degree in mortuary science from Northampton Community College in Bethlehem, Pennsylvania.

But even in his immediate family, Snyder may not be the businessperson with bragging rights, as his wife of more than eight years, Lee Snyder, is the co-founder of Benefix, a technology-powered, collaboration hub that is driving the benefits industry to provide better access and results for consumers. She remains an adviser to the company she co-founded and is the funeral home's chief marketing officer.

Together, they have two children: A 6-year-old girl, Chloe, and Charles Snyder IV, who they call "Charlie."

Looking back at the approach his dad took with him about joining the family firm, Snyder said it's one he might take with his own kids, as he wants to at least give them an opportunity to carry on the family tradition.

"Because when you are getting into the fourth generation, the pressure of carrying on another generation can also *drive away* that generation," he observed.

**Plotting a Path**

When Snyder decided to work at the funeral home, he knew what he was getting into.

"I always worked here summers and during winter breaks," he said. "Growing up in the funeral home, I was washing cars, mowing lawns, mulching, weeding, vacuuming – everything you could imagine, I would do."

He recalls playing basketball at the funeral home when he was 8 years old with one of the funeral home's staff members who is still at the firm after all these years: Mark Burkholder.

"He was finishing an internship with my dad and was 23 at the time," Snyder said of Burkholder. "He is still here now – and he's 35 years older."

He noted that numerous other employees have had long tenures at the company, which is a testament to his father's leadership – and now his. For instance, Jackie Adamson and Kelly Gramola Townsend, who work in the preplanning department, have each been with the firm more than 20 years, he said. "I am super grateful for those relationships," he said.

He also praised his mom, Doreen, for all that she has contributed over the years in customer-facing roles as well as on the sidelines. "Mom, too grew up in a family business, which is often the case being Greek Orthodox," he said. "Her parents ran a well-known restaurant in Lancaster. She was eager to help Chip with a 'whatever it takes approach' to help with the business, from supporting Chip on working funeral services and viewings with her Greek community to helping in the office and representing the funeral home at community events. Mom was a huge support system and driving force for Chip and the funeral home and her support and advocacy runs strong to this day — and I am ever grateful for that."

Upon joining the business full time, he knew he had three options: preserve the status quo, which often leads to a gradual decline, prepare the business for a sale or grow it. He made a conscious decision to pursue the third option.

In 2010, he assumed ownership of 25% of the business before becoming sole owner in 2019, buying the entire business and all the real estate from his parents.

"I realized that I wanted to work with Dad, I wanted to help the family business, and I knew there were big shoes to fill," he said. "There was nothing I had to prove to anyone other than myself – and I had that desire to help people. That pivot was toward the end of college. After graduation, I stopped fighting the idea that 'I don't want to do this,'" he said.

He also asked himself what would happen if he *didn't* join the family business, and he did not like the answer.

"I also saw an opportunity at that time," he said. "We had a corporate conglomerate competitor, and I knew we could outpace them. I also knew I could give Dad new energy and our team new challenges."

The funeral home added its first crematory in 2010 – and it now operates two more across seven locations.

"The onsite cremation is a great tool to have in our toolbox to let families know their loved one never leaves our care," he said. "Peace of mind is paramount to us, and to our team for our success."

Snyder also owns Cremation Services of Pennsylvania, an affiliate company that offers low-cost online planning for cremation starting at $1,695; as well as Heritage Monuments LLC, which assists families in creating personalized memorials, headstones or gravesite markers that will be a permanent tribute for their loved ones. The monument company is just down the road from the Charles F. Snyder Funeral Home on Blue Rock Road in Millersville but serves all the locations. Two of Snyder's aunts, Kathy Snyder Guidos and Chris Snyder Cunha, run the business, which he noted is extremely successful.

If he hadn't gone into funeral service, Snyder noted that he would have become a businessman or gotten into commercial real estate. He did an internship at Merrill Lynch, which he thoroughly enjoyed, he said.

"But I realized I could take a little bit of each of those things and apply it to funeral service," he said. "You know … to own a business, you have to be fiscally responsible and know how to financial statements for the company. I was able to accomplish those goals by utilizing my interest in funeral service."

He also has some personal qualities that have translated well to the profession.

"I have a keen eye for presentation and a natural awareness," he said. "And I think that is a great trait for funeral service."

He's naturally empathetic and can understand people's needs and get a quick read about what's happening at the arrangement table or while on a funeral service. "And I tend to naturally question how we can do things better than we have done in the past or even the week before," he said.

*Charles F. "Chad" Snyder III*

**The Right Call**

Today, the business serves more than 1,500 families per year, with an overall cremation rate in the 55% to 60% range, Snyder said. He credits much of the firm's success to the time and care it takes educating families.

"I don't think you can talk enough about that with your team and how important that is for families," he said. "A lot of families don't know what to ask for when they ask for cremation. Funeral homes – we do this day in and day out – and we always need to check with families who may be asking about cremation for the first time. We need to be cognizant of everything before, during and after cremation, so that families are aware of all options. And there is always room for improvement at every funeral home."

He thinks the profession needs to be careful with its words.

For instance, "traditional" now means cremation. "But when we use the word 'traditional,' it is a conflicting term in our profession," he said, emphasizing that cremation is the *preferred* form of disposition on a national basis – and that it's also "traditional" for many families as well, who may have chosen cremation now for generations.

A big part of the firm's growth is the result of a fresh focus on preneed, something that Snyder thought was important from the day he joined on a full-time basis.

"We were doing what many funeral homes were doing … if we had a prearrangement scheduled for 2 p.m. and three people died the previous night, then guess what? We canceled the prearrangement appointment," he said.

That left a foul taste in his mouth – and was simply not fair to families that wanted to prearrange, he said.

"But that is what happens at the average preneed program," he said. "A lot of at-need focused firms trip up over that and feel the need to serve the at-need families first. They find that more important. But I said our preneed families were equally as important. We needed to develop a better program; we cannot cancel these appointments."

The focus on preneed has driven the firm's organic growth, Snyder said. "We have also had several acquisitions that have helped with that," he said.

Every single service held at the funeral home presents preneed opportunities, he said. "Providing an experience at a funeral creates lead generation," he said. "Having the right people in the parking lot bring in guests when arrive, walking them in the door of your facilities … everything we do is geared toward providing an experience."

That includes Lunch and Learns, which the firm conducts without fail twice a month. "It's like clockwork, no negotiation," Snyder said, jeering at the notion of skipping one. It's been like that for the last 10 years, he said.

"It has been a great way to grow our business through preneed and to capture new customers in advance, providing them with peace of mind," he said, adding that unlike some other funeral homes, the price of a prearrangement is guaranteed when families do business with his firm.

He credits his preneed team as well as Precoa for much of the firm's growth on the preneed side. He also noted that a relationship with Graystone Associates has paid dividends on various fronts.

As for staffing, the business has a full team in place, which Snyder attributes to having built a workplace culture that's enjoyable.

"And our facilities are attractive," he said. "Our locations are updated, clean and we have technology at our fingertips. That is the DNA that we buy into."

That "DNA" is promoted to team members, with messages about "Decisions," "N-ergy" and "Actions," which they're expected to keep top of mind day in and day out. "It's about how we treat each other internally," Snyder said, as well as how staff members treat families.

Snyder prides himself on ensuring his business stands out from competitors.

"Our people are very special," he said. "I would say that is our No. 1 differentiator. We have an incredible team that cares about the well-being of others. Our facilities are absolutely incredible. We have two custom built funeral homes that no one else has, and we have the only funeral homes that were custom built from the ground up. We bought the land and built the funeral homes."

The fact that the firm has several locations is a big selling point, he said.

"Each of them possesses a different personality, so we have options for families to choose from," he said. "If someone wants an intimate, historical setting – we have that. If they want a modern setting, we have that. If someone wants a suburban setting, we have that. So, the array of options we have … you can't compare."

But like every funeral home owner, he faces challenges.

"Revenue," he said. "Having everybody at your company buy into how important revenue is … the cost of doing business and running a business continues to grow. It is much different than it was 20 years ago when I first got started."

The goal of getting every team member to present every option to every family is an idea he's always working toward, he said. "That is one of the reasons why preplanning is so important to us – it allows us to study our future customers," he said.

Asked about the product selection available to families, Snyder noted that while he's "American proud," everything that most of us are wearing right now was made in another country.

"I am proud to have as much as we can offer American made … but you have to do what you have to do and entertain other options," he said. "Loyalty is super important, and pricing is super important – and profitability is very important to be sustainable."

*In 2022, the firm completed its Willow Street location.*

**Taking His Responsibility Seriously**

As an owner, Snyder takes his duty to about 40 full-time employees and the community at large seriously. "I don't handle as many arrangements as I did 10 years ago," he admitted. "But I have a fiscal responsibility to the team, and they do in return to the company. When that is understood and when you work as a unit together, when you embrace and trust each other knowing that mistakes will be made and you learn from them and talk them out and serve each other …" – that is when you can achieve great things, he said.

Looking ahead to the future, Snyder sees the acquisition of additional funeral homes on the horizon. He'll continue to focus on growing the business, he said.

"I have been very blessed," he said. "Dad and I did our succession plan and executed that in 2019. He is still a very active adviser; he is an ambassador for our company, and he still comes to the funeral home because it gives him purpose."

Snyder is grateful his dad – a cancer survivor who is now 72 – didn't walk away, which he could have done.

"There is nothing wrong with walking away after doing your life's work, but with Dad, he enjoys coming in here and talking to our team members and meeting families," he said. "Even though he does not handle every detail, his presence goes far."

Watching his dad's dedication to his community brings tears to his eyes, Snyder said. "He could just say he wants to go golf every day for the rest of his life, but he balances out work and play," he said. "And people are just thrilled with his presence. I still lean on his advice."

*Visit https://www.snyderfuneralhome.com to learn more about Charles F. Snyder Funeral Homes & Crematory.*

# Alix Simplifies Estate Settlement for Families

*By Thomas A. Parmalee*

If you know someone who needs their estate settled, think twice about volunteering for the job.

Alexandra Mysoor, who once offered to settle the affairs of a close family friend, learned that the hard way.

When it was all said and done, she had spent about 900 hours on various tasks, but it was through that work that she saw an opportunity to help others. And as someone who started a successful ecommerce company and has been an adviser to numerous company founders, she knew she was the one to do it.

With a little help, of course.

After studying the problem, she connected with Hugh Tamassia, a technology and finance veteran who has held senior roles at JPMorgan Chase & Co., American International Group and Acorns.

Now, backed by $5.5 million in a seed round of financing led by San Francisco-based Initialized Capital, with support from Magnify, Scribble, American Family Ventures and Alumni Ventures, the duo has launched Alix, which Jon Fortt, a CNBC news anchor, said could be thought of as "the TurboTax of estate settlement."

The company promises to save families hundreds of hours that they would normally spend handling the estate of a loved one. Its website states that its team will reduce the time spent on settlement tasks by up to 85%.

Alix, so named because the company's founders wanted a name that evoked feelings of a trustworthy friend, is cultivating relationships with funeral homes throughout the country, said Mysoor, who in addition to serving as the co-founder and CEO of Alix is on the board of directors of Security National Financial Corp., which trades on the Nasdaq under ticker SNFCA and offers various life insurance products, including funeral plans.

"The number of funeral homes we work with changes on a daily basis," Mysoor said. "We are currently working with over 50 funeral homes across the United States, supporting funeral staff in strengthening long-term relationships and differentiating themselves in today's competitive market. We're excited by our continued growth and partnership with funeral homes, and we can't wait to further build upon this as we move forward."

The company is open to growth and expanding its impact, Tamassia said. "While we currently operate primarily in the United States, we believe Alix's empathy-driven services can provide exceptional support for families, funeral homes and aftercare providers everywhere," he said.

Mysoor, whose parents are from India but who grew up in Minnesota, was a premed student at University of California, Berkeley before she changed tracks and embarked on a career in digital marketing. She landed an internship at an agency that worked with Apple, and it was there that she rubbed elbows with the likes of Steve Jobs as "a fly on the wall" early in her career.

"After being at Berkely and exposed to all things Silicon Valley, I knew I wanted to be part of this in some way – and I had to shift in that moment," she said. "I felt compelled to get an internship somewhere, and the first one I found was at a digital marketing agency, but I had to be housed at Apple's campus."

In her early 20s at the time, she absorbed all she could relating to creating new categories and putting consumers first, she said. She'd go on to start her own digital marketing agency at age 24 before teaming up with her husband, Prashanth Mysoor, to start Generation Orange, one of the world's first environmentally-conscious baby products companies, which became one of the first third-party sellers on Amazon.com.

Along the way, she has also started other companies, such as Par Avion Tea, a luxury high-end tea and tea-infused beauty products company, and done consulting work for various companies, sometimes in exchange for equity — a move that's paid dividends.

Asked about what it was like observing Jobs, she said, "Just being in the room was super exciting for me – he really cared about hearing what other people thought, and he wanted them to have a point of view."

She became – in her words – "an accidental entrepreneur" after realizing that a contractor she supervised who worked at home and fewer hours than her, at that, was earning more money.

A light bulb went off in her head: She could enjoy a happier life and be more successful as a consultant. "I realized if they could do it, I could do it," she said.

Her co-founder, Tamassia, got his start in business working at fintech startups and ended up working for JP Morgan & Chase in various roles, including chief technology officer, before spending time at AIG and Acorns.

He worked at JPMorgan during its most exciting period – "when it really *wasn't* the best bank in the world and Jamie Dimon was putting the pieces together," he said.

When he was approached by Mysoor, he did not have much experience with estate settlement but found it to be a fascinating problem. Even better, it was a challenge he saw as "very solvable" through technology.

**The Great Wealth Transfer**

The opportunity to help families settle estates – and the role that funeral homes could potentially play in that process – cannot be overstated.

About $84 trillion in assets will change hands over the next 20 years, according to Cerulli Associates, a consulting firm. About $72 trillion will primarily go to members of Generation X (those born between 1965 and 1980), millennials (1981-1996) and Gen Z (1997-2012). Most of that money will come from baby boomers.

One of the ways to help smooth that transfer is with the proper financial technology, which is what Alix has been laser-focused on, Mysoor and Tamassia said.

"How are you going to transfer that wealth itself?" Mysoor asked.

Moreover, the idea of a company holistically helping families through the process is something that is new, Mysoor said. She observed that most executors tend to be women, often the oldest daughter of the deceased, who take on a caregiving role when family members age.

While it is partially powered by artificial intelligence and other technology, Alix prides itself on relying on a stable of advisers that work directly with family members to help them through the estate settlement process, Mysoor and Tamassia said.

"We talk a lot about technology internally, but these automations are in the back end to make our care team better," Mysoor said, noting that it has lawyers, certified public accountants and individuals with a background in funeral service on its care team.

"We have people – *humans* – who are really extending the journey of where funeral directors are working with families," Mysoor said. "It is this handoff of a baton."

Tamassia agreed, adding, "Our customers don't have to care about AI and shouldn't care," he said. "It is important to us and how we run our business, but we are leading with expertise and humans. We keep the AI behind the scenes and don't talk about it too much with our customers."

As it stands now, most families simply feel overwhelmed when it comes to settling an estate, Mysoor said. They may go online and find some type of checklist, but there are few tools that do the heavy lifting.

Alix does not just automate the discovery aspect of estate settlement, but it actually settles the estate, she said.

"You can't transfer something you don't find, but once you find it, who is going to do the work?" she asked. "We do that work. People come to us for peace of mind and certainty."

### The Details

On the Alix website, you can find a detailed list of tasks that the company handles for families – everything from searching for unclaimed assets to negotiating and settling outstanding debts, putting together an inventory of assets, preparing the final income taxes of the deceased, distributing money to beneficiaries and everything in between.

"We are not a fiduciary or a CPA or a lawyer," Tamassia said. "I think people feel like when they are settling an estate, you need those, but that is a very small percentage of the time." He added, "Most people can settle an estate by themselves without the help of lawyers, CPAs and fiduciaries. And we can do all the work that people could do on their own but should not have to do."

When a family uses Alix, no money comes out of the executor's pocket, Mysoor said. "From our team's decades of professional and personal experience settling estates, we understand every family and every estate isn't cookie cutter," she said. "This isn't one-size-fits-all, so neither is our pricing. Instead, we price our services at 1% of the estate. This ensures fair and comprehensive services, with fees deducted directly from the estate, not out of the executor's pocket, to accommodate the unique nature of each family and settlement."

Alix stands ready to help all families, Mysoor said. "We support every family that comes to us, no matter the size of their estate," she said. "When getting started with Alix, all families are connected directly with our Care Team, which conducts research into the size of the estate, the discovery process, and the needs of the family. After this is completed, we speak in depth with the family about whether Alix is the right fit for them. We are built on empathy and a shared understanding of how difficult this process will be so if Alix is not the right fit for a family at this time, we guide them through what their next steps will look like, free of charge."

The company is working with funeral homes to spread the word about Alix to families, but it does not view funeral homes as selling the product.

Rather, the founders of Alix view funeral homes as a resource that families may consult when they have estate settlement questions.

For example, someone may go back to the funeral home to get a death certificate, and they may suddenly start to think about all the estate settlement work they must do when a funeral director tells them they may need more than one copy.

That would be a great time for the funeral director to suggest Alix as an option, Mysoor said.

As to how that relationship between a funeral home and Alix looks like, Mysoor said, "Alix provides support to funeral homes through a partnership model that considers a variety of factors, ensuring tailored assistance to each firm." She added, "Like every family, every funeral home is different. We approach every partnership as a tailor-fit, considering the size, scope, and impact Alix can have on each funeral home's community when determining partnership details. Factors such as the firm's reputation and community trust play a significant role in determining the nature of support provided."

There is not a "cookie cutter way" to work Alix into the conversation with a family, Mysoor said.

"Funeral homes know their families best," she said. "We have a menu of options that may help them, but we really trust the funeral home. There are some that do a great job with aftercare and have a cadence in which they get to know families. And they know when to bring it up. The trusted referral is a tremendous opportunity for both of us."

Families can watch a video highlighting Alix during their arrangement conference. Additionally, the Alix team shares handouts that give information on what families can expect during the estate settlement process and how Alix can help.

For funeral home staff, Alix tries to make things as easy as possible – staff can simply share the resources with families during the arrangement conference and then let Alix know if a family is interested in speaking to the Alix team before they get started with the process.

"We try to figure out what you do or do not know about the estate, and it becomes threads for us to put together a plan," Mysoor explained, noting that an initial conversation usually lasts 45 minutes or an hour.

Once that plan is in place, Alix schedules a follow-up meeting with the executor. "You can download our app, but it's not for everyone," Mysoor said. "You are not just dropped into an app – we view our app as connective tissue when you are not talking or working with our care team."

There are sixteen full-timers and a handful of advisers that work with Alix, including three full-time staff with a background in funeral service, Mysoor said.

"That was extremely important to me," she said. "People have been doing this for generations, and their wisdom is super important … from day one, we have had funeral professionals by our side trying to figure out how Alix could be the connective tissue in aftercare."

Asked whether Alix plans to team up with preneed insurance companies to bundle its service with policies, Mysoor and Tamassia said they are always open to growing the business and finding new avenues to support families in need. Currently, they have focused their attention on families who are looking for at-need services but have received "a tremendous amount of interest" from preneed insurance companies, leading the pair to believe this is an area ripe for exploration.

"We actively help funeral homes by handling essential post-funeral tasks, and, in turn, have seen how our comprehensive aftercare helps funeral homes increase their preneed sales by maintaining and strengthening relationships across generations," Mysoor said. "Educating families on the benefits of preneed planning during their post-funeral interactions, we're able to drive families back to the funeral homes where they had positive experiences."

So far, the founders of Alix are excited about the reception the company has received and are bullish about the future.

A lot of people think that when you complete estate planning, everything is fully taken care of," Mysoor said. In reality, a trust or will is just a paper map that leads you on a digital scavenger hunt. It won't do the work for you. With Alix, we're taking on that burden for families."

Visit *https://www.meetalix.com* *to learn more about Alix.*

# Darren Crouch Continues to Think Big as the Chief of Passages International

*By Thomas A. Parmalee*

When Darren Crouch, 53, co-founded a company 25 years ago, he was thinking big.

If you have any doubts, simply look at the second word in its name: Passages International.

"My upbringing influenced that," Crouch said. "Being that I am from and have lived in many countries, I knew from the very start I wanted our company to have a global footprint."

The company's mission was clear from the beginning: to offer funeral homes environmentally friendly products that would appeal to a public that wanted greener options while prearranging or planning a funeral at the time of need – all while helping funeral homes earn additional revenue.

"When we looked at it, there was no one out there doing this," Crouch said.

He was never deterred by the idea that he was an unlikely character to bring an option that was tucked into the far corner of the selection room and bring it to the forefront.

"I am really proud of what we have created at Passages," he said. "When we started the company, and even today there is no one doing what Passages does. Yes, there are several companies that have eco-friendly products, but their core business is more along the lines of embalming fluids, wood or metal caskets or brass urns. We are and always have been the only company in the U.S. that specializes in sustainable, renewable, biodegradable and even fair-trade funeral products. We are in-step with the modern consumer that values more sustainable options and wants to spend their funeral dollars on affordable and meaningful experiences that celebrate the person and tell their story."

*The hardworking team at Passages International.*

**A Man Going Places**

Born in England, Crouch moved with his family to the West Indies as a toddler.

"My dad was in the hotel business and worked in Tobago," he explained, which is the smaller of the two Caribbean islands comprising the nation of Trinidad and Tobago. "And a couple of years after that, we moved to Africa.

He lived in Swaziland and Botswana before spending his middle and high school years at a boarding school in Johannesburg, South Africa's biggest city. When he graduated in 1988, he could have joined the South African Army to fight in Angola or Mozambique.

"There was a lot of change happening in South Africa," he said. "It was a good time to move back to the U.K."

So, he packed his bags and went to the Manchester Metropolitan University, following in his father's footsteps to blaze a trail in the family business: hotel management.

To earn his hotel management degree, however, he needed to spend a year working in the hotel industry, which made him think of a friend who had done his internship in Taos, New Mexico. "The hotel liked him and wanted more interns, and so I applied with three of my friends," he said.

Traveling clearly has never bothered Crouch, and so when his application was approved, he jumped at the opportunity and headed to the Quail Ridge Inn.

"It's about an hour and a half north of Santa Fe," he said of Taos. "It is a funky place in the middle of nowhere with artsy people."

And it was at the inn where he met Patricia, the daughter of Rivera Funeral Home owner Amos Rivera, who was also getting some early work experience.

"She was smart, fun to be around and her work ethic, interaction with customers and confidence stood out to me," Crouch said, who added that she also has a great smile.

"I then went to work at some hotels in Los Angeles, but I got burned out," he said.

Thinking they would regroup, the couple returned to New Mexico – back to where the funeral home is located. That was when Crouch began talking more with his brother-in-law, Tim Rivera, who was managing the business and had seen a troublesome change.

"He had families with plenty of disposable income, but they were not buying urns," Crouch said. "It didn't matter how he merchandized or priced them … they were leaving with a cardboard box – just a temporary container."

Both of them thought it was a poor business practice and not the best thing for families. "Affluent people were spending $2,000 or $3,000 on a cremation, and we both thought the last thing they should get is a cardboard box with their loved one's remains," Crouch said.

So, 25 years ago – in the summer of 1999 – the two formed Passages International.

"Our original concept was to provide families with dignified ecofriendly and affordable containers with which to hold their loved one's remains, but also allow funeral homes to earn some more revenue versus providing a cardboard box," Crouch said.

Asked how he could so bravely leave the only field he ever knew – hotel management – to start a venture in funeral service, Crouch said he simply needed a change.

"I was working really long 12-to-14-hour days, often late at night," he said, noting his last post was at a luxury hotel in Beverly Hills where some rooms cost $3,000 per night.

It was not uncommon to have superstars such as director Ron Howard or actor Sylvester Stallone staying the hotel as it was adjacent to an agency where top Hollywood agents worked. "It became very stressful to navigate and manage that," he said.

If you made a mistake and a big star stopped staying at the hotel, the venue could lose substantial amounts of money. Likewise, it was disillusioning to see some co-workers earning hundreds of thousands of dollars per year in tips when he was working for substantially less.

Crouch and his brother-in-law introduced their company to the profession at the National Funeral Directors Association convention in Kansas City, and the response was not what they had hoped.

"They did not quite get the concept of what we were talking about," Crouch admitted.

But over the years, as consumers have become more interested in green and biodegradable options, the interest from funeral directors has followed, he said.

"It has become our space – we own it," he said.

Crouch's wife, although she grew up in funeral service, went down a different path – to a career as an attorney.

"She does her thing, and I do mine," Crouch said, noting they have two great children: a 24-year-old daughter who graduated from New York University with a degree in psychology and is going on to study for her masters in Global Affairs at NYU, and another daughter who lives in L.A. pursuing a career in acting and modeling. "We are empty nesters and enjoying it," Crouch said.

Today, Crouch has dual British and U.S. citizenship, and while he never set out to live in America, ending up here hasn't taken him by surprise.

"I have traveled and grown up in many areas," he explained. "For me, I never felt like I was going to settle down in England. I felt like I would be on the move, whether it was Europe, Asia or Africa. I knew I wanted to get out and see the world."

And Passages has sure allowed him to do that – Crouch is indeed always moving.

"I do a lot of traveling to trade shows and making customer visits – and I travel internationally to work with our overseas manufacturing facilities and partners," he said.

During those visits, he inspects designs and conducts quality control, making regular visits to Thailand, Bangladesh, China and other countries.

He's always been too busy keeping his nose to the ground to learn languages other than English, he said. That is something he regrets, but it has not held him back.

"I have always felt like I am pretty comfortable in a lot of situations – whether it's speaking with someone who barely has an education or someone who has a Ph.D. or is the CEO of a company," he said. "I feel like I can hold my own in any of those situations, and it comes from my upbringing."

Moving around has enabled him to fluidly adapt to his surroundings regardless of what language is being spoken, he said. "That has really helped for business," he said.

As the years have gone by, Crouch has gone from a minority owner of the business to majority owner to full owner. Today, he's the one that runs the entire show at Passages.

"When we started the business, my brother-in-law had the controlling interest, but that flipped three to five years in, and I acquired the controlling interest. He was still involved – and then about 15 years ago, I bought him out. I am the sole owner now," he said.

His brother-in-law, he noted, turned Rivera Funeral Home from a company with one funeral home to one that operated three funeral homes, a crematory and cemetery before recently selling the business to a Salt Lake City based firm.

*Scattering tubes from Passages International sell at a brisk pace.*

**Lessons Learned**

Unlike some others who have started businesses with family members, Crouch only has great things to say about his brother-in-law.

"Obviously, there were some challenges, but he brought a lot of the history and industry knowledge to the arrangement," Crouch said. "He knew the business, he knew the players – and that was really helpful to have that perspective. He is also a shrewd and smart businessperson."

While the pair did not agree on everything, Crouch said, "I don't recall ever having any major blowups. We still enjoy each other's company, and it worked out well for all parties. I have a lot of respect for him."

The way the two men approached their partnership, however, is instructive.

"We tried to document stuff," Crouch said. "It wasn't just a handshake … we also had something in writing."

When working with a business partner, the value of good communication simply cannot be overstated, Crouch said. "One person says, 'I thought this,' and the other says, 'You said that,'" he said. "And it's good to say, 'This is what we agreed to, and it is written down here.' With Tim and I, we had everything written down. I feel we did it by the book without being overly rigid – and it helped us stay on track."

As far as the time he spent in hotel management, he has no regrets, noting that he's taken lessons he learned in that field and has applied them to what he does now – particularly a relentless focus on serving customers.

"The quality and attention to detail at a luxury hotel was pretty amazing," he said. "We did things from a service perspective that would exceed expectations."

For instance, when someone went to lunch, the host not only validated their parking but unknown to the customer would call valet parking so after their bill was paid, their car would be waiting for them at the exact right moment. "Little things like that made a huge difference … and planning ahead, knowing who is coming in and what are their likes and dislikes," he said.

Sometimes, customers may seem unwilling to pay, but that's only because they see little value in the product or service, Crouch said. By grasping that truth, he's forged more meaningful relationships with funeral home owners while focusing on how Passages can deliver value people will pay for, he said.

"Especially on the cremation side where people see little tangible value, that is why there has been a race to the bottom," Crouch said.

**Always Innovating**

One of the calling cards of Passages is that it is always innovating.

"At Passages, we talk about how our products can help a family create a memorable and meaningful – and *sustainable* – experience to honor and remember their loved one," Crouch said.

Too many times, though, the stance of funeral homes is to simply give families a cardboard box and tell them they'll need to figure it out.

"Our products allow families to do unique things and to create memorable and powerful experiences," Crouch said.

Ironically, however, the products themselves do not have much value, Crouch said. They are not made of bronze or marble or some other grandiose material.

"Where the value comes in is the *experiences* our products enable families to have," he said. "If you can provide that, people will pay for it."

Even better, it's a rising tide that lifts all boats – the experience of the family, the bottom line for Passages as well as the bottom line for funeral homes are all improved.

As one example, Crouch noted a local funeral home in Albuquerque that has grown its cremation revenue by 30% since it began offering Passages products.

It's done so simply by changing the minimum container for cremation families – it used to be a cardboard box that cost $195. Now, it's a bamboo container that costs $625, or families can opt for an upgraded bamboo container for $1,025.

Even families that prefer something basic have no complaints about the bamboo option, Crouch said. "The nice thing about the bamboo container is it's simple," he said. "There are no handles or linings. It has a simple quilt in the bottom."

It's not a particularly affluent market, but the owner of the Albuquerque funeral home has made a commendable choice: "He decided he does *not* want his brand associated with cardboard boxes," Crouch said.

Another exciting innovation that Passages is rolling out is Etern.life, which is a memorial map displaying the location of cremated remains that have been scattered.

According to the Etern.live website, "Our innovative platform allows you to honor and celebrate the lives of your loved ones through exactly locating where they were scattered and creating an online memorial. With Etern.Life you can place a pin on our interactive map to mark where you're loved one rests, thereby registering the scattering and preserving their digital legacy for generations to come."

Crouch is bullish about the new offering, observing that about 40% of families continue to scatter cremated remains – and that number shows no indication of going down. "And another 20% may be uncertain what they are going to do with the cremated remains, but will likely end up scattering them," he said. "We felt there was an opportunity to provide an additional service with our urns. So, with every urn we sell, families will have the ability to geolocate, taking note of the longitude and latitude of where they scattered their loved one's remains."

They will then be able to place a pin on a digital map and upload a memorial, which may include several photos and some information on the deceased. "It's about creating a community of people who have been scattered," Crouch said — just like a cemetery is a community of people who have been buried.

He envisions Etern.life becoming a dynamic memorial site, where people can share what they did to remember their loved one, who that person was, and the product they used in scattering their loved one's remains.

"And using the map, they can go back to that exact spot within a few feet and pay their respects," Crouch said.

It's just another way Passages is seeking to differentiate itself.

"I am aware of lots of products on the market, but I don't know of any other company that includes this feature with every urn," he said. "We see it as a huge growth opportunity in terms of growing market share – and maybe there will be some revenue opportunities as its own entity. For example, if someone scattered the remains of their loved on in the past, they could actually go on the website and buy the ability to put a pin on the map."

The company will begin to promote the option toward the end of the year, Crouch said.

*The Willow Casket has a flat top and attractive design perfect for families that desire a simple, yet dignified farewell for a loved one.*

### The Quest for Green

As someone who grew up all over Africa, Crouch has always had an affinity for the land and protecting natural resources – something he continues to advocate for today as president of the Green Burial Council.

"I became very aware of conservation by seeing the poaching of rhinos and elephants," he said. "I also became aware of turning the water on and getting water out of the tap is a luxury. We literally had 55-gallon drums that the bath water would go into – and that water would go to water the grass."

So, while Passages sells green products, it also makes a concerted effort to *be* green, and so does Crouch, who drives a Tesla. His wife does, too. "We have solar panels on our roof," he added.

But he's also practical, meaning that he often flies to conventions and for business. "But wherever I can, I minimize my carbon footprint," he said.

He also hates waste, and while he rarely argues with his wife, he's been known to give her a hard time when she buys too much food. "There are only two of us in the house," he said. "Maybe we just buy less?"

Still, he's aware of the contradictions that arise in selling green products, but he tries not to let them weigh on him. For instance, it's not unheard of for a family to desperately want an environmentally friendly casket that a funeral home does not have in stock.

In those instances, the casket is sometimes sent via airplane to get to the funeral home in time. "We've also had families drive roundtrip from San Antonio to pick up a casket in Albuquerque – a 14-hour drive!" he exclaimed. "This speaks to how important it is and to what lengths people will go to get these products."

But, he's fully aware that driving 14 hours each way to pick up a casket or shipping one by airplane may not align with what's best for our planet.

But at the end of the day, he said, families choose what is important to them and select the shade of green that best fits their needs.

These types of examples also allow him to make the case to funeral homes that believe in his message that it's all the more important to keep his products in stock.

**A Changing Marketplace**

For the first several years Passages was in business, it did not offer caskets – it mainly offered biodegradable urns.

"It was an uphill battle," Crouch said, noting that even though Walmart has long been offering concentrated laundry detergent, funeral homes at first simply did not grasp the need to offer families environmentally conscious options.

"We were saying consumers expected greener options, but at that point, green burial really wasn't readily available," Crouch said.

For years, Passages spent time and energy essentially creating the space, Crouch said. Finally, about 15 years ago, its efforts paid off, with the marketplace finally adopting green products on a mass scale.

"Most funeral homes acknowledged they needed some biodegradable options, but with mass adoption, we got competitors," Crouch said.

Passages has tried to combat that by constantly innovating. About 15 years ago, it introduced caskets.

At first, the response from funeral homes was that they didn't need to offer green caskets because there was no green cemetery near them, Crouch said.

Eventually, however, as more consumers asked for greener options, reality took hold and more funeral homes began buying products from Passages, Crouch said.

"The data today is really overwhelming," he said. "Consumer preference reports from the NFDA show many would be interested in a greener option if it were presented to them. You can't ignore what these nonbiased surveys are finding."

The data is proving relevant as casket sales at Passages continue to go up, Crouch said.

Still, the company sells many more urns than caskets, which contributes the lion's share of revenue. "For scatter tubes alone, we are selling over 50,000 per year in the United States," Crouch said. "The challenge is that most of our urns wholesale for under $200 and some of them are as low as $25. But our caskets wholesale anywhere from $500 to $1,200."

When a funeral home buys a casket, there is a lot to navigate. "We are not a Batesville or Matthews, we do not have our own trucks," Crouch explained.

Sending urns is pretty straightforward and inexpensive – that can be done via FedEx or UPS, Crouch said. "But with caskets, you are at the mercy of trucking companies," he said. "Finding the right providers to deliver caskets is a big deal for us. We are not white glove service like Batesville, which will bring it in and store it, but we work extremely hard to make it as seamless and easy for funeral professionals."

When funeral homes buy a casket from Passages, standard shipping is built into the price, Crouch said. "If it needs to be expedited, there is an additional charge, so we encourage them to get it and stock it," he said.

From humble beginnings, Passages has grown into a formidable business with 22 full-time employees and two warehouses in the United States – one in Albuquerque and one in Somerset, New Jersey.

It also operates a sister company – Passages International UK, which supplies the European market. It doesn't just ship throughout the U.K. but also into France, Denmark, Italy, Portugal and the surrounding region, Crouch said.

Although it does substantial business throughout the world, about 75% of its business originates in the United States and Canada, Crouch said. "But we do pretty good business in Australia and New Zealand. We have customers in Japan and Uruguay. And we had an inquiry yesterday from a customer in Korea," Crouch said.

While Crouch's ability to navigate different cultures has been an asset, there are some things that attribute has not been able to help with, such as the COVID-19 pandemic, which caught everyone off guard.

"We had discussions in my CEO peer group as to what it would mean, and some people were thinking it would be over in a month or two, but I was thinking it would be more serious," he said. "It was not great for our business."

Part of that is because of timing: It coincided with the rollout of a new initiative that sought to persuade funeral homes to cremate bamboo instead of cardboard.

"We had everything in place, and then the pandemic breaks out and all hell breaks loose," he said. "At that point, no one was thinking about tweaking their business – and the launch really suffered."

While the company was well positioned to have much of its staff work from home, interruptions to the supply chain made it difficult to replenish products – or if they *could* be replenished, made it much more expensive to do so.

"We were getting items from overseas that took three or four times longer to get to us and costing three or four times more," he said.

For a time, a shipping container that once cost $5,000 to $8,000 was running the company $30,000, Crouch said. "It was a huge hit on profitability," he said.

Also, by the time Passages took advantage of government incentives to minimize the pandemic's impact, they began being discontinued.

"The other thing is I don't know if there was much selling going on during the pandemic," Crouch said. "Funeral homes needed to take care of trailer loads of bodies. If a tsunami or massive earthquake hits, even though there are lots of people dying, it is not necessarily great for the funeral business."

Asked about artificial intelligence, Crouch said he's keeping close tabs on what it may mean for him as a business owner. For instance, while everyone is fixated on where they rank on Google, there may very well come a time when most people simply ask ChatGPT for the best funeral homes in a certain area code, or make an inquiry about the best plumber, etc.

"You better be in the top three," Crouch said. "And it is not only checking your website but also reviews."

If you're not ranking well in such AI results, you better find out why, Crouch said, observing that you may have positive reviews, but perhaps those reviews aren't saying something specific, such as you respond quickly.

"I am watching how it will affect websites and SEO," he said. "I may use it for some generic stuff, such as if I want a policy on sexual harassment. Or if I want a job description that may have taken me three or four hours to do in the past."

As time marches on, Crouch is looking forward to breaking more barriers, serving new customers and keeping his dress shoes moving all over the globe, trying to leave it a little better than the way he found it.

"Passages is known as a company that provides sustainable and eco-friendly products," he said "But we are so much more. We have created products and innovations that solve problems for funeral professionals that they don't even know that they have or are looming on the horizon. It excites me to know that the products we have created are providing revenue opportunities for funeral homes and meaningful, healing experiences for families, all while leaving a lighter touch on the planet."

*Visit [https://www.passagesinternational.com](https://www.passagesinternational.com) to learn more about Passages International.*

# Antonio Green Is Keeping Service Alive in Detroit

*By Thomas A. Parmalee*

If it weren't for the Sept. 11 terrorist attacks, Antonio Green might have been flying the friendly skies instead of serving thousands of families at the James H. Cole Home for Funeral Homes, which has two locations in Detroit, Michigan.

"My plan was to be an airline pilot and help out at the funeral home part time," he said, noting that he'd initially considered majoring in aviation before realizing he could still pursue a career as a pilot while earning a degree in something else.

Ultimately Green, 41, who is married with two boys and a girl ranging in age from 5 to 12, majored in communication at Bowling Green State University in Ohio before earning his degree in mortuary science from the Cincinnati College of Mortuary Science in 2006 and receiving his Michigan funeral director's license in 2007.

Along the way, he also earned a private pilot's license and has fond memories of flying out of Blue Ash Airport in Cincinnati.

Green's flight plan, however, took an abrupt detour after the cowardly attack on America in 2001. The entire aviation industry took a nosedive, and even though he was still in college, the way forward was clear: Fly high right where he was by turning his full attention to the family business.

**A Rich Legacy to Preserve and Build Upon**

Today, Green is the manager of the Northwest Chapel at James H. Cole Home for Funerals as well as the president of the James H. Cole Legacy Foundation, which gives back to the local community. He is also an author, public speaker and an executive coach.

"I still meet with families on a daily basis," Green said, noting that he's been in charge of the Northwest Chapel since it was built in 2010.

The firm, whose vast majority of customers belong to the black community, would not exist if it were not for Green's great-great-great grandfather, James Cole, who moved North after being freed as a slave from a Mississippi plantation.

"The story was his mother passed after a yellow fever or cholera outbreak," Green said, sharing the story that has been passed on in his family through generations. He noted that his great-great-great grandfather was actually the *son* of the plantation owner – a not so uncommon occurrence.

"So, upon her passing, the story is the plantation owner gave him the option to stay on the plantation or have his freedom," he said.

That was in the early 1860s, and his great-great-great grandfather would have been about 13 or 14 years old when he was freed.

"He had a short stint in Tennessee and landed in Detroit," Green said.

By the time 1903 rolled around, his great-great-great grandfather had made a success of himself, which the family knows because there is a 1903 newspaper article to prove it, calling him "the richest Negro in Detroit," according to Green.

"He had created a merchant business in the form of livery stables and was able to use that money and get into real estate, purchasing properties and renting properties and apartments," Green said. "He established this wealth for his family."

According to the funeral home's website, which delves into its fascinating origin story, it was Green's great-great-great grandfather's grandson – James H. Cole Sr. – who started the funeral home.

In 2019, the business celebrated its 100th anniversary. "It's a momentous milestone for any business but particularly for one owned and operated by four generations of one African American family," the website states.

Back then, Blacks found it hard to go to a funeral home that was not operated by someone who was also Black, Green said. The funeral home's website states, "The funeral home provided a much-needed service to the neighborhood's predominantly Black families who frequently were turned away by white undertakers."

Green explained, "(My great-grandfather) founded the business to offer affordable services to the community. We have found letters from the 1930s from families that mailed in a thank you note, saying, 'Here is the $3 payment for the funeral, and I promise to keep paying it off,'" Green said.

Over the years, families have often expressed shock when the funeral home advises them to do what is in *their* best interest, which does not always coincide with what is best for the funeral home, Green said.

Eventually, Green's mother, Karla M. Cole-Green, the youngest daughter of James H. Cole Jr., took over the business upon her father's death in 1991. She remains in charge as president, with Green and his brother, Brice, helping her manage operations as members of the fourth generation to dedicate themselves to funeral service.

The duty to work hard for what you want in life has been soundly instilled in Green. "My mom, she was always working six days a week," he said. "My grandfather was the same way – even on Sundays, he came into the funeral home."

While he always knew that he would join the family business "in some shape or form," winning the respect of co-workers was no easy task, Green said.

"I was growing up in the business," he explained. "So, I had people working there who remembered me as that little pipsqueak getting in the way. And now, a few short years later, I was at the point where I was supposed to be the boss or the person leading the company. So, I had to learn to bridge that gap to get the respect of some of the elders who had been there for 20 or 30 years. There were people who are here who I referred to as 'aunt' or 'uncle.' I had to get buy in and respect … and once they saw that I was there to *work hard* and was not there as a trust fund baby and I was just as dedicated as they were, after a couple years, I *did* get that buy in. And they gave me leeway to introduce new ideas."

A millennial, it was his experiences in the workplace that led Green to write a book on how to work with and understand members of his generation: "Talk to Me: Understanding the Millennial Mindset." **You can download the book for free at https://bizcoachantonio.com.**

"I was going to conventions and conferences, and the common theme I heard at every single one was '*those damn millennials … I can't work with them, and I don't know what motivates them,*'" he said.

The book is an effort to give business owners a roadmap that will help them understand that millennial mindset.

Green delivered a presentation on the topic at the National Funeral Directors Association's 2022 convention, which gave him his first experience on the national speaking circuit. "Ever since, I have done tons of speaking," he said, noting that he enjoys it because it gives him the opportunity to help others.

Not all millennials are the same, as Green explains in his book.

"I am at the very beginning of the millennial generation, and in my book, I break the millennial generation into two," he said. "The earlier part of which I am a member are the X millennials and the latter members are the social millennials. The X millennials will bear more resemblance to the Generation X'ers, who grew up before the internet took hold. They remember checking out library books using the Dewey Decimal system."

Those X millennials went on to high school and college, when the internet began to be more widely used and instant-messaging platforms exploded. So, they enjoyed "the best of both worlds" and are "able to switch gears," Green said.

Social millennials can be more challenging for earlier generations to understand as they never grew up without technology or without being connected to their friends, he said. "They always had that interconnectedness and do not know the old school ways," he said.

*Antonio Green enjoys sharing his wisdom with fellow funeral professionals and colleagues.*

In addition to being that "pipsqueak" that got in the way of some of the funeral home's current staff when he was younger, Green has fond memories of all the time he spent at the funeral home's original location on West Grand Boulevard, which is next to where producer Berry Gordy established "Hitsville U.S.A.," which was Motown's first headquarters and recording studio. Now, it's the Motown Museum.

"Our original building was shoulder to shoulder next to Motown," Green said. "There is literally a driveway that separates the two buildings. There was an insurance company next door."

Eventually, the funeral home bought the insurance company's building before tearing down its former location. It moved into the insurance company's former building and expanded the parking area. Today, its flagship location is still next to Motown.

His mother and grandmother lived above the funeral home for some years, and they have plenty of stories about Stevie Wonder sitting outside and playing his harmonica on the street, Green said. Other artists would often practice outside while they were waiting to go into the studio, he said.

"You'd see random acts on the front lawn," he said.

As for his role as president of the James H. Cole Legacy Foundation, a 501(c)3 not-for-profit organization, he noted that it was founded in 2019 to celebrate the firm's centennial and to support community-based groups that seek to encourage economic growth and prosperity.

Initially, the intent was to support schools and underprivileged students, but the focus changed with the arrival of COVID.

"We had to drastically switch gears," Green said, noting that the foundation provided meals to health care workers, firefighters and police officers.

Once the pandemic subsided, it turned back to students, providing school supplies and Grub Hub gift cards to older students, so they could enjoy meals after school. The foundation has also spearheaded Christmas giveaways and supported a battered women's and children's shelter.

The foundation stands ready to help smaller nonprofits or groups that focus on helping the Detroit community, Green said.

**Lessons from the Pandemic**

When the COVID-19 pandemic erupted, it hit Detroit particularly hard.

The funeral home suddenly had to contend with serving more families than it ever had to before in a 90-day period.

"Outside of New York and New Jersey, we were the hardest hit area right off the bat … it was insane," Green said.

What made it even harder is that some staff members felt uncomfortable reporting to work. They were scared.

"But we got through it," Green said, who added that there were points that the funeral home was working with only 40% of its staff.

"The No. 1 thing the pandemic taught us is there is nothing we could *not* do," Green said.

It also taught the family that it could operate leaner and meaner – in the aftermath of the pandemic, the business has made it a point to "trim a little of the fat," Green said.

Even during the hardest of times, however, faith has helped Green push through to brighter days.

"I grew up in the Catholic Church, and Mom has always been a devout Catholic," he said. "God is first in foremost in our lives. When things get hard in the business, you have to fall back on faith to get you through it."

One thing that Green has realized over the years is how blessed he is and what an important and fantastic role the Lord plays in his life.

"There are definitely times when there is no way we would have gotten through things without prayer," he said. "God will get you through it if you are doing the right thing."

*The James H. Cole Home for Funeral Homes has about 45 full-time employees dedicated to the Detroit community. In the front row are Karla M. Cole-Green with her two sons, Antonio (on the right) and Brice (on the left).*

**Boosting Business Operations**

About 42% of the roughly 2,000 families the funeral home serves per year opt for cremation, but most of them buy a casket and have a viewing prior to cremation, Green said. Only about 15% of families choose what the profession would call "direct cremation."

Helping families prearrange has become a priority for the firm over the years, Green said.

"Before 2008, we had more of a passive preneed program," he said. "My mom would do a lot of prearrangements or meet with families."

But then the funeral home teamed up with Blue Nebula Consulting, which has a partnership with Precoa.

"They were able to provide us with a hands-off preneed program," Green said. "They take care of all the marketing … we just train a counselor on how to sell our products."

The relationship has been going strong for more than 15 years, and the funeral home is happy with the results, Green said. "They have really helped us establish that preneed program – what we had before was pretty nonexistent," Green said, noting that the funeral home enjoys being able to "guarantee that market share" without the headaches that go along with overseeing the program itself.

The funeral home has also focused on aftercare with Everything After, which Green and his family learned about after the company won the NFDA's prestigious Innovation Award.

For years, the funeral home had been looking for an aftercare solution but with the volume it does, it did not find value in postcards and letters, which were cost prohibitive. "It was just not advantageous to do that," Green said.

But the text-based solution that Everything After offers has hit the mark. "We saw that and were like, 'This is perfect,'" Green said. "We implemented that pretty quickly, and it has worked out well."

In addition to following through with a personal touch, the solution has also allowed the funeral home to learn about problems and address them quickly, Green said.

He likes that the program is not overly automated. "This is an actual person," Green said. "We don't have to worry about them not getting compassion or empathy."

Another benefit of working with Everything After is it has resulted in a huge boost in positive Google reviews, Green said.

Even when a business is doing great, families are sometimes slow to give kudos unless they're asked, and Everything After has been able to push people into that positive review funnel, he said.

As far as social media is concerned, it has used Disrupt Media for years, he said.

**Staying Ahead of the Curve**

Like any business leader, however, there are challenges Green is still trying to conquer.

"I consider myself an innovator, and I always want to stay ahead of the curve," he said. "I am always trying to figure out where our industry is headed and how I can get ahead of that. How do we use technology to better the business? To improve the quality of our staff's lives and the lives of the clients and customers we serve. Those are the things I am constantly focused on."

One way Green is trying to accomplish his mission is by developing an AI bot that families can communicate with via the firm's website – something that he hopes to offer to other funeral homes on a subscription basis once it's perfected.

It will do much more than answer generic questions – you'll be able to find out what makes a stainless-steel casket better than an 18-guage or what specific services the funeral home offers, Green said. "You'll be able to ask any question you want, and the bot will be trained to intelligently answer just like a person. It won't be a traditional chat bot where you get these brief answers. We are in the final stages of training the bot and will do a soft launch on our website."

He observed that "everyone is working on AI" but few people seem committed enough to "take a dedicated step into it."

Asked what stands out to him most about being in funeral service, Green said it's those families that come back whenever they are at their lowest point.

"I have had families I have seen four or five times over the last 10 years," he said. "They continue to come back, and it is almost like they are your family – they don't want to see anyone but you." He added, "That just reinforces that we are definitely doing the right thing, and we use that to help our staff realize we are helping people. Sometimes, with the number of cases we do, it is hard to see that we are having an effect on people's lives on a daily basis."

*Visit https://www.jameshcole.com to learn more about the James H. Cole Home for Funerals.*

# Katie Dunkel, Owner of Digital Script Keepsakes, Engages Her Creative Side to Help Others

*By Thomas A. Parmalee*

Katie Dunkel stays busy managing a Service Corporation International location, Pat. H. Foley & Co. in Houston.

But when she isn't helping families honor and remember loved ones, there's a pretty good chance you'll find her doing one of two things: playing pickleball or putting in the hard work necessary to build her business, Digital Script Keepsakes, which she began on Etsy before transitioning it to a full-fledged business at the beginning of this year.

The concept is so simple that it's brilliant: "We specialize in turning your handwritten notes, recipes, and personal messages into exquisite home goods," according to the company's website. "From cozy pillows to elegant tea towels and magnetic keepsakes, we offer a range of products that celebrate the uniqueness of your story."

FuneralVision.com couldn't help but be impressed by Dunkel's go-getter attitude and flair for creativity.

We recently reached out to her to learn how she made her way into funeral service, what she struggles with as a funeral professional, what she loves most about her job and how she's continuing to challenge herself by growing her business.

**Tell us a little bit about yourself.**

I'm originally from a small town in Southern Illinois. I have lived in Houston for 10 years now. I really love Houston from all the food to the diversity it brings – it has a lot to offer.

Outside of work, you can likely find me playing pickleball with my friends several nights a week and even the occasional tournament on weekends. I also love DIY projects and using my creativity. I have an 11- year-old cat, Polly Pocket. Most of my family lives in Illinois and Oklahoma. I do have a few cousins here in the Houston area. I enjoy traveling whether it be to see family or somewhere with either mountains or a beach!

**How did you first become interested in funeral service?**

In high school, I had a friend whose older sister went to mortuary school. I was so intrigued. Honestly, I didn't know women did this. Being from a small town (Mount Carmel, Illinois), my parents knew the owner of our local funeral home- Short-Cunningham. I was able to shadow the funeral directors and embalmers there. After a few visits and gaining their trust, they allowed me to see and do even more hands-on. This led to a part-time job and has snowballed into my full career.

**Is there a particular funeral service or experience that has made a lasting impression on you and/or has reminded you of why you chose to get into death care?**

In my teens (both prior and during my time working in a funeral home), I experienced the loss of a few friends as well as my brother's death when I was 18. Looking back, I think those experiences definitely molded me and were somewhat make or break moments for my future in this industry. Going through a traumatic loss will show you how important funeral professionals are to the family and the community. It's always been important for me to help. I learned my gift of helping in this way at a younger age than most, but it's something I am grateful for.Digital Script Keepsakes offers a variety of products through its website.

**How did you end up going from Illinois to Texas?**

After graduating from Southern Illinois University and completing my internship, I was ready for a change. The stars aligned perfectly as I finished my apprentice cases in the summer of 2014. In August, I applied for a funeral director position I found in Houston. By October, I was fully moved and starting my new journey. It's really crazy to look back on how quickly it all happened. This is also where I first joined Service Corporation International. I didn't know a lot about the company back then, but not having my own family in the industry I was interested in this path. With Houston being a major city, SCI has a Care Center. I liked the idea of being able to focus more on families and services rather than embalming. I felt it was important for me, personally, as it gave me a little more work-life balance.

**At some point in your career, you began focusing more on funeral home operations, such as logistics, compliance, financial reporting, etc. What was behind the change?**

Yes, in 2017 I was promoted to be a location manager. My location is a standalone location (no cemetery attached), so I still work closely with families alongside my funeral director and the rest of my team. You are right though, there is a lot more focusing on compliance and financials.

I have always been pretty driven and knew when I started as a funeral director that I wanted to get into management. I was able to achieve a promotion fairly quickly, but I was still very young. I went from feeling so secure in funeral directing to then managing other adults. I had a lot to learn! I have since become very confident in what I'm doing and have remained at the same location I was promoted to: Pat H. Foley & Company, which was started in 1965. It's an honor to be a part of such a long heritage. I work in a great area of Houston and love the connections I've been able to make with this community. It definitely gives me that similar feeling I had in my hometown.

**What is your favorite part about working for SCI?**

SCI is a company that can afford people with endless opportunities from a career standpoint. I'm fortunate enough to work where SCI headquarters is located. That was a happy accident! In a corporation, you get to work with many different people whose roles assist us in our day-to-day helping families. Many of my leaders and mentors have been so supportive of my goals and that is really valuable to me. At the end of the day, though, I truly believe regardless of where you work, your direct leaders have the biggest impact on you. I've been very fortunate in that regard.

**What is the biggest challenge you face as a funeral professional?**

Mental health is the first thing that comes to mind. I'm a huge advocate for taking care of yourself. It reminds me of that saying, "You can't pour from an empty cup." We can't help families as well when we are struggling. My mental health journey started with going to therapy, learning who I am, and unlearning some of my perfectionistic tendencies and poor coping skills. I realized those things were actually limiting me rather than helping me.

**You recently started your own company – Digital Script Keepsakes. Tell me … was there an epiphany moment when the idea or the business struck you … or was it just festering for a long time?**

The concept initially started with my Etsy shop where I offered digital products only. It has all unfolded in many phases up to this point.

My customers would buy the listing, then provide a picture via message of the handwritten recipe or note. The handwriting is then digitally traced by me to create a high-quality image file in both JPEG and PNG formats. These files are emailed directly to the customer, who can then take them to a print shop or print at home. Once printed, they can frame the image and use it as a keepsake art piece.

I've since started my own website Digital Script Keepsakes. That is where I have now expanded the business to offer physical products, too.

**What are the main products you sell through Digital Script Keepsakes – and which one is proving to be the most popular so far?**

The main products are home décor items such as decorative pillows, pillow covers, wall art, kitchen magnets, canvases and tea towels. I still offer digital products, too: a print-from-home option that can be framed by the customer. I would say the digital product and the decorative pillow are the most popular items.

**What does pricing range from, and how hard was it to determine pricing, so that it appeals to families while also offering you a profit?**

Prices range from $15 to $60.95. It's important to me that people see the value of our products. Not only are these custom designed, they are likely very sentimental to the customer. Our pricing is based on a typical retail business model while also considering the time it takes the digital artist to replicate the handwriting. We take in every detail of the writing and make sure it is perfect before designing it on the product.

**Are you also working directly with funeral homes?**

We are mainly focused on selling directly to the public. I'm more than happy to communicate to other funeral homes and funeral professionals to discuss how we can best assist in providing this to a family.

Being a newer small business, we do not offer wholesale or personal incentives. As we expand, I am open to growing in that way.

How sweet would it be to include someone's handwriting in their own memorial program? I'm definitely open to helping funeral homes make custom products – especially with the digital product we offer. Please don't hesitate to reach out to me to discuss that process.

**How did you find a partner to manufacture your product or how does that work?**

A lot of research, as well as ordering sample products from different companies. Every product we use has been personally inspected to make sure we are offering high-quality items.

**Why do you think keepsakes with script as an element resonate so powerfully with families?**

I love this question. I think once people see that special message or recipe in that familiar handwriting on a real product … it tugs on the heart strings and brings back a particular memory for them. That's how all of this started really: My Grandma Peggy was known for her sour cream cookie recipe.

Every year at Christmastime, she would make dozens of them, and the granddaughters would come over and help decorate. There are lots of memories in those moments when I reflect back. She passed away in 2018. My cousin inherited most of her recipe cards, and she scanned all of them and created a google drive to share with the rest of us. I had seen someone digitally tracing handwriting before, and it gave me the idea to do that with her most special recipe: Sour Cream Cookies. I finished it and sent it to my cousin (who lives 800 miles away from me now). I told her she could print it and frame it especially for Christmastime. Well, she ended up surprising me with putting this image on a magnet and gifting it to me. It was the sweetest thing. It is on my fridge and I think about my grandma every time I see it. Plus it makes it super convenient to follow the recipe when I'm baking!

*Katie Dunkel is on a mission to help families remember loved ones by engaging her creative side.*

**Without getting too technical, can you share with us the technology behind how you create keepsakes with script as such an essential element?**

Sure! I upload the customer's original image to a program on my iPad. This software allows me to carefully and diligently trace the handwriting. It's important for me to share that I do not try and "improve" the handwriting. If a person had terrible penmanship, who cares! It's special all the same. I think handwriting is so unique to each human – similar to a fingerprint. As a digital artist, we have a certain skillset and tools we use to make sure the digital tracing is a perfect replication to the original writing.

**What did you wish you knew about starting your own business that you've since learned?**

Success really is subjective. No business receives tons of orders and clients overnight. You can absolutely find success in the small things!

**Is there a book or resource that you'd recommend other funeral professionals check out, and why?**

A book I'd recommend is "The Four Agreements" by Don Miguel Ruiz. It's a great book for any person, not just funeral professionals. It's about taking personal responsibility and living a more fulfilling life by breaking down these Four Agreements that the author describes. It's a great book to occasionally reread as well!

**Are there any final thoughts you'd like to share?**

This product is not just for those who have lost someone, but as funeral professionals we often see the joy and happiness that sentimental gifts can bring to people.

For anyone interested, they can visit and order from my website: digitalscriptkeepsakes.com. You can also follow us on Instagram digital.script.keepsakes or on Facebook at Digital Script Keepsakes.

*Visit https://digitalscriptkeepsakes.com to learn more about Digital Script Keepsakes.*

# Foundation Partners Group Sees Lots of Frosting in Cake Acquisition to Sweeten its Business

*By Thomas A. Parmalee*

If you're trying to grasp the significance of Foundation Partners Group's acquisition of Cake, it's helpful to understand what it's buying.

Lee Senderov, chief marketing and digital officer at FPG, explained it like this: "It's kind of like the Expedia for all things end of life."

Cake drives its top line "by promoting our affiliate partners who offer services and products that our users will appreciate, and by working with enterprise partners to create versions of Cake configured especially for their needs," according to its website. "We make money by promoting our affiliate partners who offer services and products that our users will appreciate, and by working with enterprise partners to create versions of Cake configured especially for their needs."

Partners include AARP, which is an investor in Cake; Better Place Forests; and Trusted Will. "As the largest direct-to-consumer channel for end-of-life planning and bereavement support, Cake has been approached multiple times throughout the years for acquisition." Senderov said. "As a strategic investor, Foundation Partners has been observing Cake for years. The timing was right to join forces to deliver a better omnichannel experience for families."

While FPG does not foresee dramatic changes to the Cake business model – at least not initially – it does have a slew of ideas on leveraging the Cake platform to drive preneed leads, Senderov said.

"A lot of our ideas are in their infancy," Senderov said. "We are assessing different options for how to best use and leverage the Cake assets – as well as figuring out how to best combine those assets with our funeral homes."

The company is also "assessing how much of the current model we will be keeping versus what we should change," she said.

Terms of the acquisition were not disclosed and FPG declined to reveal details on whether Cake is profitable. But Senderov noted that Cake has made "some really great strides in thinking how to monetize the space."

Cake is about 10 years old, and during that time, more than 100 million consumers have visited the website, Senderov said. "It continues to run at the multi-million visitor level year over year, and it continues to grow organically," she said. "That really speaks to the need for this kind of information."

The co-founder of Cake, Suelin Chen, Ph.D., did a tremendous job turning Cake into a trusted destination for families to get neutral information about the end-of-life space, Senderov said. Chen will be staying on as an adviser for at least the next six months, Senderov said.

Coincidentally, both Chen and Senderov live in the Boston area. Cake had six full-time employees when it was acquired, some of whom will be staying on with FPG. Everyone worked on a virtual basis, so there is no office space to determine what to do with, she said.

As to why the company is named "Cake," its website admits the word may not be the first to come to mind when it comes to end-of-life planning. "But we chose it because it's a warm, inviting symbol of celebrating and honoring life," its website states. "Proactive planning is a considerate and generous act that honors our lives and the lives of those we love. Planning also encourages us to reflect on our final wishes, which can help us live more purposefully and meaningfully in the present. When we think deeply about what's most important at the end of life, we understand what's most important now, and can better appreciate our relationships, celebrate accomplishments, and realize our goals in the precious time we are given."

*Lee Senderov*

## A Robust Library and Additional Resources

The Cake acquisition comes with a library of articles related to end-of-life across numerous categories, Senderov said.

"They have met a consumer demand," Senderov said. "As we think about innovation, that is what drew us to the partnership with Cake: Their ability to think about what is missing in the market, and how do we fill that need?"

Senderov, who sits on the board of Newton-Wellesley Hospital, which has locations throughout the Boston area, where she's a member of its Palliative Care Committee, noted that when she was getting up to speed on materials that were provided to nurses interacting with families with loved ones in palliative care, she was given a packet of articles. It was filled with information from Cake.

"They have such great content that is so informative to families," she said.

"That is how I think of leveraging Cake's content," Senderov said. "How can we use the content it has collected from so many experts in the field – around 6,000 articles related to end of life?"

Cake has already experimented with different subscription models, Senderov said, adding that for the most part, consumers don't want to pay a monthly or annual fee to belong to something Instead, they want to pay once.

"Subscription models in this space are very different … people don't want to think about when is going to be the end," she said.

Cake has multiple tools that focus on different aspects of the user journey. "One hundred thousand people have signed up to access the end-of-life planning tool, the post-loss checklist, and more," Senderov said. "Some of them also pay to access more services, like one-on-one consultations."

Cake also offers free online tributes for loved ones, which has been the subject of much discussion at FPG as it ponders how that component may mesh with its funeral homes.

"What is best for families?" Senderov asked. "We obviously have an obituary product that we provide to our families through our funeral homes, but what about families that don't necessarily use a funeral home? Maybe they used us for a direct cremation, and they are having a celebration of life at Mom's favorite restaurant. So, where should they memorialize – somewhere on Cake or somewhere else in our ecosystem?"

In addition to its library, Cake visitors can access resources related to estate planning and estate settlement as well as advance directive forms by state, a funeral home directory, information on pet loss, genealogy tools, grief resources and more.

**Preneed**

The most obvious question when it comes to FGP's acquisition of Cake is how it may play into its preneed efforts, as well as its potential to turbocharge the efforts of others engaged in preneed – even companies that may at first glance seem to be competitors to FPG.

As of now, Cake does not have any existing relationships with preneed insurance companies "in the traditional sense," Senderov said.

"But I think a lot of folks who come to the Cake website have an interest in preneed," Senderov said. "They just come in at different parts of the funnel … some may have an initial interest while others may need to be taught it exists. Others are very far down the journey and are ready to transact."

When a website is attracting millions of visitors per year, by definition, there will be people in a variety of places in the funnel, she said.

That works out great for FPG, however, as it has invested heavily in understanding what consumers want and need wherever they are in the preneed funnel. FPG stands ready to leverage its expertise in converting families who may be interested in preplanning into families that *actually plan*, Senderov said. "There are a lot of synergies there," she said.

There is also the potential for FPG to leverage Cake to drive preneed at other firms as it does not have a presence everywhere.

FPG has always made it a point to establish a footprint and grow in high cremation markets (its companywide cremation rate is over 85%), and it will continue to focus on those areas, Senderov said. "We have built our entire business model on the cremation-heavy market," she said, pointing out there are still parts of the country where cremation is lagging.

"There are states that we don't operate in, and quite frankly may never do so," she said, providing Montana as an example. "That is not a state of interest to us."

However, FPG is certainly open to thinking how it may leverage the Cake platform to help families who want to prearrange with a non-FPG firm in such states, promoting the value of funeral service while earning some money for itself as a lead generator along the way.

It may even be willing to do the same in markets where it *has* a presence, Senderov suggested. "If we don't have a premier brand in a certain market, is there an opportunity to partner?" she said. It's something FPG will need to work through, but it's a question that's worth asking.

Regardless of the company's ultimate answer, FPG is committed to providing consumers with the best experience possible, Senderov said. "It does not behoove me to turn someone away who is not in one of our markets," she said. "It is better to say, 'Here is this great firm – go work with them.'"

Asked who she considers Cake's biggest competitors, Senderov noted that it's a "highly fragmented" space with a number of players – and no one who stands heads and shoulders above the rest.

For instance, Dignity Memorial has a robust website with resources, but it's not a neutral party. Legacy.com provides the public with rich information related to life stories, but that's only one component of end-of-life planning. "The beauty of Cake is that it coalesces all this information into one resource," Senderov said.

The acquisition, Senderov said, is the first of its kind and shows that FPG is "doubling down" on its investment in digital tools for funeral directors and families to drive prearrangements, at-need services and more.

*Visit https://www.joincake.com to learn more about Cake.*

*Visit https://foundationpartners.com to learn more about Foundation Partners Group.*

# Funeral Service Events: Attendee Lists, Nametags and Other Pain Points

*By Thomas A. Parmalee*

I've often thought about writing a book on event planning, but I'm not so sure it would sell enough copies to be worth the effort.

But every once in a while, something comes up as it relates to planning an event that I feel compelled to write about, as I know there are others out there who plan events who probably grapple with some of the same issues I have to navigate, and these issues also hold implications for attendees.

So, whether or not you work at an association or organization that plans events, or if you sponsor events or if you're usually the one buying a ticket, I invite you to share your own thoughts on some of the most common pain points that I often face as an event planner.

**Attendee Lists**

When I first started planning events 20 years ago, these were not really top of mind.

But over the years, as we've increasingly become comfortable with email and communicating with each other online, I suppose, they've become a big deal.

Now, it's common for attendees to ask me for an attendee list in advance. And at the meeting itself, there is often a *downright revolt* if a list of attendees is not provided.

At first, I was reluctant to provide such a list to anyone other than event sponsors, who after all are sponsoring the event to build relationships and win a handful of new customers. If everyone gets an attendee list, would this take away some of the perceived value of sponsoring the event, I asked myself.

Slowly, I began to come around to the idea that I should at least share the list with attendees in advance – even if they were not sponsors – if they specifically asked. Often, they simply want to know who else is coming, so they can see if any friends or colleagues are on the list and to set up a dinner or two. No doubt, they are also checking to see if their competitors are coming, as well. Dan Isard, founder of The Foresight Companies, always said a line I thought was funny: *If your competitor is not in the room, you call them "a son of a bitch." If they are in the room, they are your "colleague."*

Anyhow, as the years went by, I started seeing associations and various other organizations provide hard copies of the attendee list to *everyone*, often with much more than a name and email address. Often, these lists also include a person's telephone number, business title and address. If someone signed up for an event with their home address, well, that is the address that is printed.

All this is to say that I gradually came around – based on what I heard from the attendees themselves as well as what I witnessed from others – to making the attendee list available, both in advance and at an event itself. Heck, I've become proactive about providing the attendee list instead of making it difficult.

Each event is different, but in funeral service – the space I've most often planned events for – networking is often one of the prime reasons that someone attends an event. The attendees have by and large *demanded* an attendee list, and it seems like a pretty small request given that they are spending hundreds if not thousands of dollars to travel to your event – and also paying an opportunity cost to be there as well.

Granted, I've tried to tone down the information I provide in such attendee lists compared to some others … I'm not sure everyone should be seeing someone's phone number and if they want someone's address, perhaps they should just Google it.

But someone's name, the name of their business and their email address seems to be fairly reasonable information to provide when there is such a focus on networking and meeting people face to face as part of an event experience.

**The Point …**

I'm dwelling on this because I'm really interested in hearing what others think about this, especially since I had someone recently complain to me that their email address was shared as part of an attendee list that was made available to those coming to a business meeting of like-minded professionals.

This individual was not trying to be difficult, and I genuinely appreciate that they took the time to share their thoughts on the matter ... but their viewpoint on this did strike me as being ... how can I say this in a nice way ... *out of touch*?

An email address is not a Social Security number, and the reality is – whether an attendee list is shared as a hard copy to all the attendees in a very transparent way or not – *people are getting the attendee list.*

It may only be the event sponsors, or perhaps it's being provided on request, but the feedback I've gotten over the years is also being received by others who plan events. They know just as well as I do that the attendee list has become a battleground of sorts in the sense that if you do not provide it, *attendees will fight you.*

It seems to me that most associations and organizations have gone the route of simply giving attendees (most of them) what they want and providing a hard copy or electronic copy of the attendee list or at least not balking at providing a list when asked.

My other thought is that since this seems to be a pretty standard practice from what I can see, if someone were *really that concerned* about their email getting out, they should probably come up with a "conference email" that they only use to sign up for industry events. That way, their inbox won't become cluttered with messages from people they've met along the way or who are trying to sell them various products and services.

For most, however, I *suspect* this is not a big deal.

I *suspect* that most people appreciate the value of networking so much that they may actually *enjoy* hearing from people they've met at a business meeting – even if they are suppliers, as the whole reason suppliers exist is to help individuals solve problems. And if it's someone or some company that you are *not* interested in hearing from, well, just like the junk mail you receive in your mailbox, you rip it up (or in this case, you hit delete).

Right?

Or has everyone who plans meetings – me included – got this all wrong?

Truly, I want to know.

**Nametags**

Another common complaint revolves around nametags.

As someone who plans events, I always try to get this right, but I wish people would be more forgiving on items such as:

- **Your nametag is missing**: Often, this could be because you signed up for an event late, and materials were printed in advance. That could be the reason why your nametag is missing or the reason your name is not on an attendee list (which is another common complaint – one I receive much more than an attendee list being *provided* in the first place.)

- **A mistake on the nametag**: It could be that someone actually made a typo themselves when signing up for an event, and it's all automated – that list is pulled into an Excel file and name badges are printed from there. Also, mistakes simply happen. You can choose to be gracious about it and grab a blank name tag (assuming one is provided) and print your name the way you want it with a Sharpie.

**Food**

The larger an event, the harder it is to keep everyone happy on this front.

I've often been amazed at how evaluations from the same exact conference will focus on the food, with some saying they loved it and others saying it was subpar.

The bottom line is you do the best you can, and it's virtually impossible to keep everyone happy.

The other point I'd make is that if you are vegan or vegetarian, it really is incumbent on *you as an attendee* to either let the host know of your dietary restriction, so they can try to provide you with something you can eat or get comfortable with the fact that you may need to duck away and eat somewhere on your own.

I always strive to pick food with a certain variety, but it's hard to meet the needs of everyone. You tend to pick an option that most people will be satisfied with versus an option that 50 percent of attendees will be *thrilled with* and 50% *unhappy with*.

What does that look like an action?

Well, I may love chicken smothered with barbecue sauce with a side of macaroni and cheese, but for a business meeting, I'd be much more likely to go with a selection of deli sandwiches.

I don't think many people will *love* deli sandwiches … but I also don't think many people will complain or leave unhappy with the fact that they had the choice between turkey, tuna, veggies or ham.

Coffee is always another point of contention … people love their caffeine, but you may not realize that at most hotels, it costs $65 to $85 per gallon. The costs can become prohibitive – fast.

I've walked that line generally by taking the following approach: Provide coffee up until lunch, and after that people are on their own. Generally, people seem pretty understanding of that approach.

**The Temperature**

My one piece of advice here is this: If the room is too hot or too cold, *say something*.

Often, the event staff are overworked and hustling about, and they may be sweating so much as they run around that they really do not realize that the room may be on the cold side.

Or, if it's on the warm side, they may really be too stressed and distracted to realize that is the case.

**Showing Up**

Bumps in the road always come when you plan a meeting or event – and a big one is getting your speakers to show up.

Unforeseen circumstances happen – close relatives die, people get sick, or some kind of urgent business matter comes up.

Most people are pretty understanding and forgiving about those issues, including me as a meeting planner. What certainly makes my job easier, however, is when a designated speaker at least plans to send someone else from their organization (preferably someone just as knowledgeable) to speak on their behalf.

Nothing as a meeting planner is worse than you have put in all the hard work to make an event successful and you receive an eleventh-hour call from a speaker who says not only can they not make it, but there is no one else coming in their place.

Once, I teamed up with a preneed insurance company on an event. The keynote speaker they had chosen for the event – someone they were paying thousands of dollars – called me hours before the event telling me they were unsure they could make it.

I was simply aghast as they had no backup plan and nothing going on that I would consider a crisis that would prevent them from attending the meeting. They said something about a wedding – and not theirs. In that case, I had to push back quite a bit, and fortunately they ended up making the meeting … but it was awkward.

Another time, I had a speaker duck out of an event because they wanted to attend some type of family function … it was something like a sporting event for one of their kids or they wanted to go on a family vacation, etc.

*Family first*, they said.

Fortunately, they broke this news a pretty good time before the event, so I had time to set up a backup plan, but still, it was not enough time to resubmit CEU applications and such, so attendees lost out.

It was so upsetting.

I felt like telling the person that *they were wrong* – that family is important, but you made a professional commitment and unless it's simply unavoidable, you should honor that commitment and put that before your family. No one was dying. No one *had* died. They just wanted more family time in this case.

I kept my mouth shut … but I will never invite that person to speak at one of my events again. I hope I don't sound too harsh, but that's the truth.

COVID-19, of course, was a whole different issue … it was interesting planning events during those days as I often found myself trying to cajole speakers to honor a commitment to speak at an event to save the bottom line, even when I could sympathize with their worries about becoming sick or traveling on a plane with what many of us feared was a deadly virus floating in the air.

Honestly, while I did everything I could to try to encourage speakers to come to an event during those days to prevent them from being cancelled and taking a big financial hit, I understood when they backed out, and I could not hold it against them. Those were challenging times to be in the event business.

I hope some of these thoughts have been helpful for both event planners and attendees ... I could certainly write more, but I'm more interested in hearing *your* thoughts. So, please share them!

# A Conversation with the New Chief of National Guardian Life Insurance Co.

*By Thomas A. Parmalee*

It's been about six months since Joe Celentano, who formerly worked more than 30 years at Pacific Life, took on the role of president and chief executive officer at National Guardian Life Insurance Co.

FuneralVision.com recently had the chance to catch up with him to learn more about his career in insurance, what led him to take the top job at NGL and some of the opportunities he hopes to pursue.

"I view NGL as a smaller organization that is on the precipice of blooming into a larger organization," he said. "We can be larger and succeed, not only in the preneed market but other chosen markets where we could add value."

As chief, Celentano looks forward to guiding the organization and providing the confidence needed "as we adapt our mindsets to grow in preneed and transform our technology capabilities to enable NGL to grow in any chosen insurance market."

Read more in our conversation below.

**Can you share a little bit about yourself?**

I have been married to my wife, Kathy, for 34 years. We have three adult children, who live across the U.S., including Washington, D.C., South Dakota and California. Many of my hobbies include connecting with and spending time in nature. I enjoy hiking in the woods, chopping firewood, boating, golfing and taking our dog, Zaya, for walks. Recently, I've been exploring Madison, Wisconsin, my new home and where National Guardian Life Insurance Co. is headquartered.

**You worked at Pacific Life for more than 30 years. What made you open to the idea of leaving and starting fresh at a new company?**

During my tenure at Pacific Life, I advanced my career through a variety of leadership roles and functions, including being appointed enterprise-wide chief risk officer in 2012 and chief financial officer for the Retirement Solutions Divisions in 2017 and in 2019 head of the Retirement Solutions Division. I'm proud of the outcomes that my teams at Pacific Life accomplished and the tremendous financial growth achieved during my time there.

When I was approached about the president and CEO position at NGL, it piqued my interest – and I wanted to better understand how I could play a role in thoughtfully and strategically guiding the company forward. After learning more about NGL and the preneed industry, I felt the company would be a great fit based on my expertise, its culture and vision for the future.

**Did you find NGL or did NGL find you … or did you find each other? How did this hiring come about?**

I believe in the benefits of continued growth and professional development throughout your entire career. An executive recruiter knew I was open to new opportunities and reached out to me about the president and CEO role. I was familiar with NGL and knew it was a mutual company focused on the preneed market. That initial call developed into a series of conversations that led me to believe NGL is a great company and one I would want to be associated with.

**Did you have to relocate to take on your new role? What challenges have you faced as you've made this transition?**

We are in the process of moving and establishing a permanent residence in Madison. So far, my wife and I love being in downtown Madison. We recently just closed on a condominium downtown close to the NGL office. I plan to work from the office as much as possible because I enjoy the atmosphere and seeing our team members. However, I will work virtually occasionally.

There is a lot of learning that comes with any new role. It's understanding the company's culture, processes and ways of working, and meeting many new hard-working team members. I've had to delve into NGL's short term and long-term goals and strategy. What I have learned is NGL is made up of a tremendous team of dedicated individuals and the company is well-positioned to be a leader in our chosen insurance markets while having the financial strength to deliver on our promises. Charting a future path for NGL from a foundation of strength will enable NGL to achieve our long-term strategic goals.

**In what ways did the role you played at Pacific Life prepare you to take on the CEO spot at NGL?**

With more than three decades of insurance industry experience, and through my various leadership roles, I understand the benefits, risks and tradeoffs of running an organization. Pacific Life offered training and leadership development initiatives that I took advantage of during my time there. My career trajectory encompassed roles that gave me a solid knowledge base on leading businesses and working through complex situations to achieve long-term organizational goals, all the while mentoring and developing effective leadership teams.

**How familiar were you with NGL in your previous role? Did you have any previous interactions with the company?**

I was familiar with NGL and the markets they operated in. But there wasn't a lot of overlap with my previous roles. As a result, I had limited interactions with NGL. I learned a lot about NGL through the interview process with the board of directors and conducting my own due diligence. Those experiences solidified that the president and CEO role would be a good match for me and hopefully, for NGL.

One of my first steps was gaining a thorough understanding about the preneed market and getting acquainted with our marketing partners and funeral homes. I was interested in learning how they operate and what challenges they face. It's important for me to know what our partners need because that helps create a better understanding of how NGL can support our partners and grow together.

**What attracted you to take on this role?**

There were three main factors I considered when deciding on accepting the role of president and CEO at NGL. I looked at NGL's strong position in the preneed market, the experience and diverse skill sets of the team, and NGL's overall financial strength.

NGL is a 115-year-old mutual insurance company that is known for its financial strength and stability. The team members at NGL believe in collaboration and have a desire to succeed, as well as provide compassionate service to our policyholders and partners. NGL has significant capital reserves that will allow for intentional growth in chosen markets or when opportunities present themselves. NGL is a leader in the preneed market, and we continue to look there toward future growth.

**What do you think makes NGL different from other preneed insurance companies?**

Our NGL team members are experienced, engaged and focused on succeeding and working in a collaborative environment. Our teams are empowered to utilize creative problem solving to ensure the best possible results for everyone involved. Compassion, dependability and integrity are core values that are deep-rooted in our culture and truly celebrated.

NGL is an A (Excellent) rated company by A.M. Best and has been providing insurance solutions for more than a century. Our significant capital strength supports growth through organic opportunities or acquisitions.

**How many funeral homes do you work with and how much insurance does NGL typically underwrite in a given year? What may the future hold?**

It's a privilege for us to work with and provide support to thousands of funeral homes. Last year, NGL celebrated a milestone 25 years in the preneed profession. The preneed marketplace is nearly a $3 billion a year industry; we believe there is significant potential for growth, and we are looking for ways to expand our reach and serve even more families.

**How challenging is the interest rate environment right now for NGL and other preneed insurance companies?**

Compared to 2020/2021 the interest rate environment is vastly improved. Higher interest rates reduce the risk to companies like NGL. When the interest rates climb, we can turn around and share that benefit with our partners by increasing growth rates. NGL plans for economic uncertainties, including challenging interest rates, by carefully managing our investment portfolio and investment income.

**How helpful has Kimberly Shaul, who was the interim CEO of NGL, been with your onboarding and transition?**

Everyone at NGL, including the team members and board of directors, have been welcoming and helping me transition into my new role. I've learned so much about NGL's deep and honorable history, as well as gained an understanding of current business practices and strategy. Kimberly Shaul has been extremely helpful during the transition and guiding NGL during the time she was interim CEO. I continue to look to her for advice and counsel.

**What has been something about the death-care profession that has surprised you as you've transitioned to your new role?**

I was surprised to learn how many funeral homes there are in the U.S., with a vast majority still being one or two locations that are family owned. Joining the preneed profession has given me a deeper understanding of a funeral director's role in the community. They are empathetic and caring people who provide a noble service in times of distress for families. Their leadership in communities is often overlooked when they should be recognized for their contributions. Funeral professionals dedicate their time and energy to supporting families, whether they are dealing with immediate arrangements or preplanning. NGL is proud to support the funeral profession and make it easier for them to do the important work they do in their communities.

*Visit https://www.nglic.com to learn more about National Guardian Life Insurance Co.*

# The Story of Lisa Malcore and Solace Urns

*By Thomas A. Parmalee*

Lisa Malcore, vice president of Malcore Funeral Home & Crematory and the CEO of Solace Urns, never thought of getting into funeral service – or starting an urn company for that matter. But things can change pretty fast when you marry a fifth-generation funeral director.

She met Matt Malcore while working at a shoe store in college.

"Before I met my husband, working in funeral service never crossed my mind," she said. "Actually … I used to tease him that he might want to consider locking someone down because once he introduced himself as *Matt Malcore, funeral director*, it might reduce his pool of marital prospects."

He took her advice and *did* lock someone down – her – and before she knew it, she was getting increasingly involved in the funeral business.

Earlier this year, she kicked that involvement up a notch when she founded Solace Urns, which she serves as CEO.

Already, it's picked up almost 100 funeral home customers, and business is growing. Malcore also has no shortage of ideas when it comes to creating urns that will resonate with families.

FuneralVision.com recently caught up with Malcore to learn more about how she made her way into funeral service, what led to the founding of Solace Urns and how she plans to continue leveraging her creatively to drive family satisfaction.

Edited excerpts follow.

**Tell us a little bit about yourself.**

My name is Lisa Malcore. I am 39 years old. I grew up in the tiny, yet delightful town of Luck, Wisconsin.

My husband and I have two children, Violet and Oliver, ages 12 and 10 and an excessively large Great Dane, named Evie, lovingly referred to as "Baby Moose" given her massive size.

When I'm not working, I am usually found hauling one or both of my kids to basketball, football, cross country or soccer practice. Their sports take up a good chunk of our free time. I also rebind and restore antique books and make overly large, elaborate but amateur cakes for family birthdays, baby showers and weddings.

I like to renovate. I've spent the last two years updating our Westside of Green Bay Funeral Home. Now that I'm finished, I can see the look of panic in my husband's eyes when I stare overly long at our kitchen or the bathroom at the top of the stairs. I also love to read. I will read anything that is well written. Also, I will read things that are poorly written as long the story is engaging.

**How did you get into funeral service?**

Ultimately, it was necessity that made me permanently join the funeral home staff. Ever since my husband and I were dating, I would help out where and when I was needed. In 2017, one of my husband's brothers left due to medical reasons. In 2018, his other brother decided to take another career path.

Up until that point, I had been working in the mental health field for 12 years. I took over the funeral home finances in 2018, started preneed in 2020, took my apprentice classes in 2022 and launched Solace Urns in 2024. I am hoping to end the streak of starting something new every two years and just concentrate on growing Solace to its full potential.

**Have you ever thought about becoming a licensed funeral director? Why or why not?**

Becoming a licensed director was something I considered for a brief period of time when we were really struggling with staffing. In the end, we knew that if I did become a licensed director, I would not have the flexibility necessary to be available for our kids and our overly large pooch.

We felt it was important for them to be able to have at least one parent at their school concerts, doctor appointments and be able to haul them to and from practices.

*Malcore Funeral Home & Crematory serves about 700 families per year.*

**How many families per year does your funeral home serve – what is the cremation rate, and what are the biggest challenges your firm is facing?**

We have two traditional funeral homes as well as a cremation-focused business. In 2023, we served just over 700 families. Our cremation rate is skewed because of our cremation focused business. Last year, 77% of our calls were cremations.

I would say our biggest challenge is competing with corporate-owned funeral homes. We had a very large, corporate owned firm move in a few blocks from our front door. That was when we opened our cremation-focused business. We knew that if we didn't do something to counteract them, we would lose the calls for families looking for the perceived economical option.

**You are the preneed coordinator. How have you grown your program?**

Until very recently, we have relied on our reputation and longevity to drive our preneed program. My father-in-law also teaches a learning in retirement program at the University of WI – Green Bay on end-of-life care, death education and grief support. We get a high volume of preneeds from people who have taken his classes.

We have recently partnered with Precoa to enhance our preneed program. They also provide wonderful aftercare resources. Because I, as many people do in family-owned firms, wear so many hats, giving preneed the time it deserves is something I have struggled with. I am very much looking forward to getting the program up and running.

**When did you first get the idea to start Solace Urns and why?**

Solace actually came into being because of the Elysium Urn. There was a company on the West Coast that carried that urn. However, the company dissolved a few years ago. That urn, especially the keepsakes, was something we did very well with at our funeral homes. It was beautiful, different and impactful. As funeral professionals, we always want what we are providing to be meaningful and offer comfort, or Solace, if you will.

It took us three years to track down the manufacturer to find out where we could purchase the urn, and the answer was nowhere. They made the urn specifically for the company that was no longer in operation. We talked about potential options and found out they were also the manufacturer for a couple of the other urns we carried that were, again, no longer available anywhere … ultimately, we decided to move forward and create Solace Urns.

This also coincided with a time when we were getting frustrated with the selection of urns that were available. It's seemed like our wholesalers were all carrying the same products, and those products were becoming more traditional. We felt that this was a huge missed opportunity to celebrate our client families' loved ones and make the urn part of a family's home in a unique and meaningful way.

**Where do you source your urns? Do you manufacture them yourself, or do use a supplier?**

Our main manufacturer is located in Singapore, and they are fabulous. The talent and attention to detail they have amazes me. We are very fortunate to be working with them. Watching our ideas take shape in clay and going through the casting and manufacturing process with them is, for lack of better words, so very cool. We have exclusive rights to the products they make for us, which is how you can be sure client families won't be able to find them on Amazon. Our Northwoods urn is manufactured in India.

We have spoken to a few local artists and are working to offer urns made locally in the Green Bay area. We plan to first offer limited runs to learn where interest is and hopefully add products to our permanent selection.

*Already, Solace offers a wide variety of urns.*

**I assume your funeral home offers the urns from Solace to families. How do you work this into conversation? Do you have the urns as part of your selection room?**

We do offer our urns at our funeral homes. We have our products as part of our regular urn displays right alongside urns from Terrybear, Treasure Line and Brown-Wilbert. I don't make a point of pointing them out unless I know the decedent had an interest in that area. I don't bring up the fact that they are our urns unless the family is asking questions about them. I never want anyone to obligated to choose a Solace urn to not hurt my feelings. And yes, we are Midwesterners, the people here are so nice that they might choose an urn that is not their first choice in order to not disappoint someone.

**You have some nice fishing and hunting themes in your urn selection. Why was this important for you to include?**

We are located in Green Bay, Wisconsin, and we decided to initially focus on what we knew would sell well in our area. We have a unique perspective in having our own funeral home. We know what our client families are requesting and what is currently available and unavailable. Hunting and fishing are a big part of the Midwest culture and something we receive many requests for from the families we serve.

Northwoods was brought to life from a preneed client whose favorite thing to do was chop firewood. His son asked if we had a stump that we could hollow out for him. So, raise a glass to Dennis for the creation of Northwoods.

Last Cast, which I lovingly refer to as "my baby," is an urn that I jokingly say that half of my family will end up in (though the statement may be accurate). Going through the sculpting, molding and casting process was fascinating. I do have to give credit to my brother for the outstanding name, though I wish I could take it for myself.

**What has been the bestselling urn so far – and what has been the initial reaction/feedback from families?**

Believe it or not, as of today we have a three-way tie for the number one seller in full-size urns. Last Cast, Northwoods and Final Hunt are leading the pack. Our number one selling overall product is the Northwoods keepsake, which has been flying out the door.

We do expect to have different bestsellers in different areas of the country, and I'm eager to see how the numbers will change as we move into different markets.

I also love the enthusiasm we see from funeral homes. I've had people send pictures to me of their display rooms with our urns and our brochures. People have asked for images, so they can include our products in their online merchandise and make posts to social media. My favorite is when they get the urns they ordered and call back after the delivery saying they love them, and they need to carry other ones as well.

The reaction from families has been wonderful. They are thrilled to be able to have an urn that they know their family member would have loved. Even our clients who don't pick a Solace Urn comment on them and can see how special it will be for the right person. Our goal is to eventually have something for everyone. I have encouraged the funeral homes we've worked with to let me know if there is something they think would go over well with the families they serve.

*Lisa Malcore and her family.*

**Are you looking to add additional urns to your line and/or other cremation-oriented products?**

Oh, yes. I have a new urn idea roughly every 30 seconds. The problem is keeping myself in check.

More immediately, you will see keepsakes for Last Cast, Final Hunt, Liberty and Autumn Mourning. We have the samples, and they will make the most adorable and meaningful memento of a family's loved one you will ever see. Elysium and Requiem will also have a 10 ½" size.

We have just finished the sculpting phase of a Lighthouse and a Sailboat. Both will have four-inch keepsakes as well as full-size urns. They will be made out of the UV treated granite composite material that is used to make our Elysium urn. They can be placed inside the house as part of décor or they will be able to be placed outside as a garden statue. We are hoping to be able to have these ready for sale by the end of the year.

Additionally, we are working with a local ceramics artist to offer something unique and beautiful. We hope to be able to continue expand that area and work with other local artists who work with different mediums as well.

I have many other thoughts. Within the next year or so, I'd like to have a motorcycle urn. I envision it being from the view of the rider's seat, seeing the gauges, handle bars, windshield and gas tank cap. Like all our urns, it would be a 360-degree sculpture, so there will be a view of the front of the bike and the sides as well. It will be chrome with black patina – not to get too specific.

I also see a Grambel Roofed Barn in our future. I would like a white birch bark urn similar to our Northwoods. However, I feel like white birch bark doesn't have the structural integrity needed to stand the test of time. We will need to look at artificial options and see what we can produce that still has the feeling of authenticity we are looking for.

Engraving is also in our future. We are in the process of converting our funeral home warehouse into Solace headquarters. Once we have completed ridding our building of 103 years of discarded funeral home paraphernalia, we can start engraving plates for our urns – which have an excellent base for personalization – and we can also engrave directly on the granite composite urns as well. Thinking of our first sailboat urn (name still a work in progress) to be engraved with the name of someone's one boat or their loved one's name and how much that will mean to their family makes me smile. Or the thought of having the initials or handwriting engraved on the future birch bark urn like it was carved on a tree also makes me smile.

**How can funeral homes earn money selling your products?**

We work strictly as a wholesaler and only sell directly to funeral homes. Each funeral home will price our products as they choose. We do, however, price our products so that funeral homes can sell them at prices comparable to what would be seen on more traditional urns. We feel that every family deserves the possibility to memorialize their loved one in a personal and meaningful way regardless of their level of income.

*Malcore Funeral Home & Crematory customers often pick urns with an outdoor theme.*

**How many funeral homes are you working with?**

As of today, we have shipped orders to 78 different funeral homes, and I'm happy to say the number is growing. Solace launched at the beginning of June. At this time, I have only attended one conference and sent mailings to the Midwest. I can also see the cities where people try to access our website and if it isn't an area where I have sent our mailers, I try and send them to area funeral homes. However, when someone tries to access our website in Philadelphia or San Antonio, it's hard to narrow that down to a couple funeral homes.

**How can other funeral homes offer the urns from Solace?**

By calling me at 920-621-8134 or emailing me at *Lisa@Solace-Urns.com*. I can provide the password to our website, so they can place their own order, or I'm happy to take an order via phone or email as well. As we do not have a billing department (which helps keep our prices down), I do require payment upon order via credit card. Orders placed online can be paid by credit card or PayPal.

**Do you have any other thoughts to share?**

Once again, I encourage feedback and any suggestions for any future sculptural urns that funeral directors think would do well in their area. I am well versed on the family needs on our area, but I would love to hear thoughts about what client families near you would find impactful. The capabilities we have with our manufacturer are endless, and we hope to wield this power to provide to grieving families and value to funeral home. You can do that by emailing me at *Lisa@solace-urns.com*.

*The Elysium urn and keepsakes.*

Visit *https://solace-urns.com* *to learn more about Solace Urns.*

# A Different Kind of Urn Company: Honos Caters to the Modern Home and Individual

*By Thomas A. Parmalee*

Max Lemper-Tabatsky teamed up with Miles Adams, formerly the head of operations of Tulip Cremation, to launch Honos about four years ago, which aims to redefine memorialization by offering families a selection of modern, innovative urns.

Honos is comprised of two brands: a consumer-facing business, Oaktree Memorials; and a wholesale business that sells urns directly to funeral homes, Samuel Mitchell Design.

Originally from New York, Lemper-Tabatsky, 30 (*pictured at right in the photo at the beginning of this chapter*), met Adams (*pictured at left in the photo at the beginning of this chapter*) after relocating to San Francisco. The two both worked for PJT Partners, a premier, global, advisory-focused investment bank.

"For about 10 months, we worked closely together before Miles transitioned to lead operations at Tulip Cremation, where he stayed until their acquisition by Foundation Partners Group," he said.

"In early 2020, we reconnected and found ourselves sharing personal and professional reflections on navigating loss and memorialization. Through these conversations, we recognized a gap in the market for modern memorials, and that realization became the foundation of our business."

The conversations happened at the right time, Lemper-Tabatsky said. "I was trying to see what else was out there and wanted to figure out something new," he said. "I didn't necessarily know what path it would take me down."

Adams was the perfect person to connect with to think big. "He also had an entrepreneurial itch," Lemper-Tabatsky said. And it was clear he was "really underwhelmed with the urns and memorials" available to families.

Lemper-Tabatsky felt the same way. He noted that while some companies, such as Eterneva and Parting Stone, have brought innovation to the cremation space, there are not many others offering families something new. "What you find at Amazon is really what you get at most funeral homes," he said.

Adams' frustrations with the urn selection that was readily available resonated with Lemper-Tabtasky, who remembered his mom keeping the cremated remains of his grandmother in a closet for several months after receiving an urn from the funeral home.

"She did not want a big metal container in the living room," he explained. "Really, from a décor point of view, she had modern tastes."

Adams had a similar experience when his family's golden retriever died, and his family simply could not find an urn that they liked, according to Lemper-Tabatsky.

The two friends put their heads together, and Adams shared some of the insights he'd gleaned working in death care during his time at Tulip.

"We were like, 'Maybe there is something we can do about this," Lemper-Tabatsky said. "This hit home personally, and as we did more R&D, we saw an opportunity to create something new."

**Starting a Company**

The two friends launched Honos, with Adams serving as chief executive officer and Lemper-Tabatsky taking on the role of chief operating officer.

They initially raised a seed round of capital through angel investors.

"We've raised just over $1 million with the help of angel investors and support from our friends and family," Lemper-Tabatsky explained. "This funding has allowed us to work on launching new products, set up our fulfillment center in Denver, and bring on some talented team members who are fueling our growth."

He continued, "Given how challenging the fundraising market has become, we've been careful to focus on growing profitably, instead of pouring money into advertising and burning through cash. Thanks to this approach, we've been able to grow our direct-to-consumer brand (Oaktree) and our B2B brand (Samuel Mitchell), while staying true to the investors who believed in us from the start."

The nature of the business means that even customers who come back only do so every few years – and often, they may simply be one-time customers, Lemper-Tabatsky said. "We are focusing on growing slower but more efficiently," he said. "You are forced to do that in this industry – it tends to move slower."

*A selection of urns made by Honos.*

### The Big Idea

The two men concluded that families would appreciate urns that could be in the background and that "you wouldn't even know it is an urn," Lemper-Tabatsky said. These families were an untapped market — and they had a need.

In other words, people wanted an urn that most people would think is a vase or beautiful piece of art.

"It would be something you could live with in your living room, and a friend or family member would not ask, 'Who is in there?'" Lemper-Tabatsky said. "They may say nothing at all or they may say, 'What is that beautiful piece?' You could live with it more discreetly and seamlessly – it would be a living memory you can be proud to have."

They rolled up their sleeves and did the hard work necessary to create an urn collection – pieces that are manufactured in the United States as well as in Italy and some other overseas locations.

"A few ways we've described our business include: 'urns that don't look like urns,' 'the West Elm of urns,' 'memorials made for the modern home and individual,'' and 'interesting lives deserve interesting urns,'" Lemper-Tabatsky said.

Coming up with an urn selection that would resonate with families was no easy task, Lemper-Tabatsky said.

"That was really something we had to figure out as we went," he said. "We hired design and manufacturing consultants, and with the help of advisers and a small team, we have created those manufacturing relationships on our own."

Asked to provide some insights on some of its more popular urns, Lemper-Tabatsky said its top seller is The Bleecker, which is "a stunning icosahedron – a 20-sided polyhedron – crafted from rich walnut hardwood." He added, "It comes in three sizes, and we're excited to introduce a lighter oak version later this year to complement the walnut."

Another favorite is The Hudson, which is available in six finishes and four sizes, he said. "The multicolor option is especially beloved by pet owners, symbolizing the rainbow bridge, and is also embraced by the LGBTQ+ community as a vibrant, celebratory way to honor life," he said.

The Thompson stands out with its luxurious design, featuring a soft Florentine velvet interior and a removable tray, "perfect for storing personal keepsakes like letters, jewelry, or watches," he said.

Lastly, The Amore and The Pyramid necklaces are the most popular choices for customers seeking cremation jewelry. Customers appreciate their "elegant, discreet and modern designs," Lemper-Tabatsky said.

*The Bleecker urn by Honos.*

**Reaching Out to Funeral Homes**

Once Honos started to grow market share through its Oaktree Memorial brand, it found that funeral homes and pet crematories wanted to know more about buying urns directly from the company.

So, toward the end of 2021, it launched a separate brand – Samuel Mitchell Design (which is a combination of the founders' middle names) to work directly with funeral homes and pet crematories.

"It's our wholesale brand, and it offers a lot of the same products as our consumer brand," Lemper-Tabatsky said.

According to the Samuel Mitchell website:

*We made our first urn using sustainable woods completely by hand, and we still do everything entirely by hand in that same tradition today. We have grown to include workshops in Colorado, Ohio, Italy, and England.*

*Our team brings decades of expertise to their crafts to ensure your families receive a work of art that we're proud to stand behind. At Samuel Mitchell, we are driven to create memorials that are of exemplary quality and innovative design, while remaining environmentally-conscious with the materials we select.*

Today, Samuel Mitchell Design works directly with about 100 funeral homes and pet crematories, primarily in the United States with a few in Canada as well. The team regularly attends industry conventions to build its wholesale business, Lemper-Tabatsky said.

"We have to prove to the industry that we are here to stay," he said.

The reason the duo created a separate brand to serve funeral homes is that they wanted to create a dedicated offering for funeral professionals. "We want to make sure they know we are focusing on their needs," Lemper-Tabatsky said.

Many customers order products on demand, as customers request them. "Only a select amount will hold inventory," Lemper-Tabatsky said. Products can be shipped and engraved overnight, he said.

But customers can get products to display, printed materials as well as a digital catalog, so they can sell urns to families through an online store or via a more traditional catalogue.

As for pricing, a typical example would be a funeral home or pet crematory buying an urn for $200 and selling it for $400, he said.

Samuel Mitchell Designs provides a manufacturer's suggested retail price, but funeral homes can charge whatever they like, he said.

So far, the Oaktree Memorials unit of Honos contributes the lion's share of revenue to the company – about 75%, Lemper-Tabatsky said.

Most of the company's business comes through its own website, but it does sell cremation jewelry through Amazon. "People do not go on Amazon for premium urns and such," he said. "There is so much competition – and most of the products are mostly under $100 retail."

The company has, however, had a good deal of success selling urns through Etsy. That audience "wants something handmade," he said.

Most of the human urns that the company offers sell in the $195 to $945 range. The average sale is about $395, he said.

Honos also sells a good deal of pet urns, which it sells in the $95 to $945 price range. The average pet sale is about $295, he said.

The majority of urns that Honos sells – about two-thirds – are engraved with the name of the deceased human or pet. Using that as a gauge, Lemper-Tabatsky estimates that about 60% of the urns it sells are for human family members.

As for how the company is engaging in outreach, in addition to exhibiting and attending industry conventions to market its wholesale brand, it devotes a lot of attention to Google as buying an urn is "such a high intent purchase," he said.

"We really reach people through Google where everyone searches, and we have an Instagram and TikTok account which is more organic – as well as a blog and resource center," he said. "We are really trying to be as helpful as we can."

So far, Lemper-Tabatsky is happy with results — the company has already served over 50,000 families, he said.

*Visit https://oaktreememorials.com to learn more about Oaktree Memorials.*

*Visit https://samuelmitchelldesign.com to learn more about Samuel Mitchell Design.*

# Courtney Gould Miller Shares Insights on Leadership Changes at Tribute Technology, Innovation and More

*By Thomas A. Parmalee*

On Oct. 25, Tribute Technology announced big news: Charlie Cole "mutually agreed" with the company's board of directors to step down from his role as the company's chief executive.

Cole, who previously led FTD, also known as Florists' Transworld Delivery, isn't the only one who left: Frances DeBlasio, who was chief financial officer; and Alex Cross, who was head of transformation, also parted ways with the company.

Moving forward, instead of one chief executive, the company will be led by Tribute Technology's board of directors and an Office of the CEO, composed of key executives, including Courtney Gould Miller, who will serve as president of commercial markets.

Rounding out the executive suite will be Matt Powell, who will serve as chief technology officer; Joshua Gibbs, who has been hired as chief operating officer; and a chief financial officer, which the company is about to hire, Gould Miller said.

"This experienced leadership team will ensure stability and guide Tribute Technology through its next phase of innovation and growth," according to a news release.

Gould Miller, who previously served as the company's chief customer officer, said her role will largely be an extension of her former position. "The board recognized that our funeral home customers must come first, that the voice of that customer is what needs to inform every part of our operations," she said. "It's no secret that Tribute has experienced incredible growth by being the very best at converting visitors to funeral home websites into floral and tree purchases. That's allowed us to service funeral homes through a revenue share model. We're proud of that, but the board also recognizes the need to be the best at what matters most to this profession. We need to be the best option for helping funeral homes grow their at-need and preneed services and, above all, giving them the best tech resources to serve grieving families with excellence and compassion."

FuneralVision.com recently caught up with Gould Miller to learn more about Tribute Technology, the changes at the company, how the business she grew up in and helped build – MKJ Marketing – fits into its portfolio, and more.

*Courtney Gould Miller*

**When did MKJ become part of Tribute Technology and what factors went into deciding to transition that business to a new owner?**

In 2022, my parents and I realized that partnering with Tribute Technology would be the best move for MKJ. Like any business owner knows, tech overhead can really add up, and hiring developers and website contractors was getting costly. Joining forces with Tribute let us tap into their incredible development team, complete with top-notch eCommerce and UX expertise. This partnership has allowed us to still deliver high-quality digital assets to our clients without the burden of handling it all on our own.

We are absolutely focused on expanding MKJ not only for Tribute but for our customers. At MKJ, we continue to serve the many funeral homes we have served over the last 40 years and are working with new customers all the time. We learn the most from direct communication with our customers.

**What is MKJ Marketing's place in the Tribute Technology universe ... and what's new at MKJ?**

MKJ Marketing is a premier partner of Tribute Technology, which means all MKJ clients get access to Tribute's top-notch tech, plus exclusive marketing support from MKJ's experts. What makes us unique is that our team really understands the funeral profession and knows how to connect with families in the best, most approachable way. Funeral home marketing is a very specific type of marketing that is hard for outside marketing companies to understand.

We've been expanding our digital marketing services, where funeral homes can pick the package that fits their needs and budget. From social media and SEO to email newsletters, these services are helping clients boost community engagement. We've had many clients who have produced a substantial number of preneed leads thanks to this service.

Our ideal customer I would describe as being defined by more than just case count. We have some very small firms working with us as well as large consolidators and independent funeral homes. They are all focused on implementing technology throughout their business at a very high level – and they are focused on growing and retaining market share.

The funeral homes that love us and enjoy the experience are the ones that are very excited about bringing in technology and thinking about what is next. Our profession can have those who are very afraid of technology ... we try to meet people where they are.

If you are really excited about bringing on new technology and thinking of all the ways it can streamline your service and interaction with the community, we are a great fit for that.

**What are the main operating companies of Tribute Technology and are you looking to make other acquisitions in the funeral space?**

Our brands inside Tribute Technology include MKJ Marketing, CFS, SRS Computing, Legacy Touch, Funeral Tech, Funeral Innovations, Frazer Consultants, and Ad Perfect. We have extensive teams dedicated across all these brands to ensure clients receive the best support. As for acquisitions, we are always open to expanding our portfolio by partnering with other top businesses within our industry.

We regularly look at great businesses inside and outside of the profession to assess fit for our business. We are approached all the time by businesses in the profession that recognize the expensive nature of technology and want to be part of a broader platform.

**Who are the financial backers of Tribute?**

Tribute Technology is financially backed by the Carlyle Group and Vista Equity Partners. Members of Carlyle and Vista sit on our board of directors, which is a tremendous resource because they are working with top technology businesses across all industries and bring a wealth of resources and knowledge. There are several other companies in our industry that have also received private equity investment, so we are not alone in this. We are grateful to our board members who provide many resources and strategic guidance for our growth and tech development. They help us make connections we would have never been able to make on our own.

**What do you love most about working at Tribute Technology?**

What I love most about working at Tribute Technology is how closely we connect with funeral directors and the families they serve. I grew up watching my parents work in the profession for decades — eventually helping them lead MKJ — and I've seen funeral directors' commitment to their communities up close. Knowing how important funeral service is drives me to make sure we're offering funeral professionals the very best. Being part of a team that shares that my mission makes what I do here feel meaningful every day.

**Why was there a leadership shakeup at Tribute Technology?**

Tribute Technology's leadership change was made after extensive strategic planning, including outside consultants. This planning is all about gearing up for the next chapter. The board wants a leadership team and focus that keeps pace with Tribute's evolving goals. That includes an emphasis on the connection to the profession through myself and others who have history in the profession and are also dedicated to its long-term success. By adjusting the leadership structure, we are more focused on delivering even more value to clients. It's a strategic move to make sure Tribute has the right team in place to keep building on our mission.

**Charlie Cole wasn't the only one to leave the company … what about the other departures?**

The board and leadership felt it was the right time to make changes that guide Tribute's next phase. Each of them contributed so much to getting us here, and this decision was all about positioning the company to keep growing and better serve our clients. With the new leadership setup, we're confident Tribute is set to continue growing stronger.

**Some people feel this transition was a bit abrupt … was it, or had the company been thinking about going in a different direction for some time?**

It might seem fast to some, but this direction has actually been in the works for a while. The board had been considering the best path forward, and this is the natural next step to support Tribute's goals. We're still on the same mission — this shift just gives us a new team setup to keep us moving forward and growing with our clients.

**How has artificial intelligence impacted how you and your team operate at Tribute Technology? In what ways are you using it?**

We are using AI in all sorts of ways … our development team uses AI to help them speed up their coding time, our marketing teams can produce copy faster than ever, our eCommerce and

UX team use AI for data analysis. We are using AI in pretty much every department of our company. I hope to have some new success stories on using AI for SEO to share with our customers very soon!

**How are your parents doing … and how active do they remain in funeral service?**

My parents still remain very active in funeral service — in fact, they serve on the Tribute Technology team as advisers. They both have so many insights and decades of experience that many Tribute employees call upon them for guidance and to get their thoughts on new tech features. Glenn and Marilyn are both still very involved in our MKJ Summits, too … both of them led incredible sessions at our most recent Summit in Palm Beach.

*Glenn H. Gould and Marilyn Jones Gould are advisers to Tribute Technology and remain active with MKJ Marketing, which includes their daughter, Courtney Gould Miller, who serves as MKJ's chief strategy officer.*

**Do you ever miss being a practicing attorney?**

Not at all! I am much more oriented to business. But I credit much of my professional life to law school and my legal training. Law school teaches you to think in a different way – analyze both sides of an argument, thinking about messaging and how it is received, so much.

**Are there any new products and/or services Tribute Technology is offering that you would like to shine a spotlight on?**

I'd love to talk about two new products that we are excited to share with our clients.

**Tech Turbo Packs**: Tech Turbo Packs are our all-in-one bundles crafted to enhance a funeral home's digital footprint, offering things like advanced website features and grief support. Funeral homes can pick which tier works best for their business.

**Lead Logic**: Lead Logic is the ultimate lead management tool that keeps funeral homes connected with potential families. It captures leads in real-time, making it easy to follow up fast and keep business growth on track — no missed opportunities, just smarter connections.

**What is the most interesting thing/interesting person/ or interesting product or service that you encountered at the recent NFDA convention?**

One of my favorite new products is Pressed Floral. I love how they make florals into **beautiful** keepsakes.

**What's a book or resource that you would recommend to funeral professionals?**

My favorite book to recommend is "Radical Candor" by Kim Scott. We can all benefit from having clear and direct communication, both personally and professionally!

*From Left to right: Heather McWilliams Mierzejewski, vice president of marketing; Courtney Gould Miller, president of commercial markets; Jamie Cresto, vice president of sales; and Jules Green-Fournier, vice president of customer success.*

*Visit www.tributetech.com to learn more about Tribute Technology*

# Effie Anolik Finds Her Calling as the CEO of Afterword

*By Thomas A. Parmalee*

Effie Anolik, 34, who grew up in Vancouver and Toronto, always knew she'd live in New York City. She just didn't know it would be as the CEO of her very own company … serving funeral homes.

But life as she knew it took an abrupt turn in August 2018 when she found herself planning her father's funeral. Doctors had discovered a tumor in Michael Anolik's chest five weeks earlier. He was 64 years old.

"My interest in the funeral profession started the moment I called the funeral home from the hospital and the moment I Googled how to find a funeral home on my phone," she said. "That is what I do for everything else. – any sort of purchase, I go to the internet to get information."

She did not find resources online, however, and had to arrange her father's funeral in person at a funeral home. "It was only the first or second time I ever made a purchasing decision face to face with someone," she said.

Her father had not spent time planning a funeral or engaging in estate planning, Anolik said. "He signed his will two days before he died in the hospital," she said.

But she *did know* he wanted a traditional Jewish funeral. "I didn't know what that meant at the time," she said.

His death, however, helped her get more in touch with her Jewish roots, she said. She's always thought of herself as "more culturally Jewish" than being particularly religious, so she had some learning to do as she engaged in the funeral planning process.

"I feel like our grief rituals have really brought me closer to Judaism," she said. "The structure Judaism introduces to grief is really comforting to me … there is Shiva and the 30 days of mourning. You light a candle a couple times a year."

Now, Anolik volunteers at Toronto Hebrew Memorial Park, where her dad is buried, sitting on its communications committee. She has helped the cemetery redo its website while learning more about the cemetery side of the business. In her role, she has interviewed different rabbis about grief and dying, building up its video and content library.

*Effie Anolik*

**A Winding Path to Becoming an Entrepreneur**

By the time her dad died, Anolik already knew she had a taste for being an entrepreneur. She may have been born with it given that her father owned his own business.

Several years before his death – in 2013 – she made her first foray into business, starting Fe Hardware, which has absolutely nothing to do with home improvement.

"Growing up, I always had these side businesses as a creative outlet," she said. "And in my early 20s, I learned how to make fine jewelry with an 80-year-old goldsmith. I started making jewelry pieces inspired by science, and Fe is the symbol for the element iron."

She admits she may have taken the science gimmick a little too far.

"I took product photos of jewelry surrounded by beakers," she confessed.

While the business never took off, it led her to the halls of Shopify, which changed her trajectory and made everything that came after possible.

"I was making clothing and jewelry for fun, and I needed a way to take payments," she said. "I realized I could make an online store, and then I started to help my friends and people I know build Shopify sites."

While she hasn't made jewelry in at least 10 years and by her own admission may not even be able to weld anything anymore, she learned *a lot* about building an online store.

"I had more fun building the brand side of things and the website than the jewelry," she said.

She also realized that even though she had completed her undergraduate degree in psychology and neuroscience, she'd find her passion elsewhere.

"I actually went to an event for Shopify in Toronto where I was living at the time, and I met people who worked there," she said. "I assumed that most people who worked in tech were coders, but I found out not everyone does that. I met some people with their support team, applied for a job and then moved to Ottawa where its head office is."

It was the perfect company to land a job at – and it was at the perfect time, too.

"I worked there in ton of different roles from 2014 to 2019," she said, including user experience and the product division. "I worked with some of the smartest and most resourceful people I have ever met."

She was always asking questions about what others did – and she wasn't afraid to make waves.

For instance, when Shopify customers kept calling to complain about the same problem, she adamantly made the case that the company should change the product, so there weren't so many questions about it.

"And they would tell me, 'Oh, that's user experience. It's a whole department.' And that *kept happening*. And I kept learning what other people did. It also got me interested in how you build a product from start to finish, which is product management," she said.

When she started at Shopify, it had about 450 employees. When she left, it had more than 2,000, she said.

When her father died, she also found herself a business owner once again, having inherited his bread distribution company, Best Way Distribution.

She knew absolutely nothing about the bread business, but she had to keep it afloat while working full time at Shopify.

"I'd be at the bakery at 4 a.m. and then go to work and then go back at 8 p.m. – rinse and repeat," she said. "It was never going to be a long-term thing for me, but I needed for it to be stable for the employees."

After her father's funeral, she continued her research into funeral service. She learned pretty quickly that an online planning option was something lacking at many funeral homes.

During this time, she also virtually met Zack Moy, 36, who is a software engineer who formerly served as director of engineering at Workday. She calls him "one of the smarted and most talented engineers I have ever worked with." She added, "And he deeply cares about the funeral profession."

When they first learned of each other, Anolik was living in Toronto and Moy was living in San Francisco.

"He was interested in grief and grief resources," Anolik said. "Initially we started meeting virtually every other month. We both had other jobs, but we were talking about ideas."

They began working together virtually and founded Afterword in 2020. Today, they both live and work in New York, where the company is based.

Anolik serves as the company's CEO and Moy serves as its chief technology officer.

**Launching Afterword**

When she became interested in funeral service, Anolik began talking to funeral directors and "learning about software in general," she said. "I knew that I wanted to build an additional tool, so that families who wanted to plan online could do so."

When the COVID-19 pandemic erupted at the end of 2019, Anolik shifted her attention from building online planning software to helping families with livestreaming and hosting virtual memorials.

"It was not an intention of mine, but it was something the pandemic opened up for us," she said.

The move came after a strict lockdown in Toronto.

Suddenly, Anolik had people reaching out to her asking how their families could come together virtually. After the third time someone asked, she decided to help.

"We did that for two years, but I always knew I wanted to build a tool for families to help them make decisions online," she said, noting that Afterword worked with almost 500 families in two years who wanted to livestream services.

"We did pretty well," she said. "Our version of livestreaming was a little different than others as we would send a videographer on site. They would follow the family from the service to the cemetery. They would manage it in person, and someone would manage it virtually." She added, "We no longer do that, but if someone wants a videographer, send me a note."

While COVID-19 led her to take a detour, it paved the way for her to learn about consumer preferences directly from families. "I asked them a ton of questions," she said. "It was an interesting and fascinating time."

When the pandemic eased, she rolled up her sleeves and got to work on software to help families plan online.

Fast forward to today, and Afterword is serving a growing number of funeral homes as they support families in person and online.

As for how Afterword is funded, Anolik said she and her co-founder raised some money through a friends-and-family round of financing. It recently began inviting its customers to invest in the company.

"We are not choosing to go the venture capital route," she said. "We want to keep this in the profession."

If there are funeral professionals interested in investing in the company, they are welcome to reach out to her via email at *Effie@Afterword.com*.

*A screenshot from a funeral home page that works with Afterword.*

**Products and Services**

Afterword's flagship product is its Online Planner, which uses videos to guide families through their options.

"Instead of showing families three packages and asking them to pick one, it will ask questions similar to what a funeral director would ask either over the phone or in person," Anolik said. "For instance, 'Do you want to see Dad before cremation?' or 'Would you like to witness a casketed cremation?' We are providing them information, so they can make an educated choice."

The company also offers a Digital Whiteboard product that can be accessed from anywhere as well as a Case Management product.

"Say goodbye to the days of taking photos of your whiteboard and wondering who made changes. Our Digital Whiteboard keeps everything organized, accessible, and transparent," the Afterword website states.

For Case Management, its website states, "Our reporting engine gives you unprecedented control and visibility into how your business is doing and how you can improve your core business drivers."

All of Afterword's solutions are "built in a modular way and personalized to the funeral home," Anolik said. "If they collect something specific, we will add it."

According to its website at https://afterword.com/pricing, the Online Planner starts at $179 per month; the Case Management product starts at $325 per month; and a Task Lists product starts at $99 per month. Those prices are based on a firm that serves 200 families per year, she said.

As for how those products work together, it's "choose your own adventure," Anolik said. "You might be really happy with your case management software but are looking for an online planner – and we are happy to do that. We are happy to connect with any existing solutions. I would say for the most part, funeral homes tend to end up using us for all of the things – they may start with one and end up using us for everything."

The company is working with funeral homes in 11 states as well as some funeral homes in Ontario.

"It feels as though the United States is a little faster to innovate and open to trying new things," she observed. "But the markets are pretty similar."

Most funeral homes that use Afterword's flagship product – the Online Planner – allow anyone to access it on their website. "A few will send it out as a link after they talk to the family on the phone," Anolik said.

Asked what her customers love most about working with Afterword, Anolik said the company, which leans on five full-time employees and a limited number of contractors, is always innovating as it collaborates with customers to build products. "We just take all of their feedback to heart – that is the only way we build," she said. "Our software is user friendly … and we answer the phones."

While Afterword is based in New York, she and Moy briefly ran the business above Kolssak Funeral Home in Wheeling, Illinois, which was its first funeral home customer on the software side. It remains a customer to this day, Anolik said.

When she and Moy began working with the funeral home and its owner, Jon Kolssak, they only intended to build an online planning tool. She never thought they'd end up temporarily running the business above the funeral home – it just happened.

"Before we built anything, we actually tried to understand how they actually worked," she said, noting that they went on removals with funeral home staff and sat in on arrangement meetings in the spring and summer of 2022. "We wanted to build tools to fit into the workflow."

"I consider that funeral home family at this point," she said. "We are lucky we met the right people and got to work together. We have an adviser, and he apprenticed at this funeral home when at Worsham, and he was the one who introduced us. It was not a sales call – we just wanted to get some feedback on what we were doing. And they said, 'If you build that, we will use it.'"

Afterword's biggest challenge remains the fact that it is a relatively new company, Anolik said. "Most funeral homes are really established and have been around awhile," she observed. "The last few people we have brought on had been using the same software for 20 years, and most of our competitors have been around 15 plus years."

But with that said, there are still many funeral homes that want to innovate and are excited by what Afterword can provide, she said.

"Generally, the funeral homes that work with us are supporting at least 200 families per year, but we would love to support some of the smaller firms, too," she said.

There are so many fun tools that Afterword has in the works, Anolik said. "We are working on a body tracking system for funeral homes in state that require a chain of custody,' she said. "And internally, we are building a number of AI tools to help us onboard funeral homes faster."

For now, AI is something Afterwords using more internally than anything else, she said. "We also have an AI obituary writer … but I am still leery in the ways we use it to interact with families. It is exciting, but it is in its very infancy as a technology. We are thinking about it a lot but proceeding with caution."

Anolik also hosts a podcast, "Groundbreaking: The Business of Death," in which she interviews visionary entrepreneurs redefining funeral service.

While Anolik has embarked down a path that she never anticipated, living in New York has been all that she dreamed.

"There's something about the energy of New York that really excites me," she said. "I love it here – the food, the theater, it has anything you would like to do."

*Visit https://afterword.com to learn more about Afterword.*

# Celebrate Life Co. Aims to Bring Cemeteries into the Twenty-First Century

*By Thomas A. Parmalee*

When Nicholas Allan's mom asked him to do her a favor – leave some flowers at the headstone of a beloved family friend – he said what any good son would: *No problem, Mom.*

But when the former Adobe sales operation analyst went to search for the grave, he could not find it.

There was no information on Find a Grave, no one at the cemetery office to help and no maps available to make his task easier.

He left with the flowers still in hand, unable to make his delivery with the feeling that he'd let his mom down – and a nagging thought running a loop through his mind: *There has to be a better way.*

He began looking into how cemeteries operate on a larger level and concluded that many of them have neglected to join the 21st century.

As he learned more, the 28-year-old also discovered that he had a passion for learning about the lives and legacies left behind when someone dies.

"I thought about all the people who have left an impact and who could have an impact on us – on other people beyond their families," he said.

In 2023, he founded Celebrate Life Co., which is based in Salt Lake City and aims to revolutionize cemetery care with innovative add-on services that enhance and personalize the memorial experience. He serves as the company's CEO.

According to the company's LinkedIn page, "We seamlessly blend technology with tradition to ensure that every tribute is beautifully maintained and easily accessible."

Allan stayed on at his job at Adobe for a while, operating Celebrate Life as a side hustle, he said. As it began to take up more of his time and as more clients signed on – it's now working with a few dozen cemeteries – he left his full-time job to give it his full attention.

Early on, he got a lucky break when he was attending a family gathering and reconnected with a former Boy Scout leader of his, David James.

"He had enjoyed a successful career in web development at Microsoft, and I told him about my project," he said.

A couple days later, they grabbed lunch together.

"Little did I know, I was stepping into the Shark Tank," Allan said, making a reference to the hit reality show where entrepreneurs seek funding. "He asked me about my goals, my revenue expectations and the major blocks that were preventing me from where I want to be. He became an angel investor, which has helped me get to the stage where I am – and we continue to be business partners."

As to how Allan is positioning the company, he's focusing on serving cemeteries and then helping them connect directly with consumers, which holds revenue implications for Celebrate Life as well as its clients.

"Because we sell software to the cemetery and get them organized and digitized, it opens up the door for us to go straight to the consumer," he said.

Some of the services Celebrate Life offers families include delivering flowers and headstone cleaning. Families can also opt for a flag to be placed on a grave on Veterans Day or a wreath around Christmastime. To fulfill these services, Celebrate Life can partner with third parties or with a cemetery in house.

The revenue sharing opportunity can vary because every cemetery is different, but generally, Celebrate Life will take 10% of any sales made to consumers via its platform.

"But that can be negotiated," Allan said. "For instance, we just did a deal with a cemetery that did not have much initial capital to invest in our software. So, we are taking a larger portion of business-to-consumer sales until we hit a certain threshold, and then we will go down to 10%. We can get creative in various ways to get everyone to the point of where they want to be."

While the company is still in its early stages, its flagship service is digitizing cemeteries to improve the consumer experience, which also paves the way for cemeteries to become a storefront.

By weaning cemeteries off paper maps and giving them the tools they need to provide a digital experience, Celebrate Life Co. aims to help them become more successful and profitable, Allan said.

That matters even if it's a nonprofit cemetery, he said.

"Even those cemeteries have costs to worry about, such as maintenance and buying a new lawnmower," he pointed out. "So many cemeteries are struggling to stay afloat."

Typically, the cost of Celebrate Life software is $500 per year. Cemeteries pay an additional one-time fee for Celebrate Life to digitize maps and bring them online. The cost depends on the size, quality and format of their existing maps.

"Setup costs typically range from $400 for smaller cemeteries to $10,000+ for larger properties requiring extensive digitization and mapping," Allan said. "We base it off the number of burials and digital pins that we have to place."

Once mapping is complete, families can easily find the graves of loved ones and walk to them using the GPS coordinates on a smartphone's navigation feature, he said.

The company also offers a memorial tribute option for families, which it provides for free (beyond a small storage fee if a memorial includes a large number of videos and photos).

"I am really passionate about the tributes and memorial aspect," Allan said. "Whenever someone is visiting a cemetery and it promotes that they can create a profile for someone, they do it most of the time."

Asked what makes Celebrate Life different, Allan said that competitors are focused more on the cemetery management side of things.

"While we definitely offer a tool to get cemeteries into a more digitized space, we are leaning much more into the cemetery experience," he said. "We want to create a better experience for people visiting cemeteries. So, we are more public-facing and plan for the cemetery to have a relationship with the community."

Celebrate Life serves cemeteries nationwide as well as in the United Kingdom – and Allan expects to start serving clients in Australia in the near future He thinks the future for his company is bright.

"People who have been willing to take the chance on this have loved it," he said. "We are opening the doors for them to become profitable and to help get them into the twenty-first century. We are getting them off paper maps, so that once they leave the business or pass it down so others can take over, they'll know everything is going to be OK."

*Visit https://www.celebratelifeco.com to learn more about Celebrate Life Co.*